TALKING GUITAR

CONVERSATIONS WITH

MUSICIANS WHO SHAPED

TWENTIETH-CENTURY

AMERICAN MUSIC

JAS OBRECHT

TALKING GUITAR

Published by the

UNIVERSITY OF NORTH CAROLINA PRESS,

Chapel Hill,

in association with the

SOUTHERN FOLKLIFE COLLECTION,

the Louis Round Wilson Special Collections

Library

Designed by Richard Hendel
Set in Utopia and Transat types
by Tseng Information Systems, Inc.
Manufactured in the United States of America

The University of North Carolina Press has been a
member of the Green Press Initiative since 2003.

Jacket photograph of Eddie Van Halen by Jon Sievert.

Library of Congress Cataloging-in-Publication Data
Names: Obrecht, Jas, compiler, interviewer. | University of North
Carolina at Chapel Hill. Library. Southern Folklife Collection.
Title: Talking guitar : conversations with musicians who shaped
twentieth-century American music / Jas Obrecht.
Description: Chapel Hill : University of North Carolina Press in
association with the Southern Folklife Collection, the Louis Round
Wilson Special Collections Library, [2017] | Includes bibliographical
references and index.
Identifiers: LCCN 2016039783| ISBN 9781469631646 (cloth : alk. paper) |
ISBN 9781469631653 (ebook)
Subjects: LCSH: Guitarists—United States—Interviews. | Popular music—
United States—20th century—History and criticism. | LCGFT: Interviews.
Classification: LCC ML3477 .T35 2017 | DDC 787.87092/273—dc23
LC record available at https://lccn.loc.gov/2016039783

MIX
Paper from
responsible sources
FSC
www.fsc.org   FSC® C013483

FOR MICHELLE

L'amore della mia vita . . .

CONTENTS

TALKING GUITAR

Today the guitar seems omnipresent. We see its image on magazine and book covers, posters, T-shirts, company logos, record releases, and the screens of our televisions, computers, and hand-held electronic devices. Turn on a radio, stream a song, walk through a market or mall, experience an ad with audio—chances are, you'll soon hear a guitar in the mix. Shaped and reshaped by amplification, effects devices, and other technological break-throughs, the instrument has been transformed in ways that could scarcely have been imagined at the dawn of the twentieth century. The National Association of Music Merchants, tracker of sales and trends, recently confirmed that the guitar holds its place as the "world's most popular instrument"—by a long shot.[1]

Advances in technology, culture, music, race relations, and the American lifestyle itself fueled the guitar's ascendancy during the twentieth century. The changes, subtle at first, took on momentum as recording methods improved, enabling the instrument to be better heard on records. During the Roaring Twenties a great blossoming of acoustic guitar music occurred—in jazz, blues, country, pop. Innovations of the 1930s led to the first electric guitars. Visionary players such as Charlie Christian and T-Bone Walker were quick to tap the new instrument's potential. During the ensuing decades, the palette of sounds available to guitarists dramatically expanded as pickups were added, solidbody designs came into vogue, strides were made in amplification, and a plethora of effects devices and other innovations hit the market—wah-wah, fuzz, echo, reverb, talk box, whammy bar . . .

With the rise of rock and roll, the guitar fully attained the iconic status it enjoys to this day. By the 1960s guitar styles were evolving with head-spinning velocity—folk, surf, British Invasion, pop, blues-rock, psychedelia. By decade's end, the short, carefully arranged solos of the early rockers had given way to sonic explorations unlike any heard before. In less than a dozen years, the guitar traveled all the way from Chuck Berry's "Johnny B. Goode" to Jimi Hendrix's "The Star-Spangled Banner" at Woodstock. The late 1960s and the 1970s brought the glory years for rock guitar icons and first-call studio players; superlative players likewise emerged in country, jazz, classical, and other genres.

For those of us lucky enough to have experienced this era first-hand, music served as a rallying point, a call for change, a salve, an opportunity to expand one's consciousness. Album releases were an *event*. Friends would eagerly gather around a turntable, unwrap a new platter by Jimi Hendrix, Eric Clapton, Neil Young, Led Zeppelin, the Allman Brothers, or another

1

favorite, and marvel at the sounds blasting through the speakers. "Whoa, man—did you hear *that*?!"

Some of the luckier and better-promoted guitarists found themselves on the covers of magazines devoted entirely to the instrument. The debut issue of *Guitar Player* magazine, the first in the United States, hit music stores in 1967, a few months before the debut of *Rolling Stone*. When I became an editor there in 1978, *Guitar Player* was still the only magazine of its kind. Besides the four editors on our staff, you could pretty much count all of America's full-time "guitar journalists" on one hand. Unlike today's "say it all in five-hundred words and make it sexy" style of music journalism, we were often able to publish full-length, wide-ranging interviews like those found in *Rolling Stone*, *Living Blues*, *Down Beat*, and precious few other magazines. Unlike publications such as *People* and *National Enquirer*, we focused our attention solely on the musical aspects of a celebrity's career and artistry. Because of this approach, guitarists *wanted* to be interviewed by us.

From the beginning, I saw my role as music historian rather than critic. Why dwell in negativity, I figured, when there's so much thrilling music to cover? Before every interview, I'd listen to an artist's entire catalog. I'd research his or her career, poring over reference books, record company bios, and all the previously published magazine and newspaper articles I could find. As I prepared questions, I'd put myself in the place of the interviewee's most dedicated fans and try to ask what they'd ask. It helped considerably that I'd played guitar since childhood.

The best description I've heard of what it takes to be a successful interviewer came from Ry Cooder. We'd been talking about his performing with celebrated players from around the world. "What's the attitude you approach them with?" I asked. "Like you go to a master when you want to learn or be in his presence," Cooder responded. "The thing is to empty yourself. If you're truly committed in a real way, you come across as a receptacle of some kind, a vessel to be filled up. You're not saying, 'Look at what I got. Let's see what you got'—God forbid! You come and just say, 'Imprint me with something.' And if you love the music, are with and for your practice and your ears are open, then the person knows that immediately, because musicians like that have seen everything and they know who's what. There's no faking at that level. You can always tell in a microsecond who's got the vibe and who doesn't. I always have found that people are quite happy to meet you in that spirit. And it's a great process that goes on."[2] In my experience, this same approach holds true for interviewing performers. If you're genuinely interested in learning and come across as selfless, most people will open their hearts to you.

Talking Guitar is not intended to be a complete history of the evolution of American guitars and guitarists during the twentieth century. You'd need a much larger volume—several, probably—to accomplish that feat. Instead, it's a celebration of the instrument as seen through the words, lives, and artistry of some of the century's most beloved and noteworthy players. In these pages, you'll encounter accounts of the first guitarists on record, pioneering bluesmen, gospel greats, jazz innovators, country pickers, rockers and rebels, psychedelic shape-shifters, singer-songwriters, latter-day "guitar gods," and other movers and shakers. You'll learn from the artists themselves how they drew from inspirations, mastered their instruments, found their tones, crafted classic songs, and created enduring solos. Some interviewees dig deeper still, reflecting on themes such as spirituality, the engenderment of creativity, and music as a healing force. Each conversation is unique, naturally; combined, they cover a significant portion of the scope and sweep of American guitar in the twentieth century.

■ ABOUT THE INTERVIEWS

The way musicians speak often mirrors the way they approach their instrument. Stevie Ray Vaughan, for instance, could solo so energetically that sparks seemed to fly off of him. Then, in a heartbeat, he could downshift into the softly sublime. In conversation, he was much the same way—excitedly passionate one moment, quietly confiding the next. By contrast, Eddie Van Halen, especially early in his career, could resemble a human pinball on stage and in conversation, rapidly dinging from one idea to the next. This book strives to accurately convey the exact rhythms of each interviewee's speech.

The majority of these interviews took place between 1978 and 1999, while I was a staff editor for *Guitar Player* and a contributor of guitar-related articles and interviews to *Rolling Stone*, *Living Blues*, *Frets*, and many other magazines. In their original published forms, all of these interviews were edited to various degrees. Some were recast as quotes woven into narrative features. Others originally came out in a Q&A format, but even these were typically sliced-and-diced, rearranged, edited, formatted, and trimmed to fit the available space—standard editorial procedure.

The interviews that appear in *Talking Guitar* have been carefully retranscribed from the original tapes and restored to the way they were originally spoken. For clarity's sake a few very light edits have been made—the removal of an extraneous "um," for instance, or a slight shift in the wording of an otherwise incomprehensible sentence. Naturally, not all of the information revealed in a face-to-face conversation is conveyed via words. Sometimes profound thoughts are transmitted with the wave of a hand, a long thoughtful pause, a roll of the eyes, a tapping of a hand above the heart. In the manner of a playwright's stage directions, I've used bracketed inserts to describe these moments.

Having interviewed many hundreds of guitarists during the past forty years, I had a wealth of material to choose from when preparing the manuscript. Although many are certainly worthy of inclusion, I've omitted interviews currently available in other books, such as my conversations with John Lee Hooker, B. B. King, Buddy Guy, Otis Rush, and other blues artists.[3] In instances where I have done multiple interviews with artists—Clarence "Gatemouth" Brown, Ry Cooder, Ben Harper, Eric Johnson, Carol Kaye, Barney Kessel, Carlos Santana, Joe Satriani, Eddie Van Halen, Stevie Ray Vaughan, and Johnny Winter fall into this category—I chose the conversations I felt offered the most insight and/or best served the book's narrative arc.

The original tapes used for this book, along with my other music-related papers, letters, and audio and video interview recordings, are now part of the University of North Carolina's Southern Folklife Collection in Chapel Hill. Eventually, these will all be digitized and made permanently available to authors, researchers, and fans. I highly recommend visiting this extraordinary archive, which houses the collections of several of my musical and journalistic heroes.

To set the stage for *Talking Guitar*, we'll begin our journey with a brief "guitarchaeology"—an account of the evolution of the guitar and its most important American players from the dawn of the twentieth century to the late 1930s, when the electric guitar began its ascendancy. From there, the players themselves take up the story.

At the dawn of the twentieth century, the guitar was mainly used as a "parlor" instrument suitable for small-group entertainment and serenading. The instrument was typically found in saloons, pool halls, grange lodges, barbershops, and at church services. Even then, the guitar's popularity extended across social, class, and gender boundaries.[1] While guitars were readily available through music stores and mail-order catalogs, few recordings of guitar music were available during the first decade of the 1900s, when most players learned from teachers and sheet music.

In rural areas, many young players started out on homemade stringed instruments. The most common of these, the diddley bow, probably originated in Africa. A diddley bow was typically fashioned by attaching broom or baling wire to nails in a wall or doorframe and using bottles or rocks as bridges. One hand plucked the wire, while the other fretted or glissed the string with a bottle. Many outstanding blues guitarists—Robert Johnson, Elmore James, Muddy Waters, B. B. King, Buddy Guy, and Johnny Winter among them— began this way. Others fashioned primitive guitars by attaching a tin can or cigar box to a rough-hewn neck. Those who could save enough money ordered guitars by mail-order catalog. These guitars, in turn, may offer a clue about how European-influenced parlor music came to exert an influence on the development of American blues, folk, jazz, and country music.

During the latter 1800s, the Lyon & Healy company in Chicago pioneered the mass production of acoustic guitars. By the turn of the century, their many models were sold under various names in catalogs issued by companies such as Sears, Roebuck & Co. and Montgomery Ward. Many of these catalog-bought guitars arrived with a tutorial pamphlet featuring tuning instructions and music for rudimentary instrumentals. Two of the most common of these instructive instrumentals, "Spanish Fandango" and "The Siege of Sebastopol," predated the Civil War. The music for "Spanish Fandango" required that the guitar's strings be tuned to an open-G chord (the strings tuned DGDGBD, from low to high), while "The Siege of Sebastopol" was in open D (DADF#AD). "Spanish Fandango" in particular served as a starting point for countless rural players. Its harmonic content, voice-leading chords, and fingerpicking pattern echoed in the repertoires of old-time blues, folk, and country musicians such as Bo Carter, Son House, Furry Lewis, Frank Hutchison, Sam McGee, John Dilleshaw, Mance Lipscomb, and Elizabeth Cotten. To this day, the word "Spanish" is sometimes used to describe open-G tuning, while "Sebastopol" refers to open D.

John Renbourn, the esteemed British fingerstyle guitarist and an expert on the origins of American guitar music, developed a theory of how these instructional booklets contributed to the creation of the blues in particular: "If you can imagine a field hand sitting down after work and trying to fit an arhoolie [field song] across the basic chords of 'Spanish Fandango,' then you would be close to the moment of transformation, in my opinion. In the early recorded blues of Charley Patton and his school, the harmonic language, right down to specific chord shapes but with bluesy modification usually of one finger only, is straight from parlor music. The same is true for early blues in open D compared to 'Sebastopol.' This is fascinating stuff and fairly controversial, but it fills in the missing gap between the steel-string guitar coming into circulation and the highly developed styles that appeared on recordings in the 1920s."[2] The 1897 Lyon & Healy catalog featured a budget-priced line of steel-string and gut-string guitars. In its 1902 catalog, the Gibson company listed guitars that could be strung with steel or gut strings.

Still, during the first decades of the new century, the banjo was far more popular than the guitar. Since the Civil War, the banjo had been the instrument of choice for solo performers, blackface minstrel troupes, and string bands. With its bright, penetrating sound and lack of sustain, the banjo could hold its own in orchestral settings. The warm, deep resonance of the guitar was better suited for adagios and blues and country songs, and its sustaining notes could be bent or bottlenecked. One fact was inescapable: during the era of the acoustic recording process, when musicians played into recording horns, banjos and mandolins were much easier to record than classical or steel-string guitars. This held true until the mid-1920s, when Western Electric's innovative new electrical recording process and microphones came into widespread use.

■ THE FIRST NORTH AMERICAN GUITAR RECORDINGS

The first North American guitar recordings were most likely made in Mexico City in 1904, when singer Rafael Herrera Robinson was accompanied by a guitarist on Edison cylinders. By year's end, the Victor and Columbia companies had also made forays into Mexico and recorded singers accompanied by guitar. In 1905, the *Edison Phonograph Monthly* credited "An Autumn Evening," a mandolin-guitar instrumental played by Samuel Siegel and M. Lloyd Wolfe, as "the first record ever made by this combination of instruments. It is one that, we think, will please all admirers of both instruments. The music is of a serenade character."[3]

Dick Spottswood, an expert on early recorded music, cites the Edison company's sessions in Havana, Cuba, during the winter of 1905–1906 as another key event: "Of particular interest are two solos by guitarist Sebastian

Hidalgo, who recorded a polka, 'Selva Negra,' and the popular 'Miserere' from Verdi's *Il Trovatore*. Hidalgo's two Edison cylinders (18941 and 19062) are unknown today; nevertheless, they are most likely the earliest recorded guitar solos, at least in the New World."[4] In January 1906 the Ossman-Dudley Trio recorded a half-dozen instrumentals for Victor featuring Vess L. Ossman on banjo, Audley Dudley on mandolin, and his brother George N. Dudley on harp guitar; during the ensuing months, the trio recorded three more sides for Columbia.[5]

Octaviano Yañes, promoted by the Edison company as "the acknowledged champion guitarist of Mexico," recorded his solo guitar instrumental "Habaneras" on October 19, 1908.[6] A copy of this performance survives as a Victor Grand Prize 78. Tim Gracyk, founding editor of the *Victrola and 78 Journal*, observed that "Yañes plays an instrument with at least seven strings. From low to high, it is tuned BEADGBE. Yañes keeps returning to a thunderous, unfretted low-B note, while his low-E notes are also played on an open string. He may have used a seven-string instrument of Mexican or Russian origin (the standard Russian-made import guitar in those days was the seven-string), or a converted eleven-string guitar, many of which had been produced in Andalusia since the 1890s. The bright tone suggests he is playing with his nails very close to the bridge."[7] While we may never ascertain who made the first solo guitar recording in North America, Hidalgo and Yañes deserve credit for their pioneering efforts. During the next few years, many more cylinders and 78s of guitar-based classical, flamenco, and mariachi music were recorded in Cuba, Mexico, and South America.

The next important influx of guitar cylinders and 78s came via Hawaiian musicians, who made the earliest known recordings of slide guitar. Introduced by missionaries, guitars had been popular in Hawaii since the mid-1800s. The first players of note—Joseph Kekuku, James Hoa, and Gabriel Davion—originally used materials such as bolts, pocketknives, combs, and tumblers to gliss the strings with their fretting hands; eventually they settled on steel bars as the slider of choice. Hawaiian guitarists typically held guitars flat on their laps, strings skyward. This lap-style technique came to be known as "steel guitar." Toots Paka's Hawaiians, a popular turn-of-the-century vaudeville act, recorded Edison cylinders in 1909 with Kekuku on steel guitar. These are the first known recordings of Hawaiian slide guitar.[8] In an instructional leaflet, Kekuku claimed that he "originated the Hawaiian Steel Guitar method of playing in the year 1885, at the age of eleven."[9]

Frank Ferera, the most popular and influential Hawaiian steel guitarist, made more recordings between 1915 and 1925 than any other guitarist. "Ferera was the first guitarist to enjoy success as a recording artist," Tim Gracyk explained. "His name was a familiar one in the catalogs of virtually all record companies of the World War I era and 1920s. . . . His popular records must have influenced many generations of guitarists."[10] The December 1916 issue of *Edison Phonograph Monthly* credited Ferera as "the one who introduced the Hawaiian-style of playing the guitar into the United States." The issue also described how Ferera had brought the first ukulele to the United States in 1900.[11]

Hawaiian steel guitar enjoyed a boost in popularity in 1912, thanks to the Broadway sensation *The Bird of Paradise*, with its "weirdly sensual music" played by the Hawaiian Quintette. This guitar-and-ukulele ensemble featuring Walter Kolomoku on steel guitar made twenty-four recordings for Victor during April 1913.[12] Three years later, performances by Hawaiian musicians at the Panama-Pacific International Exhibition in San Francisco provided another important catalyst for the mainland's Hawaiian music craze. The Royal Hawaiian Quartette, with George E. K. Awai front and center on steel guitar, served as the Hawaiian Pavilion's house band. Guest steelers Pale K. Lua, Frank Ferera, and Joseph Kekuku sat in with the group. More than 17 million people visited the seven-month exhibition, and with several shows per day, the Hawaiian Pavilion was considered a must-see. In our interview, Ry Cooder, one of the finest living proponents of slide guitar, describes the impact of these musicians had at the time.

By 1916, most major record companies offered extensive listings of Hawaiian fare. Hawaiian musicians—particularly duos and trios featuring a steel guitarist—became steady draws in North American hotels, theaters, and especially Chinese restaurants. A headline in the September 1916 issue of *Edison Phonograph Monthly* proclaimed "'Hawaiian Music Universally Popular," and described how the style has "taken the United States by storm."[13] Sales of guitars boomed, hundreds of Hawaiian 78s were issued, and music stores displayed Hawaiian-themed sheet music and instructional books. The Hawaiian music fad would continue well into the 1920s, when more advanced guitarists such as Sol Hoopii and King Bennie Nawahi began using metal-bodied National resophonic guitars and flavoring their repertoires with blues, pop, and Tin Pan Alley.

■ THE ROARING TWENTIES

America's first popular non-Hawaiian guitarist, Nick Lucas, emerged in 1922 with his recordings of "Pickin' the Guitar" and "Teasin' the Frets." Issued as a Pathé 78, these have long been considered the first "hot" guitar solos recorded in the United States.[14] In our interview, Nick describes how he was able to overcome the limits of recording technology to etch these performances onto wax. Sylvester Weaver, the first blues guitarist on record, doubtlessly used the same technology the following year when he played on Sara Martin's "Longing for Daddy Blues," the first recording of a singer accompanied by blues guitar. A few days later, Weaver featured the steel guitar slide technique on "Guitar Rag" and "Guitar Blues," the first blues instrumentals on record. While he's lesser-known today than Lucas and Weaver, Sam Moore deserves a standing ovation for his 1921 recording of "Laughing Rag." On this jaunty instrumental, Moore seamlessly blended a ragtime progression with hints of Hawaiian and country influences as he played steel guitar on an unusual—and short-lived—eight-string instrument called an octo-chorda.[15] "Laughing Rag" was covered later by Roy Smeck and recast by Darby and Tarlton, with words, as "Mexican Rag."

As the decade progressed, dozens of groundbreaking guitarists emerged in the genres of popular, blues, jazz, and country music. While Nick Lucas was the most widely known of the 1920s guitar stars, among the most stylistically advanced were Eddie Lang, Lonnie Johnson, and Roy Smeck. Lang made his mark as New York's top studio guitarist, playing expertly on hundreds of records by a who's who of celebrated bandleaders and singers. Lang popularized the Gibson L-5 archtop, which came out circa 1923, and was the catalyst for a major shift in the rhythm section of jazz bands. George Van Eps, who knew Eddie Lang, explained, "He was a natural talent who made love to his guitar instead of beating it to death, which is what most guitarists tried to do. Banjo players *had* to switch to the guitar after hearing Eddie. There were a bunch of die-hards who tuned the guitar like a banjo, but he forced the issue and changed the sound of the rhythm section."[16] Lonnie Johnson, who often recorded with a twelve-string, worked his magic in the areas of urbane blues and jazz, becoming, as Ry Cooder so aptly put it, "one of the transcendental people who influenced *everybody*. You can see people copying him right and left."[17] By a stroke of genius, T. J. Rockwell, an artist manager at OKeh Records, arranged for Lang, who had a profound understanding of harmony, and Johnson, who had the finest technique in blues, to record a series of groundbreaking guitar duets. These records still stand as high-water marks of jazz guitar. Roy Smeck, who idolized Lang, performed in vaudeville as the "Wizard of the Strings." Smeck's uncanny skill on guitar, banjo, steel guitar, and ukulele was on full display on dozens of 78s and two of the earliest sound-on-film theatrical releases.

Beginning in the mid-1920s Paramount Records was responsible for many enduring blues guitar recordings, such as those of Texas country bluesman Blind Lemon Jefferson and Blind Blake, the Southeast's master of ragtime-influenced fingerpicking. Tampa Red, the superlative Chicago slider, worked his magic for Vocalion Records. The OKeh Records roster included Lonnie Johnson, Sylvester Weaver, and songster Mississippi John Hurt, who'd re-emerge in the 1960s, his considerable skills intact. Columbia Records issued Blind Willie Johnson's sublime slide-driven gospel 78s. Blind Willie McTell, one of the finest bluesman of *any* era, recorded for Victor, Columbia, OKeh, Decca, Vocalion, and the Library of Congress. In the years before World War II, many regions of the South—especially those around Atlanta, Georgia; Dallas, Texas; Memphis, Tennessee; and the Mississippi Delta—had their own distinctive blues styles.[18]

Many white country artists emerged during the 1920s. Two acts who'd exert an enduring influence on country guitar—Jimmie Rodgers and the Carter Family—were discovered in 1927, when Ralph Peer, a Victor and former OKeh executive, made a series of field recordings in Bristol, Tennessee. The guitar-strumming Rodgers, the foremost country star of the Roaring Twenties, recorded the earliest versions of several country-music standards, as well as memorable 12-bar blues such as 1929's "Blue Yodel No. 5" and "Jimmie's Texas Blues." In 1930, the Weymann company introduced the Jimmie Rodgers Special model, making Rodgers the first country musician to have a guitar named after him. The Carter Family, with Maybelle Carter on guitar, helped carry traditional American folk music into the mainstream. Chet Atkins, Merle Travis, Earl Scruggs, and many others cited her as a primary influence on their style.[19]

Riley Puckett, old-time country music's foremost guitarist, was best known for his ensemble work with Georgia's most famous string band, Gid Tanner and His Skillet Lickers. On his 1927 solo recording "A Darkey's Wail," Puckett crossed over into bottleneck country blues. Other early country guitarists likewise drew from blues influences. Frank Hutchison, who'd learned his style directly from African-American musicians in rural West Virginia, had a loose, slightly inexact slide technique that surely would have sounded familiar to people used to hearing Southern street musicians. Other standout examples include Sam McGee's "Railroad Blues," a tour de force of sophisticated fingerpicking and string bending, and Dick Justice's decidedly down-home "Brownskin Blues." The duo of Tom Darby and Jimmie Tarlton made many fine slide guitar recordings and scored one of the decade's biggest country hits with "Columbus Stockade Blues." In the long run, the "white country blues" recorded during the 1920s by musicians such as Jimmie Rodgers, Frank Hutchison, the Carter Family, the Allen Brothers, Sam McGee, Darby and Tarlton, and others deserve credit for helping to inaugurate racial and stylistic integration in the blues, a trend that continues to this day. By decade's end, guitar-strumming singing cowboys such as Carl T. Sprague and Gene Autry had also issued hit recordings.

The onset of the Great Depression in 1929 devastated many American businesses. The recording industry provided no exception, especially in the field of blues records. Paramount Records, for instance, was still going strong when it held its legendary May 1930 session with Mississippi Delta blues musicians Charley Patton, Son House, Willie Brown, and Louise Johnson. By 1932, the company had ceased its recording activities, and three years later shuttered its doors. Blues artists on larger labels were impacted as well. In 1929, for instance, Columbia Records pressed 2,205 copies of Blind Willie McTell's "Travelin' Blues" / "Come on Around to My House Mama," followed by a second run of 2,000.[20] Three years later, McTell's new Victor 78 of "Lonesome Day Blues" / "Searching the Desert for the Blues" sold only 124 copies.[21] Sales of white hillbilly artists tended to be stronger, but as the Depression deepened, artists across the board were affected. As Dick Spottswood noted, "The years from 1930 to 1934 were the worst in the short history of sound recording. No company besides Victor emerged intact from those years."[22]

■ THE BIRTH OF THE ELECTRIC GUITAR

On the guitar innovation front, by contrast, the early 1930s proved to be a watershed. The acoustic instrument's lack of volume had plagued guitarists since the cylinder era. The introduction of resonator guitars by National and Dobro in the 1920s helped guitarists conjure a louder sound, as did the new larger-bodied f-hole archtops offered by Gibson and Epiphone and the Martin company's dreadnought models of the early 1930s. But unless used for comping, these all-acoustic guitars still had difficulty being heard alongside other instruments on a bandstand. That would all change with the invention of the electric pickup.

Music instrument manufacturers had primarily focused their early efforts on electrically amplifying violins and keyboards. Then, in its October 20, 1928, issue, *Music Trade Review* reported that the Stromberg-Voisinet company, the forerunner of the Kay guitar company, had developed a method for electromagnetically amplifying a guitar: "The tone amplifier is electrically operated, either by alternating or direct current. It consists of two major units—an electro-magnetic pick-up and an amplifying unit. The electro-magnetic pick-up is built within the instrument and is attached to its sounding board. The unit is connected with the amplifier, which produces the tone volume required of the instrument."[23] Lynn Wheelwright, an expert on the earliest electric guitars, clarifies that this electromagnetic pickup "was most likely the driver for a speaker. It used a metal reed, which vibrated within the magnetic field and was driven by a rod attached to the soundboard."[24] The following year, Stromberg-Voisinet ran an advertisement depicting a pair of electric flat-top guitars alongside a pair of electric banjos.[25] These guitars, however, were not a commercial success.

The electric guitar revolution began in earnest in October 1931 with the founding of the Los Angeles–based Ro-Pat-In Corporation, the first company devoted entirely to the production of electric instruments. George Beauchamp, the company's cofounder, designed a pickup that consisted of six magnetically energized pole pieces—one for each string—surrounded by a wire coil that, in turn, was surrounded by a pair of horseshoe-shaped magnets. "In concept," wrote guitar historian Walter Carter, "it was the modern electric guitar pickup."[26] In 1932 Ro-Pat-In applied its new technology to the first solidbody electric guitar, a Hawaiian steel nicknamed the "Frying Pan" due to its odd shape, which resembled a frying pan with a round body and long, handle-like neck. The prototype Frying Pan was made of wood, but the production models, introduced in the fall of 1932, were cast aluminum. "A grand total of thirteen Frying Pans were sold in 1932," Carter detailed. "Ro-Pat-In also introduced a Spanish-neck, f-hole model with a wood body supplied by the Harmony company of Chicago, and four of these models were sold in 1932."[27] (During this era, the term "Spanish-neck guitar" referred to a standard-shaped guitar played the standard way.) The following year Ro-Pat-In changed its name to Electro String Instrument Company and created the "Richenbacher Electro" badge that began appearing on its pegheads. Today the company is known as Rickenbacker.

By mid-1932 the Vivi-Tone company also began producing standard-shaped electrically amplifiable flat-top guitars. Unlike the Ro-Pat-In model, ViVi-Tone's earliest electric guitar was a "plank" model. "It had a 3/16-inch thick ply top," Lynn Wheelwright detailed, "supported by a heavy wood spine and no back or sides. By the end of 1932 ViVi had built around a hundred of these in various configurations, including violins, mandolins, mandocellos, and four- and six-string guitars. These skeletal-looking instruments were available by mid-1932, and the ViVi-Tone archtops by spring 1933. ViVi-Tone's total production reached about six-hundred instruments, the majority being electric."[28] Despite its innovative nature, ViVi-Tone was not commercially successful, and the company folded in 1936. Wheelwright explained: "I suspect that the problem with the ViVi-Tones was they would come out of adjustment easily when dropped or banged around, causing the vibration-transfer pickup to misalign and stop working properly."[29]

Soon other companies were offering electric guitars. In 1932 National and Dobro merged to become National-Dobro. Wheelwright's research into recently discovered company letters and advertisements confirms that the new company had a working electric guitar by late 1933: "This was essentially a solidbody that used direct string vibration over an electromagnetic humbucking pickup. Considering the number of survivors, they had decent production. National-Dobro also launched a line of high-quality ES archtops by mid 1935."[30] By late 1935, three other prominent companies had entered the electric-guitar market. Gibson's first pickup-equipped guitar, a small metal-body EH—for "Electric Hawaiian"—was a steel guitar in the shape of a standard guitar, while Epiphone's Electar steel had more of a tear-drop body shape. Epiphone also came out with the first of its Spanish-style electric archtops, while the Regal company's first electric Spanish guitar, as Wheelwright described, "was, for all purposes, a solidbody with no sound holes, a heavily braced 3/8-inch laminated top, and a twelve-pole humbucking pickup. It sounded incredible and had no obnoxious 60-cycle hum."[31]

In 1936 Gibson introduced the pre-war era's most successful electric guitar, the ES-150; the "ES" designation indicated "Electric Spanish," while the "150" referred to its original price of $150, including the amplifier. This instrument, and the pricier ES-250, were popularized by Charlie Christian during his celebrated stint with the Benny Goodman Sextet and Orchestra. Still, during the 1930s sales of steel guitars far outstripped those of Electric-Spanish models. According to Lynn Wheelwright, "Rickenbacker made only a handful of ES guitars, but probably over a thousand EH units. The same was true of Gibson, Epiphone, and National-Dobro, but not to such an unbalanced extent. There were large Hawaiian guitar clubs all over the country."[32] Around 1938, the Slingerland company of Chicago began offering its Spanish-neck Songster model, which George Gruhn and Walter Carter cite as "the first production solidbody model from any maker prior to World War II that comes close to postwar solidbody standards."[33]

■ THE PLAYERS ADAPT

While Alvino Rey's name is not widely known today, in the 1930s he was at the forefront of promoting the electric guitar. Lynn Wheelwright, who now owns Charlie Christian's ES-250, worked as Rey's guitar tech for many years. "Alvino is best known for his 'talking guitar' and as the father of the pedal steel," he explained, "but he was so much more. He should be known as the 'Godfather of the Electric Guitar.' He was a very early advocate of the technology. He was playing electric banjo with Phil Spitalny's Orchestra in New York in late 1928. By October 1932 he had one of the first Frying

Pans, which he put to use on his twice-daily radio show out of San Francisco. He also used his Vivi-Tone electric, plugging it straight into the radio station's console. He was the first electric guitar player on coast-to-coast radio. I would credit Alvino with putting this newfangled electric gadget, which at the time was considered an expensive parlor trick, into use and into the ears of the public. He made it acceptable and proved to other musicians as well as bandleaders that it had a legitimate place on the bandstand. Alvino was the most important electric guitar player of the early- to mid-1930s. When Gibson was looking to get into the electric market, they enlisted Alvino's help in May 1935. He was the first official electric guitar endorser for any company and one of the highest paid front men for any band—and all with an electric guitar."[34]

Soon after its introduction, the electric Hawaiian guitar made its debut on record. Dick Spottswood detailed, "The earliest known recordings of an electrically amplified guitar were made for Victor by Noelani's Hawaiian Orchestra."[35] Their initial session, which took place in New York City on February 22, 1933, produced six sides. On a few of the songs Noelani Lopez (or "Lopes," as her name was sometimes spelled) sang lead vocals to the accompaniment of guitar, banjo-guitar, ukulele, and electric steel guitar. Joseph Lopez, who'd been performing on steel guitar since at least the mid-1920s, was credited as the composer of the session's final selection, the steel guitar solo "Hawaiian Love-Waltz," which suggests that he may have been the steeler on these historic recordings. A subsequent Victor 78 of "Hawaiian Love-Waltz," by the Hilo Hawaiian Orchestra, spelled his last name "Lopes" in the songwriter credit, so perhaps he was related to Noelani. In September 1933, Noelani's Hawaiian Orchestra made additional records featuring an electrified Hawaiian steel guitar. By 1934 other Hawaiian musicians—notably Andy Iona and His Islanders and Sol Hoopii—were using electrified steel guitars.

In 1935, the first western swing records featuring electric guitars hit the market. That January, Milton Brown's Musical Brownies made stellar recordings with Bob Dunn's electrified slide guitar prominently featured in the mix. In his youth, Dunn had seen a Hawaiian group performing in Oklahoma, and he'd subscribed to Walter Kolomoku's correspondence lessons.[36] His instrument at the Musical Brownies sessions was a heavily modified round-hole acoustic. "The Martin O-series model acoustic he cradled in his lap was anything but typical," wrote country music historian Rich Kienzle. "A Volo-Tone pickup was mounted over the soundhole, and a wire ran from the pickup to a small, nondescript amplifier. The Martin's strings had been raised to permit Hawaiian-style playing. Among the songs he used it on that day were

'Chinatown, My Chinatown,' 'Sweet Georgia Brown,' 'St. Louis Blues,' and his own composition, 'Taking Off,' which has since become a western swing standard."[37] On September 23–25, 1935, Leon McAuliffe, a brilliant player from Tulsa, Oklahoma, whose phrasing could well have influenced Charlie Christian, featured both electric steel and electrically amplified Spanish guitar on the first recordings by Bob Wills's Texas Playboys. Three days after the Wills session ended, Jim Boyd also used an electrically amplified Spanish guitar while recording "Hot Dog Stomp" with his brother's band, Bill Boyd's Cowboy Ramblers.[38] From then on, electrically amplified guitars played an integral role in western swing music.

On the jazz front, Eddie Durham is a contender for being the first to record an electrically amplified solo. A skilled arranger who doubled on trombone, Durham began experimenting with acoustically amplifying a standard guitar while a member of Bennie Moten's band in the 1920s. To compete with the volume of Moten's horn players, who occasionally soloed through megaphones, Durham first used a radically modified instrument: "I got one of those tin pie pans and carved out my acoustic guitar's top and put it down in there," he explained. "It was the size of a breakfast plate. When you'd hit those strings, the pie pan would ring and shoot out the sound. I'd also use a megaphone with it. I didn't have that for too long, though, because I got a National steel guitar. It had a resonator in it, and it was usually played with a bar. I removed the bridge and put an acoustic-type bridge on it so the action was lower. I fooled around with that for a long time, and nobody else was playing a guitar like that back then. The neck was too thick, though. There was no such thing as two microphones in bands; they only had one. I used to let them stick the mike near the resonator and I'd be just as loud as anything else. I wouldn't do rhythm, though—no way. I did solo work."[39]

In early 1935 Eddie Durham joined Jimmie Lunceford and His Orchestra. At first, he recalled, "I went back to using a wooden guitar. I used to let Lunceford put the microphone up to the f-hole. Then later on DeArmond came out with a pickup, which I got, but they didn't have sound amplifiers. So I'd get any kind of amp I could find and sit it on the corner of the stage and run a cord to the guitar, and that was it. And if we were playing in a big auditorium, I'd go directly into the sound system. You couldn't play rhythm like that because it was too loud. I used to blow out the lights in a lot of places; they really weren't up on electricity like they are now. I'd just play solo work, and I think that at that time I was the only guy playing that kind of guitar in a jazz band."[40] While Leonard Feather and other jazz historians have cited Lunceford's September 30, 1935, recording of "Hittin' the Bottle" as the first jazz recording to feature an electrically amplified guitar, aural evidence suggests it could have been done with a resonator guitar. There's no doubt, though, that Durham used an electric guitar to solo on Count Basie and His Orchestra's August 9, 1937, recording of "Time Out," as well as for his 1938 discs with the Kansas City Six.[41] During this time, Durham was photographed with a National electric guitar.

Other early electric guitarists encountered problems onstage. Eldon Shamblin, who played alongside Leon McAuliffe in Bob Wills's band, recalled his 1938 effort to electrify his archtop: "We had a man right here in Tulsa, Bob Ridley, build an amplifier, and I used a little crystal mike on my Gibson Super 400. I had to cut a notch in my bridge to slide that little crystal mike under. This was the most horrible thing that you ever heard in your life! This would nearly make a man go commit suicide. One night you'd play it, your E string would be hotter than a pistol, and you couldn't hear your B or G [strings]. The next night maybe your B was hot, and the others wouldn't sound. I think about that point Gibson came out with an amplified guitar. I had a Gibson guitar and a Gibson amplifier. I don't remember what model it was, but it was one of the first ones to come out. It wasn't very good, really."[42]

On the blues front, the vast majority of 1930s recordings featured acoustic guitar. A few performers, notably Blind Willie McTell and Lead Belly, preferred twelve-string guitars, while their counterparts in the Mississippi Delta and other regions favored six-string instruments. The first person to play an electric guitar on a blues record was probably a white, sixteen-year-old studio musician in Chicago, George Barnes. On March 1, 1938, Barnes backed Big Bill Broonzy, a fine guitarist in his own right, on "Sweetheart Land" and "It's a Low Down Dirty Shame." Immediately afterward, he accompanied Curtis Jones singing the same two songs. Barnes highlighted his sophisticated performances with unusual string bends. Within a few weeks, he had also played electric guitar on sessions with Hattie Bolton, Blind John Davis, Jazz Gillum, Merline Johnson, and others. On October 18, 1938, Lonnie Johnson, who Barnes credited with teaching him how to play blues guitar, used an electric guitar for the first time during a Peetie Wheatstraw session. Tampa Red began recording with an electric guitar that December, followed by Big Bill Broonzy in July 1939. In 1941, Memphis Minnie became the first woman to play electric guitar on blues records.

It would take Charlie Christian, an extraordinary twenty-three-year-old from Oklahoma City, to demonstrate the full potential of the electric guitar in a jazz setting. In 1939 Columbia Records producer John Hammond arranged for Christian to audition for Benny Goodman. At this time, in Hammond's estimation, there were essentially two electric guitarists in jazz: "One was Leonard Ware in New York. I had him on my third Spirituals to Swing concert, in 1938, but unfortunately the machine in which he recorded had a 'wow' in it, so we were never able to put those things out. He was very good, but he was not in Charlie's class. Charlie was an original. There's never been anybody like Charlie on the guitar. He was a complete revolutionary. The other jazz guitar player was Floyd Smith, but he played a Hawaiian guitar, you know. And Hawaiian guitar is bad enough, but amplified, it was excruciating!"[43] Ware, who didn't do much recording, used an electric guitar on several 78s cut with Sidney Bechet and His Orchestra in November 1938. Floyd Smith made his mark in jazz history on March 6, 1939, when he recorded "Floyd's Guitar Blues," played on slide guitar, while a member of Andy Kirk and His Twelve Clouds of Joy. Leonard Feather wrote of the release, "A minor sensation, it was the trigger for the whole fusillade of new guitar styles to be issued only months later by Charlie Christian's arrival in New York. With the advent of Christian, the guitar came of age in jazz."[44]

Christian's solos on 78s and radio broadcasts with the Benny Goodman Sextet and Orchestra rapidly made him the best-known electric guitarist in jazz. Players across the country studied his solos and longed for guitars like his Gibson ES-150 and ES-250. Forty years after Christian's death in 1941, Benny Goodman still had unabashed enthusiasm for his former bandmate: "He was unique! A brilliant musician. Inventive. He was way ahead of his time, and a joy to listen to. He was rather shy, but by gosh, when he sat down and played the guitar, he was something! He was an amazing player to listen to. He contributed a great deal to jazz, and a lot of people were influenced by him, including me."[45] And, as leading Christian disciple Barney Kessel says in our interview, "The music Charlie made changed the world."

During the Roaring Twenties, Nick Lucas and the steel-string guitar seemed nearly inseparable. By July 1922, Nick had already secured his place in music history by waxing the first hot guitar solos released in the United States, "Pickin' the Guitar" and "Teasin' the Frets," both of which he composed. Framing his warm, pure tenor with agile guitar parts, Lucas scored his first major hit two years later, "My Best Girl." With his many recordings and frequent radio appearances, this warm, effervescent Italian-American helped introduce a generation of listeners to the sound of a beautifully played flat-picked acoustic guitar. Lucas went on to win rave reviews on Broadway, give command performances to European royalty, and costar in the 1929 Technicolor film *Gold Diggers of Broadway*. In one of the film's highlights, Lucas crooned the biggest hit of his career, "Tip-Toe Thru the Tulips with Me," accompanying himself on his ornate Gibson Nick Lucas Special, the first artist-endorsed guitar. By then "The Crooning Troubadour" was America's most famous guitarist. His smiling, tuxedo-clad image adorned stacks of sheet music and guitar instruction books. Music stores featured displays of Nick Lucas guitar picks, which were offered in a wide variety of materials and styles for decades to come.

As Nick's influence and popularity were eclipsed by others—Eddie Lang, Django Reinhardt, and Charlie Christian among them—he soldiered on, making records and playing nightclubs. He was featured in several 1930s Vitaphone shorts, and during World War II starred in four Soundies, which were the forerunners of MTV-era music videos. His later years found him gigging in casinos, playing conventions, and appearing on television. When pop sensation Tiny Tim married Miss Vicki on the *Tonight Show*—to an audience of 40 million—Nick was there, performing "Tip-Toe Thru the Tulips" in the background.

In the late 1970s, I learned that Nick Lucas was alive and well, living in semiretirement at The Fontenoy apartments on North Whitley in Hollywood. From his sixth-floor apartment windows, he could watch guitar-carrying students make their way to the nearby Guitar Institute of Technology, unaware that they were walking past the man who laid the groundwork for everyone from Eddie Lang and Charlie Christian to Eddie Van Halen, Joe Satriani, and Steve Vai. Nick was happy to receive my telephone call and quickly agreed to do an interview. Our conversation took place on September 3, 1980. Early on, I asked Nick about how guitar recordings were made during the era of wax masters and the big recording horn.

Are you up for doing an interview now?

Oh, sure. I'm ready to go.

I hope you don't mind going back in your career a little bit.

Well, all you gotta do is ask questions. Everything you have in mind, why, I'll be glad to answer 'em. How far back do you want to go?

To about 1906, with your brother Frank.

[*Laughs.*] Yeah!

Learning mandolin?

Yeah. 1906 was just about the time. I was in grammar school; I was just about eight, nine years old. First of all, before I started with my brother Frank, he wanted me to study music without an instrument—solfeggio, which I studied from a Sicilian maestro, they called them in those days. That's all they did is teach music without an instrument. They taught the fundamentals of the music, of timing, and things like that. I studied that for about a year, and then he put me on the mandolin, because in those days mandolin was the dominant instrument with the Italians and with the general public. Of course, it wasn't a commercial instrument; it was mostly for house entertainment—playing weddings and christenings and things like that. This was in Newark, New Jersey. That's where I was born.

Was your name originally Nick Lucas?

No, my original name was Dominic. My baptismal name was Dominic Nicholas Antonio Lucanese. That's an Italian name. Antonio was taken after some of my relatives; I guess they always like to include them. So actually I had four names. My first name was Dominic, I understand, due to the fact that I was born on a Sunday. "Domenica" means "Sunday" in Italian.

So after that, after I had a little knowledge of the fundamentals of music, he put me on the mandolin. My brother Frank was a very versatile musician. He was a thorough musician. He played the accordion, and in those days the accordion was *it*. It was a very, very popular instrument. And he wanted me to play the mandolin so that I could go with him on different occasions. I played weddings and christenings, because we did come from a very, very poor family. In those days, money was scarce and the wages were very poor. However, the living in those days was very, very inexpensive also, so there was no problem there. My father was working, of course. My brother would take me along with him, playing at weddings and christenings and saloons, passing the hat around, which I did. And we played in streetcars and passed the hat around. We played on street corners—anything to make a dollar, so that we could help the family along.

So Frank was a couple of years older?

Yes. I might say Frank was about five or six years older. He was born in

Italy. They migrated from Italy in the early 1890s, because I was born in 1897. And he was the first. Then my sister, who passed away about a year ago—she was eighty-five—she was second, and then I was third. I was number three. There was another sister, and then there was three more brothers. Two of them are alive now. There's only three left in the family—my brother Lib and my brother Anthony, they're both alive. They're musically inclined, but not professionally.

So my brother took me around to play all these Italian weddings and christenings, and we got the big sum of a dollar an hour. All this work that I did for him gave me all the practice I needed, especially on the right hand, to get that tremolo and that technique. I had to study the mandolin under his tuition, and he was very stern. He really helped me. He gave me all the musical education that I ever needed. After that we parted, because he went into vaudeville with an act called The Three Vagrants. And then after I graduated school I was on my own, and I got a job in a nightclub in Newark, New Jersey, called The Johnson's Cafe. This was in 1915.

Were you playing guitar yet?

No. Believe it or not, I was playing . . . they wanted more volume than a guitar, so I got myself a banjorine, which is a mandolin with a banjo head on it. And in order to get volume, I played the mandolin. That was my basic instrument. My brother, in the interim, he thought he wanted me to play a guitar, so there would be more volume as a background, because the mandolin is primarily a lead instrument. He also started me on the guitar, so I became as good on the guitar as I was on the mandolin. But when I first started, I played the mandolin in the nightclub and bought myself a banjorine. They were available in those days—anything that sounded like a banjo.

So I played with this big orchestra that consisted of three men [*laughs*]— piano, violin, and the banjorine. And we played the revue. They had nightclub revues—like, they had a soprano singer, a comic, a line of girls, and a male singer. And that was the revue. The show lasted about two hours. And we played just with three pieces until eventually it went haywire—they put in a drummer! This was in Newark, and of course Newark is a short jump from New York. Naturally, I got all the work in town, because there was only very few musicians available in Newark who qualified to play for these nightclubs. You had to be a good faker. You had to read quick, you know. And most of 'em was fakin.' They'd say, "Oh, play it in C or play it in D, put it up in F, put it down a key," and if you couldn't do that, the music didn't mean a damn thing. When I went to the musicians' union, I had to take a regular musical test, pass an examination, so I could get my union card. Of course, they don't do that today. They give you a card. Just pay your initiation fee, and you're in.

This is where I got all my experience. I was there two years, working with this outfit—the piano, violin, banjorine—and I doubled on the guitar when we had to play waltzes and things like that. The guitar just came in handy. From there, I went on to another nightclub in Newark called The Iroquois with another combo. I had the great experience of playing with one of the greatest jazz pianists of that era, Blanche Merrill. She played that boogie-woogie piano. She used to live in New York too. We also had violin and drums. Oh, this was giving me all the experience and the qualifications of becoming a great jazz musician—unbeknownst to me.

Was the money good enough to survive on?

I'll tell you, the salary on the first job I got in Newark when I played in a nightclub was $20 a week. And I thought that was good then. I was in demand in Newark, and Newark was a wide-open town in those days. They had nightclubs all over, and everything went—gambling, prostitution, everything was wide open. Then when I got another job at The Iroquois, they gave me $25. I bettered myself from $20 to $25.

And then we formed a unit called the Original Kentucky Five. In those days, they leaned on the South, like Dixieland jazz bands were very famous. So I got myself a group called the Kentucky Five, and I toured the Interstate circuit and the Keith circuit as a backup to the Ziegler Twins—they did a vaudeville act. I had a violin, and I had alto sax, piano, drums, and myself. I would say that was in the years of 1919 and 1920. I got married in 1917, then my daughter was born in 1918, so naturally I couldn't stay on the road too long. I only stayed on tour with this Kentucky Five, which I originated, for about a year because I had to come home. My wife had my only daughter, and I had to get myself a job around town. So I got myself a job in New York with Sam Lanin. And at that time Sam Lanin was the kingpin of New York. He did all the recording dates—well, I wouldn't say all, but most of it. I was working with him at the Roseland Ballroom. I played tenor banjo. I got myself a tenor banjo.

So the volume could cut through the orchestra.

Yeah. And I had the guitar alongside of it at all times for when we played waltzes. It was very difficult to play a three-quarter beat on the banjo, so the guitar came in handy. It blended better with waltzes. I had such great musicians as Jules Levy—that goes way back—on trumpet. We had two bands on the stand. One would stop, and then immediately the other would continue. Those were the days when it was five cents a dance, ten cents. You remember that, way back? You buy tickets and pick up a dame there and dance with her, and that's how they survived. The other band was called Mel Hallett, who was very popular up around the Boston area. And there was a fellow playing piano there with Mel Hallett by the name of Frankie Carle. He became a great pianist.

How did you break into recording?

I did all of Sam Lanin's recording dates. In fact, sometimes I'd do two a day. The sessions were from 9:00 until 1:00, and then from 2:00 to 5:00, and then I still did my job at night. And I had a contract with Sam, getting $90 a week. And the phonograph dates, all they paid was $20—that was the scale then. So I made $40 a day, and I practically worked there every day—four or five days a week—making those record dates. I was making a pretty good salary. $200 or $300 a week—that was a lot of money!

What was a recording session like in the early 1920s?

We always had trouble with the recording dates, because in those days they had the old cylinder wax. They had a big box in the back, and they keep all these waxes in the box always heated up. And the wax was pretty thick. We only had one horn to catch all the music into the cylinder to record. We didn't have microphones—this was the days before microphones. And we had the conventional combination, like three saxes and two trumpets and a trombone, piano, tuba, and a rhythm banjo. Guitar was unheard of. And we—that means the tuba and myself—had to sit way back in the studio, because when you blow notes out of a tuba, if it's too loud, that needle would jump off the cylinder and they'd have to start all over again. Very sensitive. And the banjo was the same thing, because it was a penetrating instrument. So I thought of an idea one morning of bringing my guitar to the studio. And Sam says, "What you gonna do with that?" I said, "Well, Sam, I'm having so damn much trouble with the banjo, let me try the guitar." He said, "Well, Nick, they won't hear it." I said, "Well, put me closer to the horn." So he got me right under the horn.

Now, this is a great big horn. Visualize a great big horn, like you see advertised by the Victor Phonograph Company, the great big one with the dog. Well, that's what we had. So he put me under the horn, and the instrument was there. The rhythm was more smoother, and we didn't have any trouble with the needle jumping out of the grooves. So he said, "Gee, Nick, that's all right. Keep it in." So that was the beginning of me playing guitar on record dates. Now, I would say that was around 1921 or '22, something like that. I still worked with Sam for a while, then I worked with Vincent Lopez at the Peking Cafe on 45th Street. That was a hot spot, and in those days, Vincent Lopez was very, very hot in New York. He couldn't do anything wrong.

Did you record "Teasin' the Frets" around this time?

No. "Teasin' the Frets" was done while I was working with Sam with a different group, with a fellow called Don Parker. And on "Teasin' the Frets" and "Pickin' the Guitar," I did that all by myself. That was on Pathé Records. The sessions were from about 10:00 until 1:00, and I was all by myself. All I had was the musical director and the technicians in the studio. Nobody else. They were recorded in New York at the Pathé Phonograph Company on 42nd Street.

Did you compose those tunes?

Yes.

I've heard that those are the first recorded guitar solos.

I seem to agree with you on that. Now, I haven't done any research work on it, but I think they were the first ones.

Do you remember what kind of guitar you used for them?

Oh, yes. The guitar I started on, which was called a Galliano, made in New York by the Galliano Company. It was a small company located on Mulberry Street. I wasn't associated with Gibson until later, when I left New York. I went to join Ted Fiorito, who was an old friend of mine from Newark, and he had a band in Chicago called the Oriole Terrace Orchestra. He was at the Edgewater Beach Hotel there, and he sent for me. He asked me if I would be interested in coming out there, and he offered me $150 a week. And so my wife and daughter and I got in the car and drove out there. This was in 1923. It took us about four days to get there, because in those days they didn't have the route numbers. It was town to town—next town, next town. Of course, that was only day driving—I never drove at night because you'd get lost. You wouldn't know where the hell to go.

At that time I still had my Galliano. And when I went to Chicago, naturally we were a big hit there at the Edgewater Beach Hotel. We were booked for two weeks, and we stayed there almost three years. That was where I got my big break on radio. In those days, radio was the only media of entertainment. WEBH, Chicago—that was the studio. In the interim between sets, I used to go into the studio, which was right adjacent to our bandstand, and fill in some time with my guitar and sing and kind of croon. And that's when I started to get mail from all over the country. This wasn't a network by any means; it was just that they all had these crystal sets and they would tune in and get me all through the night. I got loads of mail, and I started to become very, very popular.

How did Gibson's Nick Lucas model come about?

The Gibson instrument company, which was located in Kalamazoo, approached me. This was in 1924. They wanted me to play their guitar, but

I said, "Geez, I got a great instrument now. I'm very happy with it and it sounds good. However, if you can make me a guitar to my specification, I'll be glad to make the change." I had no ties or contract with Galliano by any means, because I bought it for $35. So Gibson said, "We'll do anything to make you satisfied." At that time, the guitar was practically obsolete—it was going out. They had to do something. But by the same token it was coming in, so they made a guitar for me called the Nick Lucas model.

What was distinctive about it?

Well, the distinction was this: the neck board was a little wider. They made the neck board in those days—and they still make 'em today—a little bit too narrow, because you can't get a true tone out of some of your chords because the strings are so close together. I don't have an exceptionally big hand, but I wanted more room between the E and the B string, especially, for when I played a G chord or a C chord. See, then all the notes would come out distinct. I wouldn't get any interference with my flesh on the fingers. So they made a little wider fingerboard.

What happened to the original Nick Lucas guitar?

I still have it! I still play it! I still use it! It's a gem. It's been fixed about forty times, but I still use it. I wouldn't part with it. And I also said that I want a little wider body than the usual, and I want it black, and I want it so it don't shine, because the spotlight would shine on a guitar and it would glare all around the people in the audience. So they came up with this Nick Lucas model, which was a beauty!

When did you make the transition from guitar star to singing star?

With the Oriole Orchestra I was becoming very popular through the radio. I wasn't getting any money for it—this was all gratis. So that was my first stepping-stone to becoming a success as a singer and a performer. And then Brunswick Phonograph Company, which was located in Chicago, heard me and they signed me up to record. And I made a record there called "My Best Girl" and "Dreamer of Dreams," which was my first vocal recording—all by myself, in the old horn, no microphones. I sang in the horn and I made this recording, and it was a terrific seller. And then I left the band to go on my own. At the time I was with Dan Russo and Ted Fiorito, and I left them in December 1924. In the interim, I made the record, and the record was catching on all over the country. I was in demand. They wanted me to make personal appearances all over the United States. My first big theater engagement was at the Chicago Theater in December 1924. This was as a solo act. A friend of mine, Bert Wheeler, heard me sing and told his New York agent about me. He said, "Come out and catch this guy—he's great. I know he's gonna become somebody." So he did. We didn't sign a contract, but we had a

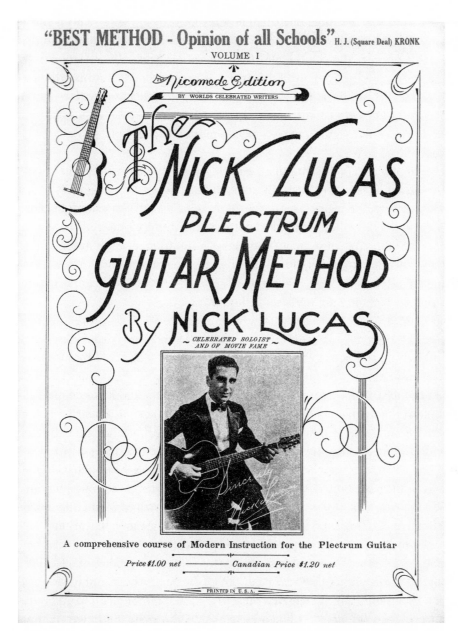

Nick Lucas guitar picks and instructional books were commonplace in music stores for decades. (Courtesy Jas Obrecht)

handshake, and we were together for about fifteen, twenty years. From then on I played vaudeville.

My next big break from there came when I played the Palace Theatre in New York. That was the epitome of all. That was tops! I went into the Palace of New York, and I was a big hit there. Now, England was big in those days. I played at the Cafe des Paris, and the Prince of Wales and the Queen of Spain were in to see my show one night. Then they had me entertain for them privately about two weeks later. That's when I got publicity all around the world, and from then on, I couldn't do anything wrong. When I came back to America, naturally I had all the work I wanted to, and I continued to play in vaudeville, because that was the only thing around. Vaudeville was it. I played the Orpheum, Keith—I played all the circuits. I was making $3,000 a week. That's like $30,000 today—maybe more! All by myself. All I was doin' was singin'!

Your wife and family must have been happy.

They sure were! As I said, this all came unexpectedly, because in those days, entertainers were far and few between. I used to play a lot of solos, but in those days they wanted to hear me sing. And today they still want to hear me sing. My voice, thank goodness, is still in excellent condition. Because I quit in 1965. I was working steady. I worked for Harrah's Club in Reno and Tahoe for eight years, had my own group. But that was too tough on my throat, so I quit in 1965. My voice today is better than ever. But the people in those days, and even today, they want to hear me sing. The guitar is a part of my act. See, nobody can play for me. When I sing, then I play for myself. I improvise, I play runs in between, and I play a little solo. Like I'll play "Baby Face," and maybe I'll play sixteen bars on the guitar.

In those days, the entertainers that were successful and very famous, I could count them on one hand. There was Eddie Cantor, Al Jolson, and Bing Crosby. And I was in that era. I was before Bing Crosby, but I wasn't before Eddie Cantor, though. He was way before me, as was Al Jolson, because I was practically a schoolboy when they were around. But my ambition was to be as good as them, but I never try to copy anybody. Never try to copy anybody. I try to be myself. When I record, I use my own ideas, and I felt I was a little unique due to the fact that my guitar and my voice blended. It was one.

My voice is me. My guitar comes second, but the guitar is the one that made me. Without the guitar, I wouldn't be what I am today. Lucas without a guitar wouldn't be Nick Lucas. I'm not saying this in the spirit of conceit, by any means, but I feel that most of these contemporary guitar players studied from my books. I had two books on the market. They came out around '26 or '27, right after I became popular on records. Then when I got to 1929 and played the Orpheum Theater in Los Angeles, that's when I got my biggest break, with the *Gold Diggers of Broadway*. I was working there at the Orpheum Theater, and this was big-time. I was on the bill with Sophie Tucker and Jack Benny and myself. That's pretty stiff company, isn't it? But I was learning as I was going along, watching these performers. I was very observative, and I learned how to get on and off stage, and that wasn't easy.

It took me 15 years to learn how to take a bow. Today they do it overnight. So that's where I got my biggest break, with "Tip-Toe Thru the Tulips." In fact, on April 15th of this year, the Variety Arts Club that I belong to gave me a big testimonial honoring fifty years of "Tip-Toe Thru the Tulips." I never dreamed that a song would become synonymous with my name all these years. And still, no matter where I go, it's "Tip-Toe Thru the Tulips."

And it's such an optimistic song.

Oh, yeah. I only hope to write another one like it. You see, you never know, when you're in show business, about a song until you sing it to the public. I might think it's great—every songwriter thinks every song he writes is great—but not until the public decides upon it, because they are the ones that buy it.

Many famous guitarists have credited you with inspiring them to play.

I feel that I helped all these contemporary guys way, way back. Gene Autry said, "Without Nick Lucas, I wouldn't be playing the guitar."

Merle Travis also said he was influenced by you.

Merle Travis—he's a fine guy. I'll tell you another one—Barney Kessel. He's a great musician. And even Roy Clark said that he studied from my books. Now, I'm ignorant of that until they tell me. The first book was for beginners, and then I had a little advanced one. It was a beginning book for ordinary musicians, because contemporary guitar players in those days, they didn't know from nothing. They wanted to become guitar players, and they picked up my books. They happened to be very popular in those days. In fact, when I played Australia for six months in 1937, there was a group of natives waiting for me at the boat—this was right outside the Fiji Islands—because they all had my books and my guitar picks. I had to give them a concert and play every damn thing I knew on the guitar, because they all had guitars.

Now today, as you know, every girl and every boy wants to play the guitar. There's a big guitar school around the corner here in Hollywood, and I see 'em every day, walking around the neighborhood with guitars. So I think I started something. I don't commercialize on it. I don't go around telling people about it, but after I analyzed the whole damn thing, I started to realize the guitar is getting more popular now then ever. Somebody told me there's about 30 million people playing the guitar—not professionally, but they all have a guitar, like having a piano in their home.

This has been a great interview, Nick.

I'm telling you the truth, the whole résumé of my life from the beginning, when I played the guitar, when I was eight, nine years old. I'm eighty-three now, you know. [*Laughs.*] I hit it August the 22nd. I don't like to publicize that too damn much. What do you think? Does it spoil the illusion? Use your own judgment on that. And I'm in good shape physically. My voice is in terrific condition, and I still can play "Pickin' the Guitar" and "Teasin' the Frets"—that's not easy! That takes a lot of fingering.

I still work. I play choice engagements, but I don't get out enough. I don't socialize enough to get acquainted with some of these musicians today that made it big, which I'm happy for. And I had my turn. I had my success, and I thank the good Lord that I still can sing and I still work. I played a lot of fair dates and casual dates. Just recently I played three days in Indianapolis at the Shrine show, and I was there last year. They want me back because they enjoy it. It makes me happy to know that I'm still able. As long as my health keeps up, I'm gonna keep on doing it until I can't do it any longer!

CODA: Nick Lucas enjoyed our interview and stayed in touch with me for the rest of his life. I always enjoyed his upbeat personality and loved getting his phone calls, photos, and letters. Nick Lucas passed away on July 28, 1982.

O n slide guitar, Ry Cooder is the man with the *perfect* touch, a player so gifted he's able to jump genres without sacrificing his identity. He's played barrio bottleneck behind Tex-Mex accordionist Flaco Jimenez, loping slide with Hawaii's Pahinui family, gutbucket blues with John Lee Hooker, gospel music with Pops Staples, electrifying rock with Little Village and the Rolling Stones, and transcendental improvisations with musicians as far afield as Ireland's The Chieftains, Cuba's Ibrahim Ferrer, India's Vishwa Mohan Bhatt, and Mali's Ali Farka Touré. His playing graces the soundtracks of *Performance*, *The Long Riders*, *Crossroads*, *Primary Colors*, and a dozen other big-budget films. He has a shelf full of Grammys, including back-to-back Best World Music Album awards for his collaborations with Bhatt and Touré, and another for his beloved 1997 collaboration with Cuban musicians, *Buena Vista Social Club*.

I've done several interviews with Ry Cooder, including three *Guitar Player* cover stories focusing on his slide playing, film scoring, and work with world musicians. My favorite, though, happened unexpectedly. Researching Blind Willie Johnson, the sublime prewar gospel-blues slide guitarist from Texas, I was struck by how magnificently Cooder had recast Johnson's landmark instrumental "Dark Was the Night—Cold Was the Ground" in his *Paris, Texas* soundtrack. I sent Cooder a note asking if he'd give me a quote. A few days later, on February 25, 1990, the phone rang and it was the man himself. After talking about Blind Willie Johnson, Ry suddenly moved on to another Johnson—Robert—and shed light one of the great mysteries surrounding the legendary Mississippi Delta bluesman. Read on.

You come closer to sounding like Blind Willie Johnson than anyone I've ever heard.

God almighty!

How do you think he physically played the instrument?

Well, I'm playing his music the way I know how to play bottleneck, which is to hold the guitar upright, wear a bottleneck on your finger, and fingerpick the thing, and play in the tuning that I'm certain that he used. But I have no idea how he played what he played. I mean, who knows? It's so far back into the distant past that anything is possible. I've seen this guy, Rev. Leon Pinson—he's a blind preacher from Mississippi—play holding a bar in his finger and thumb on his left hand, reaching around underneath like you would, and fingering the thing that way. And getting a very similar vibrato to Blind Willie Johnson. He has the quality of never quite coming up to the note and hitting it. In other words, that's a very inexact technique that I just described, but it does give you the quarter-tones and all of the strange nuances. When I'm playing, I'm so used to playing the very note. Look, it's sad that no one ever thought to take a picture of the guy while he was playing, because he played in two styles. He played normal guitar, just strumming and rhythm, which you can hear him doing with his thumb. I don't have any idea how he played, and I don't know what he looked like when he played. You know, two seconds of observation would answer every question you could ever have.

People who knew him from playing on the streets of Beaumont in the 1940s said that he played with the guitar on his lap and used a pocketknife.

Played flat?

Like a Hawaiian guitarist.

I can't imagine how he could have played what he played doing that. There is one thing about when you play that way—the same with this guy Pinson, who's playing not flat, but holding the thing, rather than wearing it—there's something that happens when you wear it, and there's something else that happens when you hold it. Now, Blind Willie Johnson had great dexterity. He could play all of these sparking little melody lines. There's fabulous syncopation. He'd keep his thumb going real strong. But when I saw this guy Pinson down South last summer—even though he's nowhere near the guitar player Johnson was—I had an ear to what he was doing that sounded like Johnson. I don't know, it's just a different sound, and I can't quite say why. But I have a feeling when you play bottleneck and you're wearing the thing, your hand is there on the strings, either damping them or not damping them. It's more of a controlling sound when you hold the guitar and nothing but the bar or the knife blade, maybe, touches the string. The guitar tends to ring more. It tends to keep the strings released and open, see. And more sound is happening. Because Johnson's sound is very active.

I never could figure out how in the world he got such a busy sound playing so little. I used to think, why are all the strings going all the time? Because the recording is so horrible—the quality of the recording is the worst in the world, on one of those horrendous little machines which is eliminating all but the most spikey sound that the guy is producing. You're not hearing any of the real aural ambient effect at all. I'm sure that in person, this guy sounds a thousand percent different. All the recording is showing us is the lowest-common-denominator type of sound, the most direct thing. The struck notes are all that you're hearing. But even through that, you can hear that the strings are moving all the time. And I used to think that he's making a lot of work to move all these strings around. And I know that old, primitive players, street guys and blues players, do nothing to work too hard. It seems

RY COODER

32

like, to me, when I met these guys, the few that I've met, they're very efficient in the style. If it takes too much effort and physical work, then you're doing something wrong. So when I was young, I didn't know. I used to go to tremendous efforts to try to do this stuff, only to realize later that I was probably barking up the wrong tree.

Are you suggesting that he didn't damp behind the slide?

Oh, I know he didn't. Now, he could have used his picking hand. Because if you're playing flat, you can, with the side of your hand in the manner of steel players, stop resonance just by approaching the strings, barely touching them. But you can do a lot that way. But I personally cannot see how. . . . Of course, I don't play flat.

Another account says he held his guitar normally and used a jackknife for his slide.

I don't know, because I haven't researched or read—I'm sure you've looked into this way further than I have—but I have a feeling that all of the primitive players who were not in Mississippi and who played slide played flat. Lead Belly played flat. Guys from Texas did play flat. Because when the Hawaiians came through in an early World's Fair [the 1916 Panama-Pacific International Exhibition], everybody saw these guys and everybody was influenced. There was tremendous impact. And they all played flat. So most people would have said, "Right, I play flat." Now we know Blind Willie played regular, because there's that one picture of him. And you know that that's the way that the guitar was used. But then when you go to play the sliding style, why, then you're playing flat. It's just natural that everybody would have done what the Hawaiians did. It's just human nature—except in Mississippi, where for some crazy reason they didn't. In Mississippi they seemed to play regular, but with bottlenecks and bones and things. Some people held a jackknife between the fingers, as though it were another finger. But outside of Mississippi—and I don't know about any scholarship or historical investigation that bears this out—but you can hear the difference. And you can hear when people are playing flat. It's probably true that Blind Willie Johnson played all that stuff flat, and it is quite amazing, but it would account for how he gets around on the strings.

Of course, I've tried all my life—worked very hard and every day of my life, practically—to play in that style. Not consciously saying, "Today is Tuesday, I will again try to play like Blind Willie Johnson," but that sound is in my head. And really when you come right down to it, you can sit down and play some of his tunes, and the single-string melody thing that he did, which is so great. He's so good—I mean, he's just so good! Beyond a guitar player. I think the guy is one of these interplanetary world musicians, the kind of person they talk about in that Nada Brahma book, where the world is sound and everything is resonating. He's one of those guys. There's only a few. Being blind and all, maybe he asked what's going on, maybe somebody described it to him.

I wish we had some notion what people thought of these Hawaiians— they must have looked like Martians coming through with their grass skirts and things. And God knows they're good players. Because they were so good at what they were doing, why, Mexicans picked it up, and the South Americans picked it up. We know that they sold steel guitar from then on, and the stuff was made to be done that way. And along comes a guy like, say, Robert Johnson, whom I *hope* didn't play flat!

Johnny Shines told me recently that he did not.

It's just unthinkable, because there's too much going on. When you play flat, you can't do so much. Well, that accounts for some of the simplicity and purity of Blind Willie's thing, and I cannot do it. I cannot play flat to save my life. I can't coordinate my body that way. It's fine with me that he did. When I saw this guy Leon Pinson down in Mississippi, I went home and I found me a metal bar like he had and started trying to do it. It was awkward for me, but after a couple of days I started to see where you could play all this Blind Willie stuff that way. It didn't occur to me to think, "Therefore he must have played flat." It's just what Pinson has gone and done. But if you did, you'd even be closer to that sound. I can see that it's probably the case.

Was Pinson's hand coming around the neck of the guitar the way you normally would?

Yes, because he plays regular too, like they all do. They all make a clear distinction between slide playing and regular playing. They don't mix them together. Very few people did in those days, or do now. So he says, "I'm now gonna play slide," and he takes out his bar, tunes the guitar down to a chord— same one as Johnson, same D tuning—and goes on doing this thing, not fretting at all. If you wear the slide, you can fret, but he's not. He's just playing the note and very few chords. Now, Blind Willie played hardly any chords. It was years before I realized that my brain was imagining the chords—he wasn't playing them. He was just playing two or three notes and getting a suggestion of a chord once in a while. He was playing in that modal feel, not wanting to disturb that tonic drone. He didn't need to. He was doing a different thing. And when you hear this old guy Pinson, you hear him strictly playing quarter tones and not playing the notes straight up and not wanting to create these stacked-up triads and regular harmonic intervals. It's dissonant all the time. Now, that's what these old recordings of Blind Willie John-

Ry Cooder, early 1970s. (Courtesy Warner Brothers Records)

son don't show us because you can't hear anything. You don't know to what extent this was dissonant or polytonal in that way.

Didn't Johnson have a remarkable left-hand vibrato?

Oh, the best! The absolute best. Very light touch—real light and really fast. It's just a thing that you can't talk about, almost, because it's just so perfect. But that vibrato, you can go and do it by wiggling that bar just right. I'm trying to do it these days. I hate doing it—it feels terrible—but I can see that you get a different sound, and that's the only explanation that I can think of. I'd also like to know what kind of damn guitar he had. He probably used a little guitar. They didn't have big guitars in those days. Hillbillies did, later in the 1930s when Gibson started making those big jumbos, but back in those days, all those players had smaller instruments.

What's your attraction to "Dark Was the Night—Cold Was the Ground"?

I think that's the most transcendent piece in all American music, the way he used his voice and the guitar. This other tune that I love so much is "God Moves on the Water." Oh, that thing is like a roller coaster, man. He's got an energy wave in there that he's surfing across the face of that tune so mighty! He hits the chorus, and to me it's like ice-skating or downhill racing—it's an awesome physical thing that happens. But "Dark Was the Night" is the cut—everybody knows that lick. You can throw that lick at anybody nowadays. I threw it up inside *Paris, Texas*, you know, and everybody relates. And now you play that lick, and everybody knows what it is. It's like an unspoken word. It's really amazing.

I'll really tell you, Blind Willie Johnson is in the ether somewhere. He's up there in the zone somewhere. But if he played flat . . . And at this point, after talking with you, I'm starting to feel that really would account for it. Because I know that if it was regular, I could be doing it. I can do what he did—I can play those notes now. I mean, I have learned. My coordination and understanding have developed to the point where I am capable of executing those passages, but it sounds really different when you play flat.

Which of the first-generation bluesmen did you observe first hand?

Skip James I barely got to see, because he was sick all of a sudden. But I saw him, and I didn't know what to make of him because his records really impressed me. When I saw him, he was having such physical trouble and he was so strange as a person that I recoiled from him. I didn't know what to do. I was pretty young, and the vibe really killed me. But his records I listened to quite a lot. We used to see [Mississippi] John Hurt, of course. And then, for me, the big was to see Sleepy John [Estes] because I liked his records so much. When I got mobile, I got a little older, I went down South to see him, and we used to sit with him. I'd go see him in his house up in Brownsville,

Tennessee. Take him money and things. By that time I was kind of doing things. But as a teenager, I used to see him come through here.

Well, the whole thing about guys like that was you weren't ready for them as citizens of the world. You know, for middle-class white kids in Santa Monica, sad to say, you don't really know any people like that. Or Rev. Gary Davis—you just don't know what's going on. I had these records, although they weren't easy to get in those days, but people had given me tapes or some 78s. I used to listen to these things and think, "Well, what could this all be about? Who are these people? What are they saying?" It's a mysterious journey here, like in *Alice in Wonderland*. And then, not understanding anything about the historical, social, economic conditions that produces music—there again, being pretty young and all—all of a sudden, in the folk boom, on the scene in Hollywood, in this folk-music club, there appear these guys. And they walk to the stage, walk through the audience. I was thunderstruck! I couldn't breathe, you know. They got up onstage, sat down, and commenced to do whatever it was they were able to do. And of course that really killed me, because I thought, "This is beyond my understanding."

After a while I began to gather up courage and go up and talk once in a while. You could sit down and say, "Can I understand this?" or "Can you show me this or that?" It was hard for me, but I did. And then I found out it was good, because they didn't mind. They liked talking; it was not unpleasant for them. I didn't bother anybody or badger them, like people do these days. But I was always curious and always trying to understand. Then it became obvious that it wasn't so much the music as it was the people. If you could figure out where the people were and how they were as beings, why then the music was very clarified. Because what's totally mysterious on record and inexplicable, why, in five minutes of watching a guy play, you got it. You understand body rhythm and how the instrument is approached, which is *entirely* different than how I'd seen it done. It was not linear, it was not patterns—they'd play out of patterns. They don't play the horrible boom-chicka-boom thumb-finger, thumb-finger thing, you know. Everybody I knew did. That mad adherence to a mechanical thing that you set yourself up like a robot and play and think that's what it is. I don't know how that ever got started—banjo, maybe. But these guys didn't play patterns, they didn't play tuned. They were probably mostly out of tune. The whole thing was a revelation in what the instrument really could do in terms of personal expression. It's a great gift to be able to have seen those people. Poor people today can't see anybody.

Back in the earlier days, there wasn't the attention to Western musical traditions of timing and tuning.

Not at all.

This is evident on The Bristol Sessions *and other early country recordings—no studio sync-up here.*

Oh, forget it. They're coming from an entirely different way of life, an entirely different background. It's just so radically different. If you go to Mississippi today, even, it's a different place. You feel it's a Third World country, a whole other scene. And back then, think of what it must have been like.

What first impressed you about Sleepy John Estes on record?

Well, he had a great group—that piano player and the jug and the harmonica and him, all playing in different rhythmic emphasis. Everybody has a different take on what the rhythm is. Some of it's half-time, some of it's double-time. But the jug band idea, I think, is the greatest idea in terms of ensemble, applied in whatever way you want to apply it. In other words, primitive guys playing what they think is right and what they probably heard on somebody's uptown record and trying to do themselves. Or just what they hear music as sounding like, see, because they all listen to records too. Robert Johnson trying to sound like Lonnie Johnson makes perfect sense. And then saying, "Well, this is my version of Lonnie Johnson. This is what I think's going on."

Sleepy John Estes, of course, was a natural. He just put his hands on the instrument and opened his mouth. And then somebody would play piano and make it up out of nothing. I mean, out of nothing at all. Having no education, musically. It's not like New Orleans, where everybody was schooled and there was a standard of reference. God almighty, down in the country, there is not standard of reference. You just did whatever your body would do. That's the beauty of it. And Yank Rachel on mandolin—the whole thing is just fabulously interesting to me. From the sound point of view, I just used to bathe in those records. It's like sit down and let it wash all through you. Pretty fascinating. Jesse Fuller—same thing with him. He used to come in, set that stuff up, and then sit down and play it and just wind it up. It would just unspool at you. It would take you away from your environment, that's for sure.

Did Gary Davis ever give you tips on playing?

Oh, I used to sit with him. He was a guy who gave lessons, actually. Now, how he got started and what made him turn to doing that in his age, I don't know. But it was known that if you wanted to pick up from him, why, all you had to do was give him five or six dollars and go sit with him. So I used to go to where they put him up in some little house down here in L.A., someplace near Hollywood, when he'd come into town. And I'd sit there and say "I like this song" and name one of his tunes—because he had songs. He wasn't just

playing 12-bar blues, he was playing songs, and they had structure and all. Of course, he had this bizarre chordal sense and crazy right hand, and that was interesting. So we'd sit there for an hour or however long he wanted to stay—because when you're in the company of a master, time is not a thing of the clock. The clock is not ticking, necessarily. If you want to stay all day, that's okay. If you get tired, you leave. It's kind of that sort of a thing. So we used to sit there. I never could play it back to him. A month later, it would come to me, what he had shown me or what he had done. He would just play, and then you would try to remember. I'd stare at his hands and try to figure it out. But I couldn't make anything sound like that, and I never could play his way. I found that it was beyond my ability to do the thing that he was doing.

From a physical standpoint, what made it so difficult?

I don't know. I mean, he had a bizarre technique. And you had to commit to it. It's not a technique that flows into another person's technique. In other words, Gary Davis is all by himself, in my experience, and if you committed to learning and being a student of his and a follower of his guitar mannerisms, you had to do that regardless, and everything else was secondary. I didn't want to do that. I was really interested in something else at the time, and I felt that this was out of my range. I used to love to play his tunes, but I didn't play them with any deep satisfaction because I realized it wasn't working. This is not doing what he is doing. This is turning out like something else, and I'm not really crazy about it. Although he had some nice chord changes that used to thrill me, and I used to like to play the tunes just to hear those chord changes go down. But it was impossible.

In the prewar blues genre, do any other people stand out as being transcendental?

Gosh, sure. I mean, so many people. Blind Blake is a great player, a great musical figure. He's another mysterious figure. In the years where he was on top of his thing, I think he was fabulous. I think Lonnie Johnson has never been recognized as one of the transcendental people who influenced everybody. You can recognize Lonnie Johnson in just about anybody, with his voice and his elegant style. The stuff he did with Louis Armstrong was just incredible. So there he was. And he recorded with guys like Eddie Lang and all that. What he must have sounded like to country black people—they must have thought, "Well, this is somebody else!" You know, he's up in town, getting this fabulous tone, and he's real elegant and real top-hatted. It's a whole other thing. It's pop music, really. You can see people copying him right and left. Oh, it's amazing. When I was very young, I heard some of that stuff, and it came through and really killed me. I used to sit and try to do that all the time. Still do. If I want to warm up, get my hands working and discipline my body, I will try to play some of his instrumentals. I can't imagine what the hell he was doing, but I'm trying for it all the time. It's just a way of using the instrument, right?

Did you hear many influences in the music of John Hurt?

That he had heard? Well, who knows? There's a guy from Mississippi who's playing in an un-Mississippi style. Very linear, melodic style. What did he hear? He must have heard Geechee music, maybe. Maybe he heard stuff from the Piedmont area. Maybe he thought it up all by himself.

Explain what you mean by Geechee music.

You know, the way the Sea Island people sound. That island thing all in the Piedmont area where Gary Davis, Sonny Terry, and a lot of those people sort of are from. It's a very melodic style, syncopated in a different way. They play major chords and things, unlike a guy like Skip James, who plays crazy polymodal things and it's a more open sound. Then Furry Lewis and John Hurt are far apart—maybe that's Memphis. I don't know what that is.

Now, Furry Lewis was in medicine shows. Medicine shows were interesting because they took music all around. They would leave regional areas, which were so distinct in those days. The musicians in the minstrel shows would travel to other areas and influence and be influenced. They were like a rock-and-roll tour is today, you might say. I mean, the fact that Joseph Spence traveled through the South in the '20s in medicine shows is mind boggling! I mean, that's just absolutely *amazing* to me. And God knows what people thought of him, and yet if he went in the Piedmont area, there must have been places where he recognized music like his own. That's a real interesting thing to think about, because guys like Furry Lewis were on medicine shows most of their early life. Jesse Fuller was travelling in medicine shows. That's one of the things you could do to make money.

Were these shows designed to sell snake-oil liniment?

Oh, yeah. You know, they would come into town on a truck, depending on how prosperous and how big they were. We're talking about a countrified version of a minstrel show when minstrelsy had already either died out or was unknown in the countryside where there wasn't a theater. Out in the countryside, in these little bitty towns—which was most of the Deep South—these damn guys, these quack doctors, would come in with a show and go ahead and do it. They would have a musical interlude, like Blind Peg Leg so-and-so would do his thing. Can you imagine what some of those shows must have been like?

Have you ever seen this film called *Louie Bluie*? There's a little piece of footage about the jug band that's in there, from like about 1910? That's your medicine show. That's hotter than fire. That one guy with the hat plays so much jug, he looks like he's about ready to blow up! It's awesome looking. That kind of thing just kills me, because I know they were out there and they were doing this, and it was *hot*. We think of the old men who could barely do it, but this was not so back in the '20s and before. This stuff must have been *cosmic*! All we know is what we've got on records and a few still photographs. It's really a shame. But I think to myself, "Well, that guy [director Terry Zwigoff] found that piece of film footage. I wonder what else is out there?" We'll never know what it's like—or in the alleys off Beale Street. And just everywhere. I mean, music was all over the place. Country suppers and parties and picnics, and then there's all that piano music, and then these guys get together. Blind Blake played all over the place with all kinds of people, including Johnny Dodds. It's just really something. Or the zither player who played with Lead Belly.

But as far as old Blind Willie Johnson is concerned, he just missed the media, even when he died. If somebody would have been paying attention, but nobody thought about it much in those days, I guess.

It's just like nobody thought about Robert Johnson. What happened was the engineer who made those records died, and no one ever asked him what kind of guitar did he play. And I'll tell you something else about this. You know how they talk about how he was nervous and wouldn't face the room [during his recording sessions]? I don't believe that. You think that man is nervous? I'll tell you what he was doing. They say he sat in the corner. Do you play a guitar?

Yes, I do.

Well, find yourself a plaster corner sometime—all those hotel rooms [where blues sessions were recorded] were plaster. And I don't mean wallpaper or curtains. But you go and sit in the corner, with your guitar, tight up against the corner. Face the corner and play, and see what it sounds like. Now, what you do there, what you get there, is a thing they call "corner loading." That's an acoustic principal. What that does is it eliminates most of the top end and most of the bottom end and amplifies the middle. The same thing that a metal guitar does or an electric guitar—it mostly amplifies the midrange, which is where that metallic, kind of piercing sound is what's left. Now, you take and record that way, and you'll sound different. Because Robert Johnson sounds funny—let's face it. It doesn't sound like anybody playing an acoustic wooden guitar. But it's not a metal guitar. But if you sit in the corner and stick your face up into the corner and listen, you'll hear that sound. It ties the notes together. It compresses the sound too, and his sound is very compressed. See?

So I don't believe—I think it's silly to say—that a man who if we believe that's him in that ["dimestore"] picture, and if we listen to his singing and his forceful personality—this is a guy who was afraid of the audience?! Hell, no! This is a chew-them-up-and-spit-them-out kind of a guy. I think he was sitting in the corner to achieve a certain sound that he liked. In other words, if you'd have said, "Robert, I'm gonna boost the midrange, take off . . ."— because it's a dry sound, the acoustic guitar, finally. It's a boring sound for

Robert. He wants to hear *wang*! He wants to hear the electric. He wants to hear that kind of boosted midrange. And I'll bet you that if you could have done that for him with equalizing and headphones in the modern era, he'd have been very glad. I'll bet you if you'd have given him a Marshall amp to play it through, he'd have been extremely glad! But sitting in the corner, he could achieve something like that.

And with the sound on those records, the voice and guitar is being mooshed together. It sounds like it's being compressed—and early field recording did compress a lot. If you look at some of that primitive equipment, being tube and not having a lot of headroom, it does tend to compress. I've never fiddled with that. I wanted to try it for the movie [*Crossroads*]. We found the machine that they were gonna use to shoot the scene with—they got it out of a museum. I said, "Alright, let me take the machine into the room and load up the corner and see if we get that sound." As interested as Walter Hill, the director, was in that idea historically, he didn't have time to mess around. Someday I'm gonna try it, because I just know in my heart it will work. Because I have done it—I have sat in the corner, with earphones, and listened to the sound, and it sounds like that. And it's a great thing, because all of a sudden the whole projection of the instrument is changed radically by a simple thing like that.[1]

I mean, these are the things that Don Law or whoever made those damn records could have answered in two seconds, for Christ's sake. But nobody asked him. And if you weren't there, you don't know. How big was Robert Johnson's guitar? Somebody said it was big, a Kalamazoo or Gibson—I've heard that said. Those are large-bodied guitars. They push some air around. And his hands look funny, bending at the top joint like that. I'm starting to believe that's him in the ["dimestore"] photo.

Were you a fan of Tampa Red?

Oh, yeah! Love Tampa Red, of course. Now, if you were to say, "Do you think you sound like any of these people?" I would say it's easier for me to sound like Tampa Red. I think I've got that wired. I don't think I'm so good at these earlier guys, because they're so idiosyncratic, but Tampa Red ironed out all the kinks and made it a little more accessible. He played it with a little more with a modern, big-band feeling, like a soloist, almost. Very linear, and really, really good. He put it all together, as far as I'm concerned. He got the songs, he had the vocal styling, he had the beat. I really think that it's a straight line from Tampa Red to Louis Jordan to Chuck Berry, without a shadow of a doubt—a straight line through those three guys. You really can feel it. And he wrote some songs—or assembled them in the manner of traditional music, where you don't write so much as you assemble or reassemble—like "It's Tight Like That" and "Sittin' on Top of the World." That's a mind who sees how to refine and flesh-out, drawing from all sources. He's drawing from sources like the Chatmon brothers and the Mississippi Sheiks, Papa Charlie Jackson.

Tampa Red put it all together, he really did. He changed it from rural music to commercial music, and he was very popular as a result. Look how successful the guy was—he made hundreds of records, and they're all good. Some of them are incredibly good, with Washboard Sam and whoever was on piano—that stuff is fabulous! You gotta say, "Okay, that's where it starts to become almost pop." It's a very straight line—him, Louis Jordan, Chuck Berry. The development is clear in my mind when I listen to that stuff. It's good. And he had a great guitar technique too, for sure. Ooh! Non-threatening. I mean, everything about him was fun-sounding. He wasn't scaring anybody. He didn't sound like he was gonna eat you alive. He just sounded like, we're all having fun here, like "Jim Jackson's Jamboree" and all that stuff. I really love all that.

What did you think of Robert Wilkins?

Well, he's a great player, a songwriter. That "Prodigal Son" song is a hell of a song. [In 1929, Wilkins recorded "That's No Way to Get Along" and later renamed and expanded it as "The Prodigal Son."] When you get these guys who write from a spiritual reference or point of view, it's really interesting—like Washington Phillips and all that. Washington Phillips played dolceola [a small keyboard instrument]—different bag, but he had some pretty scary tunes too. Oh, there's so much. The list goes on and on—it's amazing, isn't it? It's a one- or two-generational thing, coming from almost nowhere. There's no background for the blues to even exist.

There's no reference to real blues before 1900.

Yeah. And where would it have come from, unless it's that cane-fife stuff, wherever that came from. You know, fife-and-drum bands down in Mississippi, like that guy Napoleon Strickland. That stuff seems pre-blues to me. And that seems to be the only thing that I can think of that is.

In parts of antebellum Mississippi, laws were enacted that forbade the playing of drums, which had been used to spread messages among slaves during a revolt. Maybe this helps account for the differences between the development of black music in New Orleans and Mississippi.

Yeah, sure. They had a whole schooled musical tradition in New Orleans. Up until a certain point, the kids all learned regular serious music. They learned how to read music. They also had country bands, like in the South Carolina area, those jump bands playing on broken Confederate horns they found in the field, playing hymns and things. That's a whole other bag. Do you know the Music from the South series that Frederic Ramsey put together on Folkways? One of the volumes was called *Country Brass Bands*. He went down there and he recorded two country brass bands, which were kind of loose organizations of guys who knew each other and would play on the weekends or for dances.

Apparently, this started after the Civil War. The Confederate armies all had brass bands and marching bands as part of the morale building. And when they lost, these guys just laid their instruments down in the field and left them. Then after the war goes by and the black people return to the field or their homes, and they actually found these horns in the dirt or left in sheds or I don't know where. In time, they became handed down in families, broken, full of holes, tied together with tape. And they didn't learn to play like the guys in New Orleans, with proper fingering. They knew only the bugle mouth and a little fingering, all wrong, but they liked these things and so they started playing in bands. You gotta get that record. He found two of these bands—there are about ten guys in each group, and they play some kind of hymns that they know in this style, on broken instruments. They have no chops, they've got no mouth embouchure at all. But they play this so it's strictly from the guts. It's the life vibration that they live in, a pure expression through a horn rather than, say, a guitar.

Also, in those days when Ramsey was doing this work, in the '50s, he did an early news magazine show on CBS called *Omnibus*. You must see this—it's strictly important. Ramsey did one called something like, "They Took a Blue Note." It was an hour show of jazz. They came to Ramsey, being the expert at the time, and he put it together for them. It shows him going down into Alabama. You see a little of New Orleans—that's a really nice funeral there. Then you're out there and there's Horace Sprott, who was one of his discoveries, playing the harmonica and plowing the field—that's kind of stagey and dumb. But all of a sudden, around the corner come five guys behind a barn, and they have these beat-up horns. They stand up and play this stuff, and you just fall on your knees. I'm telling you, you will have a transcendent experience, because it's right in front of your face. It's a thing that you can barely believe, but it's one of the great documents of pure soul. These guys are field hands in the 1950s, they're all middle-aged men, hard-working guys, and they play these horns in some crazy way. The sound that comes out is utterly mind-boggling. It's just too good.

I had given up all hope of ever seeing this—I figured, well, that's gone—but there are still some of these jump bands, as they're now called, down in the South. I heard one at the Atlanta Blues Festival, called the Old Morrisville Brass Band, from South Carolina, and they play this way. They can't finger these horns and they can't change keys, but they'll blow you right out of your seat. It is good.

Try to make the effort to get a hold of the CBS footage—you won't be sorry. It belongs in everybody's collection. It is something else to see. You're talking deep country here, where some of these scenes were filmed—now it's probably a mall. Man, that thing with the brass players is hot! It's riveting. You need to see that, because that's a pre-blues instrumental expression from the countryside, and that's Civil War-vintage type of understanding on your instruments.

Besides the fife-and-drum tradition, do other pre-blues forms still survive in the country?

I think that the marching band music is one, because it's all based on nineteenth-century music. I think the cane-fife thing is a voice there. And then, of course, we have Joseph Spence, who was a voice from the nineteenth century—he's dead now. He was in medicine shows, and he was playing hymns. And have you heard this [1930s] group called the Heavenly Gospel Singers, with Jimmy Bryant on bass? Well, I believe they are Geechee, Piedmont-area guys. If they don't sound like Joseph Spence, then I'll eat my hat. He does the same thing with his voice. And I know in my heart he heard that group, because that group was hugely popular. And Jimmy Bryant on lead bass was a unique expression [*sings one of Bryant's deep bass parts*]— that's what Spence is doing all the time. He's singing that part.

Apparently Jimmy Bryant used to make women fall out and they'd throw their handbags at him and the rest. And he got out in the audience and did the number. So I have a feeling that that minstrel-type gospel shout thing, which we now refer to as quartet style, is a nineteenth-century style as well. And it sort of survives in pockets down there. There are a few people who still relate to that, but it's hard to hear anymore. It's really died out since the era of the soloist kind of wiped it out. But that was a thing that you found in minstrel and church styles way early—I mean, some of those gospel quartet records are way, way early records. So I figure that sort of survives, because church things tend to change slower. People keep their church traditions. And if you went down in the Sea Islands today, where a lot of that music came from, and down around the Norfolk area, you'd hear some of that stuff. I just know you would. It isn't blues, but there's blues in it.

And the blues singers listened to church music too, because almost every black was raised up in church. I don't care if they end up the meanest, nastiest blues singer, they were raised in church. So they were hearing this stuff as a youth, and it's got to mean something, especially to country people. What else do they have to do but go to church? There's a strong musical voice in all black music that comes from their experience in church, whatever that may have been. In the case of country people it's the singing—they didn't have anything else. That's why a lot of early records were of preachers.

Around 1902, the Dinwiddie Colored Quartet made some of the first recordings of African-American spiritual music. Have you heard these?

Yes, I have. They sound like a quartet—it's quartet style. It's typical church music. Look, it was the simplest thing for the recording scouts to say, "Well, we know there's music in the church. We'll go down the road to find the church, and we'll ask who's good and have them come in and sing." They did that all the time.

Why do you think it took so long for record companies to seriously focus on black musicians?

Nobody thought of them as a market, because they didn't have any money. They're poor. You don't count them. This is a technological thing, and technology is linked to affluence. And then somebody was smart. Ralph Peer was one smart guy who went into the hillbilly hills and figured that these people will buy their own music. That's really a leap of genius. First, you had to sell them the record player. What's the point of having the records unless you've got the record player? So it became a product that furniture stores sold— that's a known fact. And they actually used to make the records in the back of furniture stores. It was a very concentrated idea. Later on, you had centers of recording, and that's a whole other story. But I don't think it was until they began to realize if you can sell something to somebody, go and make it, go and do it. But naturally, technology on any level is linked to where they think they can make money off of it.

Do you think liquor was commonly supplied at country blues sessions?

Yeah, because first of all, you do take people into strange, problem-ridden situations, which is to say, "Mr. Charley says sing, I guess I better sing." And there's plenty of that that went on. I can only imagine that these records, on up into modern blues, were made under the most nervous, uncomfortable circumstances imaginable. Because these damn guys weren't psychologists, they were businessmen. They said, "Boy, you sing." "Oh, well, alright, sir." And unless the guy was drunk, maybe he couldn't. Maybe he was too goddamned scared of white people. Who wouldn't be? "If I don't sing, they'll cut my hands off." I could believe that, so I figure booze was a way of dealing with a primitive person—get him drunk. Not so much in the case of the church people, who have their religion to kind of shield them, but with blues singers it apparently was true. It's a thing that's puzzled me—you know, why liquor was such a deal. Is it because their life is oppressing and hard and they're unhappy and they drink? I just don't know why people drink like they do, because I don't like it myself. So I have a hard time understanding that. But on the other hand, they sing about it and talk about it so much of the time that it must have been about the only fun thing that you could do. That's why in the modern scene, when you go down to the ghetto, what do you got? You got liquor stores. So that's obvious. So yeah, they probably used it freely. Said "Here, drink this and play."

I heard that they frequently put pillows under blues guitarists' feet . . .

To have them stop stomping their foot, because that pushed so much air around. I'm sure they did. They went to lengths to kind of balance it out— that must have been hard, too. But the genius of some of those records is beautiful. Some of them are terrible. It's a question of the engineering capability—where they were, what kind of room.

Plus what kind of 78s survive.

Yeah, man. The 78 is a high-fidelity medium, in a way. It's going around so fast that it does sound good, except that when they get scratched, they don't sound so good!

This interview has been a great help, Ry.

Well, good. Do what you want with it.

CODA: In its September 18, 2003, issue, *Rolling Stone* magazine ranked Ry Cooder eighth on its list of "The 100 Greatest Guitarists of All Time." Ry has continued to release solo albums since then, notably 2005's *Chávez Ravine*, 2007's *My Name Is Buddy*, and 2011's *Pull Up Some Dust and Sit Down*. His first book of fiction, *Los Angeles Stories*, was published by City Lights Books in 2011. These days, his performances often feature his son Joachim Cooder on drums.

I n August 1939 Charlie Christian departed Oklahoma City to audition for Benny Goodman, who led America's most famous swing band. Playing the electric guitar, then a fairly new instrument, Christian quickly proved that he had the tone, imagination, and finesse to create long, flowing solos equal to those of Goodman's horn players, who were among the finest in jazz. Within weeks, the twenty-three-year-old guitarist had recorded "Flying Home," "Stardust," "Rose Room," "Seven Come Eleven," and other classics with the Benny Goodman Sextet. He performed at that year's Spirituals to Swing concert at Carnegie Hall and won his first of three consecutive Best Guitarist awards from *Down Beat* magazine. Players across the country eagerly awaited each new Goodman recording featuring a Charlie Christian solo.

Christian's time in the spotlight proved short-lived. During 1940 and early '41, he recorded influential instrumentals such as "Till Tom Special," "Gone With 'What' Wind," "Wholly Cats," "Air Mail Special," "Breakfast Feud," "Blues in B," and his specialty number with the full Benny Goodman Orchestra, the magnificent "Solo Flight." After hours, he often headed to Harlem to jam at Minton's Playhouse, where Thelonious Monk and Kenny Clarke played in the house band and Dizzy Gillespie, Charlie Parker, Lester Young, Ben Webster, and Coleman Hawkins were regulars. It was here, witnesses insist, that the foundations of bebop were created. In May 1941, a young jazz enthusiast recorded Christian playing "Swing to Bop," "Stompin' at the Savoy," and other forward-leaning compositions. Two months later, the hard-partying guitarist, who'd been diagnosed in 1940 with tuberculosis, was admitted to Seaview Sanitorium on Staten Island, where he passed away on March 2, 1942.

Through the decades, Charlie Christian's influence has resounded through a who's-who of jazz guitarists. One of his foremost disciples, Barney Kessel, went on to become a mainstay of the Hollywood studio scene, a charter member of the Wrecking Crew, and a highly regarded jazz artist and educator. Such was his renown that for many years the Kay and Gibson guitar companies sold Barney Kessel model guitars. In the late 1970s, when I became an editor for *Guitar Player* magazine, I was assigned to edit Barney's monthly column. Through his writing, I learned that in his youth he'd met and jammed with Charlie Christian. I called Barney in late 1981 and asked if he'd be willing to discuss his hero. Whereas in previous conversations Barney had occasionally been critical of other guitarists, he spoke of Charlie Christian with unabashed respect and enthusiasm. Barney jump-started the conversation.

BARNEY: I'm very happy to talk about Charlie Christian with you because, first of all, it is a matter of personal love. I have just a great, great personal affection and regard for Charlie Christian and for what he stood for. And getting to meet him, as well, and being from the same part of the country—I'm actually living right now in the city where he came from to join Benny Goodman. The fact that I played with so many people when I was growing up that had played with him, and listening to his music now, and even being more moved by it now than I was even then, it's a great pleasure to do this. And I feel really glad to be the one to be talking about it with you.

Why should a young person who's learning guitar listen to Charlie Christian?

Well, it wouldn't matter whether it was a young guy or not, Jas. It's just anyone that's interested in music or any art form—it wouldn't matter what it would be—you gain an awful lot by studying those people that preceded you. And not only to study them, but to study them in a kind of sequential form, chronographically, the way it occurred. It helps to get a better understanding of where we are today and how it came about. Charlie Christian's contribution to the electric guitar was as big as Thomas Edison's contributions and Benjamin Franklin's contributions in terms of changing the direction of the world. He changed the guitar world. He changed it not so much by being a superb guitar player, but rather the music that he made. And anyone that would study him can see where all the other guitar players who came after him evolved, that they came from his fountainhead. They came from that and went their own way, according to their own tastes, but he was a way-shower. He was as much a way-shower as any philosophical giant that other people have come along and patterned themselves after.

His contributions were so strong in several departments. One is there have been very few people on *any* instrument that have come since him that have had his sense of time, his ability to play in time in the way that he plays, the spacing of his notes. That's one of the things. The other thing is he was years ahead of most of the people he was playing with in terms of the lines he was playing. They involved certain chord changes that were not existent then.

Could you give an example?

Just his playing, just his chords. If you listen to any of the blues that he played, you will hear in the line that he has spelled out harmonic changes that none of the others on the record are playing, not even the background. And yet they're refreshing and they fit. He's playing more chord changes in his lines, and also interesting ones, different ones than existed at the time. Any record would be an example of that, any record. In addition, his tone was more the concept of what is being used today in jazz, and all along. It is more of a velvet sound. It's just the antithesis of a rock-and-roll sound, or a pop-rock or punk-rock sound. It is more an *electric* guitar sound rather than an *electronic* guitar sound. And a lot of people don't understand this either. I have people that come up to me and they think that what I want now, and what Charlie Christian wanted then, is simply to amplify the natural sound of the guitar and just make the natural sound louder. That's not true. That's a different sound entirely. The electric guitar as he played it had its own sound.

So we've got three different sounds, really, we're talking about: One is we've got a regular acoustic guitar where you put something on it, and it doesn't change the sound—it only makes it louder. Now that's one thing. Another is the actual sound of an electric guitar coming through a particular pickup that sounds like an electric guitar, which is different. And then you've got things that people are playing today in the rock and pop, etcetera, which is really an electronic sound.

So Charlie Christian's tone was more hornlike. It's more like the velvety sound of some of the saxophone players and trombone players. It was more horn. As a matter of fact, many people that heard him play that didn't know him didn't even know that they were listening to a guitar. They didn't know anything about it. They just were simply going to this club where he might be playing, and they'd hear the music from outside, and they didn't know that there was such a thing as an electric guitar. Almost all of them thought that it was a tenor saxophone.

Really?

Yeah—from a distance. I mean, it was a combination of not knowing that Charlie Christian existed, not knowing to expect an electric guitar, or not having heard anyone play it—good or bad. Just hearing this sound from a distance, being outside the building and hearing it with a band, they'd think it was somehow a rather slightly percussive tenor sax, maybe even someone that is slap-tonguing it a little bit.

But those are the main things. Those are his strengths. And he was the first guitar player, to my way of thinking, who in sitting down with a bunch of horn players to play, that the content of his music was on just as high a level as theirs, if not higher in certain cases. Whereas in the past, before Charlie Christian, any time I'd ever heard anyone play the guitar in the company of various horn players—be it Benny Goodman or Jack Teagarden or Tommy Dorsey or whoever these guys might be—the only thing you could say is that that guy might be one of the best of guitar players. It's kind of like he's the best of what's around, but it isn't as good as what the horn players are playing. He's playing good to be a guitar player. See? So it was that kind of thing.

Charlie Christian was the first one that played single lines more like a horn plays them—without being a part of the tradition that preceded him. Almost all the players before him—especially the older ones, especially ones that had been playing from the 1920s—came to the guitar from a banjo orientation. Most of them. So when they came to it—with no disrespect to any of these people, because they made beautiful music—but that's why when you hear George Van Eps in those days, when you hear Allan Reuss, you hear Dick McDonough, Carl Kress, etcetera, what you're hearing is a guy who for one reason or another—maybe the economic pressures of the day—was forced to change from banjo to guitar. Maybe the orchestra leader insisted that he change from banjo to guitar, or he decided to do it. Very much like the change that went through in the late '50s and '60s, when many string bass players found that in order to keep a job, they had to switch to electric bass, whether they wanted to or not. And some of them did, and some of them didn't. So those guitar players, when they played guitar solos in those days—the 1920s and 1930s, like with Paul Whiteman and Bing Crosby and all those people, Joe Venuti—they were banjo players that had switched to guitar. And the music came out that way.

Now, Charlie Christian did not have that banjo background. As a matter of fact, there are different rumors around that he at one time played the trumpet a little bit and he played saxophone a little, and for health reasons he couldn't play a blowing instrument. He had an inclination—he and his whole family—towards developing tuberculosis. And so he couldn't involve himself with anything that would affect his respiratory system. But yet he had those things in his mind. So it's kind of like a guy that has played tenor, or wants to play tenor, but he's playing the guitar.

So he thought like a tenor player.

Yeah. Well, Lester Young was his ideal. Lester Young was *his* inspiration.

How immediate was Charlie's impact?

Extremely immediate! But it was not only immediate nationally when it broke, but it was immediate locally wherever he went. I think there are three basic things that were involved. One is that the instrument itself had never been heard. I mean, there just weren't guys around playing the electric guitar. That in itself is a novelty. And then there was the fact that he played it in the *style* that he played it. Had he come along and played the amplified guitar, but played it like everybody else was playing it, that would have been fairly novel in itself, in that you'd never heard anyone play the electric guitar. But he wouldn't have been playing it *differently*. But here he comes along and not only plays a new instrument, but he's playing it in a different way. That is, he's playing single lines like a horn. And now even that would

*Barney Kessel,
1980s. (Courtesy
Barney Kessel)*

not have counted for the impact that he had, because you could have been playing horn-like figures. You could be playing clichés that horn players are playing, and you're not really playing anything new. The only thing you've got going for you is that the things that you're playing have been around for years, but never on a guitar. The third is he was playing new things and was playing his own personal talent. So those are the three things: you were listening to a new instrument played in a new way and played extremely well. So it did make a big impact immediately.

But in those days, Jas, economically we were not living in the superstar type of life, so he had this fame among musicians, but not among the public. There wasn't a lot of hype going in those days. Gibson didn't come to him and take out ads, and there were no NARAS [Grammy] awards. There wasn't all the hype that goes on. And so the public was not as aware of him. And also his money was not commensurate with his talent, whereas today people with less talent can make even far more money. This is because they are more organized—they've got a manager and they do things to expose themselves and market their project better.

Besides yourself, Barney, who have been the foremost players to come out of the Charlie Christian school?

Well, I would say Herb Ellis. Now, I must tell you this: there are certain people that *say* that they were influenced by Charlie Christian. There are others that don't say that they were. I really believe that almost everybody that plays the electric guitar today has been influenced by him, whether they know it or not—in just the same way that when a guy turns on an electric light bulb in a room, he may really be so dumb that he doesn't know that Edison invented it. But he's still using it, and he's involved with it, even though he doesn't know where it comes from. So I think that Charlie came so early and contributed so much so early, that he made a big enough impact that it just became a *way* of playing. It's just like Charlie Parker's not the only one who plays alto, but his *way* became a way, and a big way. It's kind of the definitive way.

Many guitar players either will not admit that they've been influenced by Charlie Christian because they don't really realize that they have, or their ego may be involved to where they don't want to consider anybody's influence, that they've got it all together themselves. And then there's others— I've read about certain people without getting into names—that say they were influenced by Charlie Christian, but as I listen to them, I honestly cannot see what it was that influenced them, because I don't see the things that Charlie had so abundantly. I don't see those particular things in these players. Even though the players themselves might be good, they're good in a different way than Charlie Christian was. So I'm amazed that they say that they were influenced by him.

But to get back to your question, Jas, people that come to mind that I can feel their influence are Herb Ellis, Joe Pass, and Jim Hall in the beginning, although Jim Hall has moved away from it. Now, some of these people have moved away from it or they've diluted it. Their experiences have led to learning other things as well. In the learning of other things, they've branched out and kind of got away from it. But it's still in some of them slightly. I think of Chuck Wayne, Remo Palmieri. Now, there might be some more. But, as I say, when I listen to some of them, I cannot tell that they were. I would say that outside of myself, Herb Ellis would definitely be one, and there was a guy years ago who wrote "Cement Mixer"—Slim Gaillard—who was affected by him. Tiny Grimes was too.

What would you consider to be the essential Charlie Christian on record?
All of it!

Where would be a good place to start? Could you name a half dozen cuts?
For one thing, it would be very easy just to get a two-record album on Columbia called *Solo Flight: The Genius of Charlie Christian*, which actually was not made under his name, but was repackaged by John Hammond. Now, that's one. But that does not by any means contain all that he made or necessarily all of the best. I would say if you could get that album, and get another album on Columbia, Benny Goodman's Sextets—I don't know the name of it, but Columbia albums that have been repackaged from singles, because Charlie never made an album. This might be under Benny Goodman's name. There might be other takes on these things. Then there was a jam session that was recorded on a Wilcox-Gay recording machine at one time. One label it came out on was called Vox. I don't know if that is still under that name, but the record is available. And I know that if you buy it, on one side there will be that jam session at Minton's, and on the other side it's an example of early Dizzy Gillespie playing with Monk. The album I'm talking about is where he was jamming all night, and one of the songs on there is called "Stompin' at the Savoy."

Now, in addition to that, there are about four sides that he made that would be part of some album—someone has collated these things—but he made four on acoustic guitar with a clarinet player named Edmond Hall. It's the Edmond Hall Four. Edmond Hall played clarinet, and I think Meade Lux Lewis was on celeste, of all things. And then there was a string bass, and then Charlie played non-electric guitar. And that's really the body of his work, because he died very young and did not record very much.

Can you remember the very first time you heard of Charlie Christian?

Yes. I had heard about him in several ways. First of all, I'm from Oklahoma. I'm actually living in the city right now where he came from when he joined Benny Goodman. He was born in Texas, but the life that he lived before he joined Benny Goodman was in Oklahoma City. That's about 150 miles from where I was born. And I was playing with a fourteen-piece black band, orchestra, and most of them had already heard of him and knew him. They knew his playing. They were always telling me about him. So I'd heard about him, but I'd never heard him play. And then I had a friend of mine back then who had heard him play, and he was a guitarist, and he told me about him too. So that when I finally heard him, I'd already heard a lot about him.

The first record that I heard was with Benny Goodman, and Charlie actually didn't really have a solo. He just sort of played in the group, and he had a couple of little fills that he played with them. I wasn't able to tell much, but already I could tell that he was sounding different and good, but I had no idea of the impact he'd have. The first thing I ever heard was a thing called, uh [*sings the riff*], "Soft Winds." That's the first thing I heard. And then the next thing I heard was "Flying Home." Well, when I heard it, the only way I could say it so that people that are very, very young today would get an idea of what I felt—it *really* knocked me out! It just thrilled me. Probably it had the same effect on me—of course in a different way, and I'm not talking about the quality of the music, I'm just talking about the emotion—that the way maybe a guy your age, if you were sixteen years old and into pop at the time, felt when you heard Elvis Presley for the first time or saw him for the first time on television. Or the Beatles. It would be that kind of an impact. It embodied *everything* that I ever loved about the guitar—and more—because I didn't realize you could do all of that. And it was beyond me. It really knocked me out! I mean, I just immediately became a disciple of it.

I would go down to the record store and just bug 'em to death: "Do you have a new Benny Goodman Sextet record? Would you call me, or would you let me know when you get one in?" I'd go down there, and even if I didn't have the money to buy it, I'd just take it into the booth and play it over and over and over. They would have to literally force me out of the record booth and force me out of the store. That's the impact. And I tried to learn *every* note I could—not so much to call it my own, and not so much to copy it. The reason I tried to learn every note is I loved to hear it so much that I figured that if I was in a place where I couldn't get to a record player and I still wanted to hear it, if I learned it, I could take out my guitar and play it. And therefore I am acting as the medium or the agent that allows me to hear that song. In other words, if at that time I'd been able to carry around a portable

Charlie Christian jamming with alto saxophonist Sam Hughes (left) and tenor saxophonist Dick Wilson (right) at Ruby's Grill in Oklahoma City, Oklahoma, early 1940s. (Courtesy Oklahoma Historical Society)

record player, I would probably have been playing the record over rather than trying to play it on the guitar. I was playing it in order to be able to hear it—not so much of trying to show other people that I knew it.

That really points to an enormous impact.

Yeah! Wanting to recall it to myself, wanting to be able to do it, and finding the only way that I could immediately have access to this would be to play it, and therefore I heard it. And what knocked me out was all of the things that I told you, that I thought he was strong in. His *time* knocked me out. His *clarity*. The fact that *everything* that he played made a statement—there wasn't anything like throwaways. There wasn't little fills to create a little side effect. I mean, everything was a *statement*! Everything was a statement. You can go back and listen to these things now, keeping in mind that there was no high-fidelity then, much less stereo. When you hear him play, even back in those days—sometimes they were using only one microphone—he knew enough to get his solo on that record with a lot of presence. And there was no mixing. I mean, they just made it! That was it. There was no mixing down or being in different channels and "We're gonna bring you up and we're gonna bring the bass down." It was just there. But if you listen to his records, when it's time for him to play, he is on the scene!

From observation, what can you say about Charlie Christian's technique?

Well, when I think of technique, really I think of control. I don't think of technique in the same way that a lot of people do, so I don't really think of technique as being only speed or dexterity. I think that if you have certain things that you want to say and you're able to say them, then you have the technique that you need. The only time you would be at a loss, technically, is if you needed to do something and couldn't do it. You know what it's like, really? It's like how rich are you or how poor are you that when you want a meal or to buy a new suit or buy a new car or take a trip to Europe, that there's always enough money to do it—not a lot more than that and not a lot less. So are you really poor or wealthy? It's kind of that way with technique: if you can do what you need to do, then you've got enough technique. He certainly did not have the kind of technique that people have today, or even a lot of people during that day, because he didn't concentrate on that. It wasn't a big thing. Another thing is he played almost exclusively—probably 95 percent—downstrokes.

Did he use a pick?

Yes.

How did he hold it?

He held it in his thumb and first finger of his right hand, very tightly, and he rested his second, third, and fourth fingers very firmly—I mean, not in a relaxed way, but very, very, very tensely—on the pickguard. They were anchored there. It wasn't like a light anchor. It's not like some guitar players you see, where they're kind of rubbing maybe just their little pinkie finger against it. Have you seen guys do that?

Sure.

Yeah. He had them firmly entrenched on that pickguard, almost like there was no break in the finger joint. It was like a straight, solid, long finger that was right on there, and he played with the first finger and the thumb holding the pick. And the pick was a very stiff pick, and it was a triangular pick.

A big triangle or a smaller one?

A big one.

Did he use all of the fingers of his left hand?

He almost exclusively did not use the fourth finger. Almost not ever—almost.

What did Charlie Christian look like when he played a solo? Was he serious and concentrating, or did he seem enthusiastic and look around?

No, he didn't look around or anything. He was pretty intent on it. He'd play a lot with his eyes closed. Or sometimes his eyes might be open, but they'd be kind of moving toward the top of his head. He was pretty much into it. And he did not move around too much. He wasn't moving. He didn't look around, either, but occasionally he'd look up. He'd kind of look up and just kind of look around, and then sort of go back into it again. Yeah.

You've mentioned the importance Charlie placed on swing.

Swinging—yeah. See, but even when I say that, there's a lot of people that still don't know what I'm talking about, because they would think that it means swinging your body or kind of grooving and boogying all out, and all that. It's got to do with the pulse in your playing. It's got to do with the fact that you play in such a rhythmic way—and I'm not talking about whether you rush or drag. I'm talking about if you play a stream of eighth notes, that you play it in such a way that your *time* is so flawless that you wouldn't need a bass or drum for someone to sense what the tempo is. It's got such clarity and it's so articulated that without any rhythm instrument there, you definitely hear what the tempo is. Whereas with a lot of people, they don't play evenly. They don't play that way, so without a bass or drummer, the tempo is not clearly stated.

Did Charlie beat time with his foot or anything?

I don't know.

Do any of Charlie's physical characteristics stick out in your memory?

Well, he was a pretty inarticulate person. He really kind of spoke—at least to me, in the three days that I was with him—he didn't have very much of a vocabulary. He didn't even talk hip. He didn't say a lot of hip phrases or clichés, and he didn't use a lot of words. And he kind of grunted. For example, when he talked about Benny Goodman or Lionel Hampton, he addressed them as "the Benny" or "the Lionel." That's the way he talked. He didn't say "Lionel" or "Mr. Hampton" or "Ben" or "Benny." It's like if you're talking to me, and you said, "I was just talking to the Barney." So he said "the Benny" and "the Lionel." And he didn't get into a lot of philosophy and he didn't get into a lot of teaching. I just had the feeling that he probably was just kind of streetwise. And he was so young, and at that time he was working hard and just scuffling to make a living before he joined Benny Goodman, just working for peanuts. And I just don't think he was well educated. I don't mean that he was simple or anything; I just meant he was not a man of letters. He was not well read and all of that. At least to me, he did not express himself as well through words as he did through his music.

He had definite ideas! Let me just tell you one of the things. For instance, we were jamming and a guy came up with a tenor saxophone and took it out, uninvited, unannounced, and started to play with us. And he wasn't very good. And Charlie, he didn't get angry or anything. I didn't know what he was gonna do. But he just got his guitar and packed up. He just packed up and looked like he was getting ready to leave. Well, when he packed up, the tenor saxophonist saw that Charlie was going to leave, and so the saxophonist himself put his own saxophone in the case and left. Now, the minute the saxophone player left, Charlie took his guitar out again and began to play. And I was so young—a lot of times young people don't know any better, they'll ask questions that you shouldn't ask. Like young kids come up to me and they'll say, "How old are you?" or "How much money do you make?" They're so young they don't really know that those aren't too cool to ask. So they don't know any better. So I asked Charlie why he did that. And he said, "I don't ever take the guitar out of my case unless I'm either going to learn something, have fun, or make some money." Now when you stop and think about it, there's probably not any other reason to take the instrument out of the case! So that's what I mean: at the same time he was kind of inarticulate, if you analyze what he said, it's pretty practical. See?

What was his favorite equipment?

I don't know. I wouldn't know if what he played was because he didn't know any better to get something better, or if it was convenient, or if that's all he could buy because there wasn't much else around. I really wouldn't know. But what he was playing was a small Gibson amplifier—if there was such a one called a 150 or 185. I don't know, but it looked to me like either a 10" or 12" speaker. I'm not sure now, but it was one of those old Gibsons that was in what was called "airplane cloth"—you remember that? With the three orange bands down it. And the amplifier, I think, was in the case, but you could take it out, because it would get too hot. [*Barney is probably referring to a Gibson EH-150 amp, which Charlie was known to have used.*]

You said he played louder than you were accustomed to.

Yes, but not by any means, in any way, like Deep Purple, Blue Cheer, or something like that. Yeah.

Is it true that Charlie Christian didn't appear onstage with Benny's big band because he was black?

I don't know. I don't know. I do know this: he told me that he appeared at the White House with the Sextet during the administration of Franklin Delano Roosevelt. So he did play at the White House with Benny Goodman in a mixed band. And he also told me a funny story that at the time he was playing, the people weren't just listening to it—they were dancing to the Benny Goodman Sextet—and some lady came up to him and really didn't recognize the electric guitar but had heard him play some solos. And she said, "You're the best banjo player I ever heard!"

Is there anything else you'd like to add, Barney?

I'll tell you this: when I was a kid, I listened to a lot of different musicians. And as time has gone on, when I listen back to them, many of them don't sound as good now as they did at the time. Or I'll say, "Well, that was okay then, but things have kind of moved ahead." There are a few that sound just as good as they did then. And very few of them sound better to me now. And of those that sound better to me, I have to try to figure out why this is so. What's happening? The only thing that I can think of is that that music actually was great. It was great all the time, and it sounds better to me now.

The music itself hasn't changed—I've changed. And it must be that simply by having acquired more insight and more education and more experience, I am in a better position to appraise it and see more wonderful things that were always there but I couldn't see it. And with Charlie Christian right now—as I'm talking to you now—it honestly sounds better to me now than it did when I was a kid listening in Muskogee, Oklahoma. It sounds better. It's *classic*—not classical, but classic, in that it weathers the deterioration of time. Time in itself removes fads. Remember when you were a kid, there was Howdy Doody buttons and there was Davy Crockett caps. My own kids, they had Davy Crockett hats. I told them the day would come when nobody would be wearing these caps and nobody would know about Davy Crockett—they couldn't believe it! How about when Hopalong Cassidy was such a big thing? And Hula-Hoops and all these things. Well, the point I'm trying to get at is that in time, some of these fads do not stand up. Not only do they not stand up, they die. They die and they never come back again.

But classic music—and again, I don't mean classical music—but the very nature of what is classic means that it holds up and transcends time in a very graceful manner. Paintings have done this. Literature has done this. I mean, Shakespeare today is no less than he ever was. Charlie Christian stands up. When I listen to him, I'm aware that he doesn't have a great chordal knowledge. I'm aware that he's not the fastest guy in the world. I'm aware that he plays certain figures that he played before and that it's a limited kind of repertoire. I'm aware of all of these things. I'm aware that he didn't really play much on a very fast song. But you must listen to people for what they are, and not what they aren't. It's really just like looking at a banana and hitting it and beating it for not being an apple. It can only be a banana. We're all what we are. Segovia doesn't play Charlie Parker songs, and Chet Atkins doesn't play bebop. And Tiny Grimes isn't playing a transcription of "Clair de Lune" on a guitar. We all do what we did.

And as I listen to Charlie Christian, it isn't all that's going on in jazz, but it is the personification of jazz. His contribution represents one of the examples of a high standard of excellence, along with Lester Young, Billie Holiday. To me, it's not all that's ever happened and it's not all that's going on now, but it represents so much of what led to other things. And not only that, but it stands up well right now. Even though they play a lot of notes, I don't hear that many people on the guitar or other instruments playing with his kind of time. I don't hear people making statements. I certainly don't hear people being themselves. When I hear Charlie Christian, I always know it's Charlie Christian. I hear a lot of people playing instruments, and I don't know who they are. There's no identity. I don't think of him as a guitar player. I think of him as a person who possessed a great amount of feeling for expressing jazz, and he happened to choose the guitar.

CODA: After a long and successful career as a recording artist and jazz educator, Barney Kessel passed away on May 6, 2004.

Soon after World War II, a tough new style of electrified blues guitar came crackling over radio airwaves and jukebox speakers. At the forefront of the movement was Aaron "T-Bone" Walker, who'd recorded his debut 78 in December 1929 and had been Blind Lemon Jefferson's "lead boy," as helpers were called, earlier in the decade. Like Charlie Christian, whom he knew, T-Bone was quick to adapt to the electric guitar, which he first featured on his 1942 Capitol single "I Got a Break, Baby" / "Mean Old World." By the end of the 1940s, Walker had recorded dozens of swinging, sophisticated records. In the process, he became, as Johnny Winter pointed out, "pretty much the father of the electric blues style. He influenced *everybody*." Nowhere was Walker's influence more pronounced than in the early recordings of Clarence "Gatemouth" Brown.

Gruff, direct, and fiercely individualistic, the Stetson-wearing, pipe-smoking Brown had a rich singing voice and spirited, horn-like approach to the electric guitar, which he played bare-fingered. Unlike T-Bone Walker, who unabashedly declared himself a bluesman, Brown took umbrage at this classification. "I'm a *musician*," he once growled at me, "not some dirty low-down bluesman. I play American and world music, Texas-style. I play a part of the past with the present and just a taste of the future."[1] While Brown was rightfully regarded throughout his long career as the greatest living exponent of the swinging, sophisticated blues school inaugurated by T-Bone Walker, he was equally adept at R&B, Cajun, bluegrass, and country.

My first encounter with Gatemouth Brown took place on June 13, 1978, when he and his wife Yvonne invited me to visit them at their temporary residence near San Jose, California. It had been a couple of years since his previous album, the small-label release *Blackjack*, and he'd yet to sign with another label. After speaking with me about his life and music, Gatemouth performed a few songs on his fiddle. Soon after saying goodbye, I pulled off to the side of the road and jotted down my initial impressions: "Closing his eyes and drawing a bow across the strings, Gatemouth Brown could fiddle you a Louisiana lullaby so sweet it would melt your deepest cares into dreams of a mystical, fading Cajun twilight. Or he could strap on an electric guitar and play the clean, polished lines once blown through the sweaty trumpet of a 1940s Swing Street jazzer. A veritable Renaissance man of American music, Gatemouth can claim the names bluesman, Cajun fiddler, country picker, and jazz man—they all fit, but none of them begin to encompass the man or his music."[2] These words, it turns out, would hold true for the rest of his career.

You started recording in 1947, right?

Yeah, 1947, right.

With Maxwell Davis?

Yeah, that was the first band that I ever recorded behind, Maxwell Davis. Yeah.

How has the blues changed over the years since then?

Well, in this way, I would say: the blues took a toll in a very disastrous way, simply because the good blues people was made ashamed to play it. You might say the new breed come out, and good blues was considered. . . . What they did, they took from the backward blues and linked it with the good blues and made the guys that could play good blues ashamed to play it because they called it the wrong kind of names. Being honest about it, they called it "nigger music." That's how people used to come up and refer to it as, and the artists resented that, most of them, and they went into something else to try and shield themselves from that category of music.

Who do you think were the best practitioners of good blues at that time?

Well, I would say T-Bone Walker was one. They had people like Tampa Red, people like that. As far back as I can remember, Tampa Red, when I was a small kid, used to be a blues artist. And then when I first heard of a lot of blues, T-Bone Walker was doin' it, you see.

When you first start listening to blues music, was it from Louisiana or Texas?

No, I'm a Texan. I listened to all kinds of music for a long time, then I decided to go and invent a style of my own. And I did so.

How old were you when you made the decision?

Oh, about twenty-two.

Had you been playing by then?

Yeah. Not long, professionally. I had been playing since I was five years old.

Tell me about that.

The kind of music that I played when I was five years old wasn't blues. It wasn't jazz. It was country, Cajun, and bluegrass. That's what my father played, see? He played fiddle, guitar, banjo, mandolin—all those instruments. But not professionally, because my dad was an engineer for the Southern Pacific Railroad in Orange, Texas. Of course, that's where I grew up. He would only play on Saturday nights for house parties, that sort of stuff.

How did you start playing?

I started strumming guitar behind him at the age of five. The guitar was bigger than I was. When I got to be the age of ten I started on the fiddle.

What kind of songs were you playing behind your dad?

Tunes like "Boil Them Cabbage Down." Let me see, what else? Oh, I heard one the other night on a tape some people from the Ozarks sent up to me, some nice bluegrass music. I've got some stuff that I'm gonna redo up, a tune like "Bully of the Town" and all them real *heavy* mountain music. Of course, that music mean more to me than any other music, because I'm more familiar with it. And jazz and blues just came automatically.

Do you remember any of the advice your dad gave you?

Yes! He said if I was gonna play any music at all, the first thing I must learn is to tune my instrument. [*Laughs.*] And I did that first, before I could play very well. And the second thing, say, "Don't overplay. Play what you can, but play it well." And I've tried that. And the next thing he told me, "Don't get stuck in no one bag." Said, "Learn to play some of *everything*, and that give you a widespread repertoire."

When did you first start playing in public?

Well, when I was about sixteen, around Orange, Texas. A little old band there. Our leader was a guy called Howard Spencer. He was a mailman by day and musician by night. He played the alto saxophone. And the funniest thing, I didn't know any different. Take, for instance, a tune like "C Jam Boogie." Now, I'm telling you what key it's in. He would always play it in B-flat. Start us in B-flat. In fact, everything he ever played was in B-flat. It was funny. After I grew up and learned about music, it was real funny how them guys used to do. Oh, he was a card.

What kind of band was it?

It was a little swing band. A little swing band.

Did it have a name?

Yeah. They called it the Gay Swingsters at that time. I didn't name it! I didn't like that name. I didn't name it. You know, that's what they called it. It was funny.

What were you playing in this band?

Now, you gonna flip over this—I was the drummer! That's right. And I furthered my career—after I grew up, I was a drummer with a twenty-three-piece orchestra in San Antonio. Hort Hudge, he was Caucasian, had a twenty-three-piece orchestra at that time. He gave me a chance to be a drummer. And they called me "The Singing Drummer" because I would do vocals and drum at the same time.

So how long did you play with the Gay Swingsters?

Oh, like, five, six years, I guess. I can't remember. I never did make no money. I never will forget this. These guys used to take us, like, to Beaumont, a place called Chain's nightclub, upstairs, and we played *hard* all night and get three nickels apiece. And the guy who was handling the thing took all the money. That's what you consider paying dues!

Where did you go from that band?

Well, from that band, I joined an old road band called W. M. Bimbo and the Brownskin Models, out of Indianapolis, Indiana. It was an old road show. I'm not even eighteen yet. I'm about sixteen, seventeen—something like that. Went all the way up to Norfolk, Virginia. He took all the money and the bus and stranded *everybody*—all the kids, the youngsters—and went back to Indianapolis. I was the only one who was able to get everybody out of there. I got a job in a club they called the Eldorado Club on Church Street in Norfolk, Virginia. I never been away from home that far in my life. I was playing drums with this little band, whatever band—I don't even know who they were. But the guy owned the club was named John Ireton. And that's the biggest money I ever made in my life [until then]—gave me $125 a week to sing and play drums with the band. And I sent all these other kids home, one by one, every weekend, until 1941. When the war broke out, my mother sent me a letter, said I had a questionnaire, so I caught a train and went home. I went in the service and stayed five months, ten days, and a few hours. Got out and went to San Antone [San Antonio], Texas, and got my first break with Hort Hudge's band at the old Keyhole on the corner of Highway and Pine. Don Abbott used to be a big band leader, owned the club at the time. And I worked there two years and for very little money—say, fifty dollars a week.

What were you playing?

Drums. And so Don Robey from Houston, one of the big club owners and tycoons in the theatrical business, was a friend of Don Abbott's. So he heard me and he asked me to come to Houston. T-Bone Walker was the hot stuff throughout Texas on guitar at that time, and nobody knew I play the guitar. So I hitchhiked from San Antone to Houston and went in this club and was sittin' downside the bandstand. T-Bone Walker, he was sick with the ulcer or something. He laid his guitar down and ran to the dressing room that was about, oh, thirty steps from the bandstand. The bandstand was real long—he had six hundred people in there. The Bronze Peacock. And so just out of nowhere, I got up from there, walked up on the stage. I picked up his guitar and invented a boogie right there on the stage and made $600 in fifteen minutes in tips. All-Negro audience.

Were you playing by yourself?

No. A band was playing behind me. And the band was called—oh, what was this fellow's name? Skippy Brook was the piano player—later on he was in my band, my big orchestra, for a long time. Oh, my gracious, I can't even think of this guy's name. Anyway, I started this tune, and it happened to be my first recording, "Gatemouth Boogie." And some of the words, they, "My name is Gatemouth Brown / I just got in your town. If you don't like my style / I will not hang around." And it was coming to me just out of the clear blue. I was making rounds. And the women and the men and everything was just throwing money down my bosom and everywhere. And I made $600 in that period of time. So all of a sudden T-Bone Walker recovered and come down and snatched his guitar away from me, on the stage, in public. Kind of hurt my feelings. And told me as long as I live, never touch this instrument again. So I said, "Alright." By that time, Don Robey heard all the commotion and the people screaming right up on the stage. He come down there, told me to come to his office. The next day he bought me a $700 Gibson L-5, bunch of uniforms, and I been goin' ever since.

Was that your first decent electric guitar?

Yeah. And I recorded for that company for seventeen years.

Was that Aladdin Records?

No, that was Peacock. I started with him, and how Aladdin got in, he knew nothing about recording. But he tied me up on a contract. He flew me—the first time I ever been on an airplane—he flew me to Hollywood, California, to Eddie Mesner. And they recorded my first four sides. 1947. He [Robey] was a very smart man. After he learned about the business, he snatched me away from Eddie, and we formed the Peacock Recording Company. And that was our company for seventeen years. Mm-hmm.

Did you keep playing at the Bronze Peacock?

Oh, yes. Oh, yes.

How did your relationship with T-Bone Walker develop?

Well, it never did really develop too good. He always had a sore spot about me because, you see, I'm the one invented swing guitar—what I call "Texas swing."

How did that come about?

I had a little country oriented into the blues. That's what I did. I mean Caucasian country music, because that was my trend anyway. And so that changed a whole trend, and thousands of guitar players followed me after then or gave me credit for it. Like Johnny "Guitar" Watson. I notice in your magazine, many times when these guys be interviewed, they always use my name. Yeah.

How did you wrap up the 1940s?

Well, in the '40s I decided to get me a big band. Kept a twenty-three-piece orchestra for a long time.

What did you call it?

Just Clarence "Gatemouth" Brown and His Orchestra. I had a good band.

Clarence "Gatemouth" Brown plays the Monterey Jazz Festival, September 17, 1977. (Jon Sievert)

I had some fine musicians, like Al Grey, who's now with Count Basie. Johnny Board, Nathan Woodard, the trumpet player. He went to school at the Boston Conservatory of Music. Fred Ford was a *tremendous* baritone player, and Bill Harvey out of Memphis, Tennessee. He was my first tenor. I had Pluma Davis on first trombone. Paul Monday was my pianist. I just had a good orchestra.

Who did the arrangements?

Well, I head arranged most of my stuff. I arranged a lot of my music. Then some of the guys in the band wrote up a lot of it for me.

How long did you stay with the band?

I kept the band about twelve years.

Did you go on the road quite a bit?

I stayed on it. And then when I saw that rock and roll was becoming a fad thing, like everybody else I had to get rid of a big band. It was a sad moment, but I had to do so. And I broke down to small groups. I saw in the future it would be hard for big bands to come back. And so I used a small group for a long time. And after that I decided to back off of recording in America, and I did—back in the late '60s. So I freelanced around awhile and wasn't nothing happening. Because people at that time, they wanted different music. These old doo-wop bunch was out there doing acrobats and this old hard rock and roll. I couldn't stand the music, so what I did, I just went to playing small clubs 'round Nevada and Colorado and Texas. I had a trio and that sort of stuff, and I did that for a while. I got tired of clubs, because I really don't like clubs too much. So what I didn't know was that the French that was over in Europe had been looking for me for seven years and couldn't find me. They didn't know where I was. But they finally located me, and I started going to Europe and started recording albums. This was around the middle '70s. I been goin' ever since. I got about ten albums in Europe now. I always look forward to going overseas someplace.

When you had your twenty-three-piece orchestra, what kind of crowds were you playing for?

Auditoriums. Four, five, and six thousand, eight thousand, ten thousand, twelve thousand, depending on the size of the place. It was fine days, man.

Were you playing alongside other bands?

Yeah, we would have what they call "cavalcade." See, this promoter I had was very smart. He would have what they call "The Battle of Guitars," "The Battle of Bands." He'd put my band up against many people. He did that against Duke Ellington, and caused a lot of hard feelings a lot of the time. I guess show biz is show biz.

Were you playing mainly guitar?

Yeah. Guitar.

When you transitioned into the rock-and-roll period, what kind of a lineup did you have?

Well, I didn't actually get into rock and roll. I kind of refused getting into it. Because, to me, it's not the kind of music that's tasteful. It's either loud or off. I never could stand that irritating music. I never could. And it has ruined a lot of musicians in more ways than one. But everybody do what they want to do, but me, I just won't do it.

So what kind of music did you go off into?

I started easing back into what I always love—country, Cajun, bluegrass. See, because the clubs I was working was all Caucasian clubs, and that's what I started getting back to. I got to where I just didn't want to play rhythm and blues.

I read a quote where you said that you've been places where if the blues were played right, there would be fights.

Yes.

Tell me about that.

Alright. There is a type of blues, like anything else. . . . Alright, let's go back. What cause people to get in a turmoil? Excitement—too much excitement of one thing. Now, you can get on one of these backward blues like, "Oh, my daddy had bad luck in Mississippi and my mama don't have no food"— I'm just using that. If you use that long enough and keep pushing that one point to an audience, the next thing you know, someone, perhaps, in that audience witnessed this type of life. And when they do, they get really up- tight. And maybe somebody in there they don't like, and that's where it's on. I've seen it. Take, for instance, like T-Bone Walker. I've seen him play blues and cause many fights. But if you play different styles of music throughout the night, you won't have that trouble. People don't have time to work up no emotions. You work up emotions, but it's all a happy medium, you see. That's why I mix up all of my music. If you notice, my record is all mixed up—Cajun, country, bluegrass, jazz, blues, and ballads—everything. And the next thing, you don't play one tune too long. That will get it. I found that out. I've watched people play, man—at least some blues artists now—what they consider "Chicago blues." Well, there's no such thing as Chicago blues. It's blues brought from Mississippi into Chicago. They're ashamed to use the word "Mississippi," so they use "Chicago" to label that music up in Chicago. That's what I tell people—there's no such thing as Chicago blues.

Do you agree with the observation that Mississippi blues and Texas blues are different?

Sure, it's different. If you notice the lyrics, Texas blues don't have the heartbreaking hardship lyrics like in Mississippi. You have to listen to both sides to see the difference. And even the phrases are different, tonality. Everything is different.

How influenced were you by the early Texas blues people such as Blind Lemon Jefferson?

I wasn't.

You just weren't exposed to it, or you didn't . . .

Well, I heard it, but I just didn't like that caliber of music. My blues is based on orchestration. I was influenced by people like Count Basie, Duke Ellington, Lionel Hampton, Ray Brown, Woody Herman, Hoagy Carmichael. You know, by listening. I've always liked the style of music of the big band. I don't like just a real primitive-type blues. I have nothing against nobody doing it. I could play it easy, very easy, because there's actually nothing to play. It's just a couple of chord changes and that's it.

As a songwriter and arranger, how do you work up orchestrated blues?

Well, in the first place, your tonality with your instruments is way different because you can name any one of these hardcore blues singers, put him with a big orchestra, and you'll see that it don't fit. It don't fit. Because their changes are not like the orchestra.

Take the Kings. If you put an orchestra behind B. B. or Albert . . .

No, it will not work. It's terrible.

It doesn't have the same emotion?

No. You got to be able to phrase. See, actually what I'm trying to say [is] I don't play guitar like guitar. I play my guitar like a horn.

Charlie Christian style?

No. Different from that. I play *horn* parts—actually, tenor parts. I can play trumpet parts, make it sound the way trumpet would sound, or a tenor.

Do you read music?

No.

How do you learn the trumpet parts?

I know how a trumpet's supposed to sound. I know how a tenor is supposed to sound. That's why I say I can head-arrange a whole entire orchestra. It's just something I can do. Just a gift I can do. If you ever heard any of my records, then you can understand it. And I was taught a lot by some of the guys that was in my big orchestra. See, I was the only guitar player. And I was the first guitar player that ever led a big band in America. The first.

How has your guitar style evolved?

Since I started? Well, it went a long way—I can tell you that! It was my determination that every year it would be something new. I would never sit down in the grass and allow my feet to be stagnant. I can't be stagnant.

How would you make the change?

Well, in the first place, you got to *think* music in order to play it. If one don't think of new things to do that would fit . . . see, music is like a puzzle. If you put one puzzle together and never put another one together, you don't know anything about another. So what you do while you're playing music, if you got any brains at all, you must be learning more. If you don't, you should quit. That's what's the trouble with most of us—we'll get on one thing. If you notice, a lot of records out there, these guys, if they can do one thing, they wear this one thing out. In fact, you can see it, you hear it, in *every* tune.

How do you avoid that?

In the first place, I cannot stand to hear the same sound coming back at me. So therefore I got new things going all the time. But I can go back and play the same thing. Whatever's on my album, I can play it. Yeah. I got a bank up here [*points to forehead*] that hangs in on that stuff, I guess.

Do you ever hear other musicians and force yourself to learn how they did it?

No. That's the next thing. I will not copy off of no man. No! That's a bad thing to do. I've seen people spend half of their life trying to do what somebody else do. I don't care about doing what nobody else do. I always tell people in all my interviews around the world: Do something *you* can do best without copying what someone else has done. Because when you copy what someone else has done, all you're doing is helping them. You're not helping yourself.

When do your new developments come to you?

Twenty-four hours a day.

With instrument in hand, or without?

Without, with—it makes no difference.

Can you play anything you can hear in your head?

If I want to, yes.

Do you still play the Gibson L-5?

No. Today I'm playing one of the finest guitars—I consider—in the world. I don't know exactly the date of it, but it was built in the '60s. It's a Gibson Firebird. I love this guitar.

Anything distinguishing about it?

Well, yes. It's me. It thinks like I do and everything. In Durango several years ago a leather craftsman made me a leather pickguard for it, wrote my name on it, and it's a beautiful guitar. I was offered $1,500 for it, and I refused.

Have you made any other changes to it?

No.

What kind of strings do you use?

Oh, I use just strings—no strings in particular. I used Black Diamonds for years, but they got to where they would break too easy. Then I went to Gibsons, and I use balled ones or whatever.

What gauge?

All different gauges—it makes no difference. I like a medium string. I don't like too soft a string, because I like certain tones.

Do you ever use a pick on guitar?

No, I never used a pick in my life. I use my hand. I can't use no pick.

How many fingers do you use?

I might use four, I might use two, I might use one. I might use all five.

For playing a rhythm part, what do you use?

I play overtone rhythm with my thumb and I use this finger [*indicates middle finger*] a lot of time for picking.

What kind of equipment are you using with the band?

For myself? Well, I like my Gibson guitar crossed with a Twin Reverb Fender amp. That give you the best sound in the world.

Do you use any effects?

No. The only thing I ever use, I put just a taste of reverb on my amp, because I like that tone, and I use a phase shifter, but with just a slow motion to it. And it gives such a beautiful quality to my instrument. On my album, you can hear it very little. I mean, just enough to give that beautiful tone.

Do you remember the make of the phase shifter?

MXR—the yellow box. Mm-hmm. It's very, very beautiful, and a good phase shifter.

Have you been predominately an electric guitarist?

When I was a kid coming up I had an old flat-top guitar. I don't know what it was. And I had one with this big old metal thing in it [most likely a National resophonic]—it weighed six ton. Just one thing or another. My first fiddle I tried to make out of a cigar box and screen wire, and it didn't work out. First set of drums I played I got a big whuppin' behind it, because I sneaked one of my mom's washtubs out and got me two tree limbs and took my time and trimmed them down. I was in the backyard, wailing away, and my mama come out there and tore this tub all to pieces. Of course, she tore me up too. That was my first encounter with a set of drums.

In your current five-man band, how do you determine which instrument takes what part? And what spot do you leave for yourself?

Oh, well, I usually open. I play my solo. I always play a couple of courses [choruses]. I don't play too many courses—I don't like that. Every man plays a couple of courses when it's time, depending on the speed of the tune. Now, fast jazz—a couple of courses apiece. I make take three, that's about it. But it's going so fast, it's not long. And like that, the music don't bore you.

So you alternate between rhythm and lead.

Yeah. See, when my guitar player is playing, then what I do, I play block chords behind him. I do the same thing behind the pedal steel.

So you're more with the bass at that point.

Yeah. The bass, the drummer, and myself and one of the pedal steels working together, with block chords. And it sound like a full orchestra, like a complete full orchestra. I can take five pieces and make it sound like *ten*, whereas I've seen a lot of people take ten pieces and sound like five.

What's the . . .

Secret in that? Well, use heavy chord changes. Not loud, but *deep* chord changes.

For an example . . .

Alright. Take, for instance, if you're playing a tune, instead of everybody playing way up on the neck, which sounds shrill, real shrill, don't do that. One person back off and play deep notes. He be in the same key, but he'll be an octave [below]. That's right. And so that fills in a spot and give the body. Just like some bass players nowadays don't even sound like bass players. They sound like lead guitar, and that's sickening, man. A bass weren't meant for that, because you've got no bass. And some drummer, instead of using his bass drum, he's all cymbals. And that takes away from the body of the music. So I don't have that.

You aim for a strong foundation.

Right! That's it. And I get it. I can take a trio, and you think it's five pieces.

That would highlight the solo work more too.

That's right.

How strictly do you structure your lead work?

Very strict. Very strict. You must be accurate, on time, and *out* of it.

Some bands will jam on for ten minutes.

I don't do that. I don't do that. Three, five minutes is the most. That's when you feeling real good. That's long enough for any tune, man.

Is there music aside from your own that you like to listen to?

Yes! I like to listen to some good classical. I like to listen to some good country, good Cajun, good bluegrass. I love it. I do not like free jazz. I do not like rock. I do not like soul what they playing today. I don't. One-chord change. I've seen these bass players get on one note, man, and they hang on that note from the beginning of the tune to the very end. Well, that's what the young people are playing. There's nothing to it, man. It's not music. But I'm fighting real hard to try to give them a taste of good music. And many other people are doing the same thing.

In the whole panorama of American music, where do you see yourself?

Well, it would take time, but I see myself as a teacher of quality. I do. It take some time for that, because you know as well as I know our youngsters have been brainwashed into filth and they think it's music.

Filth?

Yeah, filth. Punk rock and all that sort of stuff is no good. But you see, that's what you call fad stuff. It runs out fast as it get in, just like a sieve. If you notice, all these fad bands, every three months—ninety days—they have to come up with new idea in order to pick up for this loss. But good music don't have to do that. What's music all about? Something you can understand and use your imagination. That's music. Music is really imagination. If you don't have no imagination about it, it's no good. That's why I said all this punk rock and free jazz—how can you go sit through some free jazz? These guys all hopped up and play a tune an hour and ten minutes—one tune. How can you have any imagination?

How would you answer critics who say that rock-and-roll and punk music are a natural evolution of the blues?

No, that's far from being the truth. *Far* from being the truth. Now, in the first place, how can rock and roll or how can this other stuff have any close, close relation to blues when it don't have none of the phrases of the blues? Maybe every now and then they might accidentally slip up on one.

A lot of people have tried to figure out in a scholarly fashion where the blues is from.

Well, it's not that hard to figure out! The blues, the real blues, came from hardship, from slavery. And it came from spirituals. Blues is a takeoff from spirituals. People being forced to work against their will, and they had a little chant to keep their sanity. And that's how blues come about. Because if you are forced to do something, you constantly got the blues.

Where do your blues come from?

My blues come from me, because I wasn't ever forced to do anything.

What advice would you give someone who wanted to become a full-time musician?

Don't do what *I* do—do what you can best, and do it right. These things you have to watch out and not do: Don't get into narcotics. Don't get into alcohol. Leave them women alone and do your work. Get as much rest as you can. And when you're not playing music, go anywhere or do anything and don't look at no music.

What do you do to get away from it?

When we're home, my wife and I, we love to plant. We plant flowers, shrubs and things. Do all our own private landscaping around the house. That's right. What other hobbies I have? Fixin' things. I love to cook—*anything.*

Any practical advice about how to play?

Yes. Number one. Don't relate on being on an ego trip. Don't relate on being loud. Make sure every note that you do is understood. Make your music so that people can relate to it. That's it.

How often do you practice?

Very seldom. I practice in my head. I'm practicing all the time, but in my head. That's right. And it comes out in my fingers. When I'm home, if I stay home two months, I never pick up my guitar. I lock it up and leave it. Never pick up the fiddle—unless the wife and I sit down and decide do something, she and I. But as far as, like, going and jamming with somebody—I don't do that, man. That bores me. It's boresome. Because in the first place, half the people you jamming with can't play. In the second place, they play them too long. Very seldom I might jam, very seldom. And when I do get on the stage with somebody that can play, I play the same regular way like I do anyway.

What do you want to do with your music in the future?

I want it to be remembered. I want it to be remembered. You see, once you put it on record, you don't lose it. Them tunes will be remembered for thousands of years. Three hundred years from now, you'll play my music—and I'll be long gone—and that will touch on many, many, many souls. I don't care where the music goes, that will be there. That stuff will always last.

CODA: Soon after this interview, Clarence "Gatemouth" Brown recorded a new album, *Makin' Music*, with Roy Clark. He then produced three fine albums for Rounder, winning a Grammy Award for Best Traditional Blues Album for 1981's *Alright Again!* After a pair of albums for Alligator Records, he capped his recording career with five albums for Verve/Gitanes. In 2005, Brown's home in Slidell, Louisiana, was destroyed by Hurricane Katrina. Deeply shaken, he moved back to his boyhood town of Orange, Texas, where he died on September 10, 2005.

The Staple Singers recorded some of the most transcendent gospel and inspired pop of the twentieth century. With his gentle voice and sublime guitar style, Roebuck "Pops" Staples anchored the family quartet that featured, at various times, his son Pervis and his daughters Cleotha, Yvonne, and Mavis. Although the Staple Singers were based in Chicago, Pops's Mississippi Delta roots influenced his music throughout his life.

Roebuck Staples was born in 1914 in rural Winona, Mississippi. When he was eight his family moved to Will Dockery's plantation in Sunflower County, where he labored in the cotton fields. He had fond memories of hearing a cappella gospel singing in church, and was drawn to the blues as well. He remembered seeing Charley Patton, one of the first Delta bluesmen, play in front of Dockery's general store, and watching a young Howlin' Wolf play for tips in front of a train depot. Acquiring a guitar, Pops learned the local non-bottleneck blues styles. At 16 he joined the Golden Trumpets, a Methodist quartet. He married his grade-school sweetheart, Oceola Ware, and the couple had their first child, Cleotha, in 1934, followed soon afterward by Pervis.

Seeking a better life for his family, Pops moved to Chicago in 1935 and found work in the stockyards. His wife and children joined him the following year. Staples became a member of the Baptist Church, where his brother Chester was a minister, and began singing with the Chicago-based Trumpet Jubilees. His daughter Yvonne was born in 1938, followed by Mavis in 1939. During the ensuing years, Pops was too busy raising his family to play guitar—in fact, he didn't even own one. As Mavis recalled, "I was about seven when I first saw my father play guitar. He had gone to a pawnshop and paid $30 to $35 for it. It only had three strings on it, and he had to save enough money to buy three more. He played the three-string instrument as best he could, then called us kids into the room and gave us parts to sing along with what he played."[1] And thus was born the world-famous Staple Singers.

By the late 1940s, the original lineup—Pops, Pervis, Cleotha, and Mavis—was singing in churches. They launched their recording career in 1953 with the Royal single "These Are They" / "Faith and Grace," which they sold at concerts. A friend took them to United Records, where they did their first session to piano accompaniment. At subsequent sessions, Pops's electric guitar sound, with its gentle and one-of-a-kind vibrato, provided the group's foundation. In 1955 they jumped to the Vee-Jay label, recording their classic "If I Could Hear My Mother Pray Again," followed in 1956 by one of the best-selling gospel singles of the year, "Uncloudy Day."

The Staple Singers went on to record pop music and soul for Riverside and Epic, but didn't hit their commercial peak until after they signed with Stax in 1968. They struck gold in the early 1970s with a series of inspirational soul/gospel singles—"Respect Yourself," "I'll Take You There" (#1 in April '72), and "If You're Ready (Come Go With Me)." When Stax's fortunes began to wane, they signed with Curtis Mayfield's Curtom label in 1975 and scored two more Top-10 hits with "Let's Do It Again" and "New Orleans." The Staple Singers appeared in three notable 1970s concert films: *Soul to Soul*, *Wattstax*, and *The Last Waltz*. The group's final appearance in the R&B charts came in 1984.

After Mavis left the group to go solo, Pops flirted with acting and made the rounds of blues festivals, where he usually sang gospel songs. In 1992 he realized his long-held dream of recording a solo album. Featuring the Staple Singers, Bonnie Raitt, Jackson Browne, and Ry Cooder, *Peace to the Neighborhood* was hailed as a masterpiece of love and hope. Soon after its release, I met with Pops in a San Francisco hotel room, where he was happy to talk about his life and music.

I hear a similarity between your music and Muddy Waters's in that you both understand the power of keeping it simple.

Yes. In fact, that's the best way to try to execute and explain yourself and what you're trying to do to the people. I'm trying to play my music to something constructive and trying to get peace here between the United States and the people—what Chicago call the "melting pot," all nationalities. I just can't figure out why there's a difference in people in this United States. Some have, and some have not. Some get the privilege, some don't. I'm trying to sing songs that together we stand and divided we fall—that's just not in a family, that's in the whole United States. If we stick together, we will stand. If we don't, I'm afraid somewhere down the line we gonna fall. It might be a long ways. If you're keeping one nationality down, you're gonna be down there with 'em. The only way to get up is to carry the people along with you. If I'm down here and you're up here, you gotta look back down here to try to bring me up. I don't care who you are or how big you are—I think the onliest time you should look down on a person is when you're lookin' down to pick him up. That's the only time.

Everybody is somebody—it doesn't make any difference whether you are the president or whether you're a drunk walkin' the streets, sleepin' in the streets. Everybody is a human being. God love all of us the same. There ain't no big guys or little guys in the sight of God. So I would just like to try to get a song over for the people to listen. And the song's trying to say don't use cocaine, because it's detrimental to your whole body and soul. It's no good for you. That's all, that's all. I'm not trying to preach to nobody. I feel good. I live good, and I feel good. I'm seventy-seven years old and, shoot, I feel good because I don't worry about nothin'. There's no use to worryin'. So that's my main emphasis—just try to help somebody along the way.

Throughout your career, going all the way back to the Vee-Jay material, it seems your message has been that music is a healing force. Music can bring a person closer to what's really important.

Yes, yes. Right. I believe that it's a healing to the soul. It's a healing to the feeling of the people. Talkin' to a lady the other day—she was riding down the freeway, and she was very depressed. Didn't know why, didn't know what to do. She was just depressed. And driving along playing the radio, one of the Staple Singers songs was put on. That song was sung through, and when it was finished, she said that it was like a load was lifted off her. She says, "Pops, that went on for the day!" That gave her all kinds of jubilee, made her feel good. And I feel good when people like that are gettin' the message.

A little child come up to Mavis: "Mavis, you talk about you 'take us there.' Say, what y'all talkin' about? Where y'all gonna take us to?" And Mavis say, "Well, what do you think?" She say, "Well, I don't know, Mavis. I don't know no place you can take us. The only place I know you can take us is to heaven." So Mavis says, "That's just what I'm talking about." They listen, you know—they be listening. That's what we talkin' about—we gonna take you to heaven. Come on and go to heaven with us.

Respect yourself.

"Respect Yourself"—now, that's my favorite! Respect yourself. If you don't have no respect . . . When I was a boy, I had to respect my parents. Not only my parents, but my peers' parents. Any older person, you would have respect for them. But now, we don't have no respect for one another, nobody. That's bad. But back in those days, it was a better world. We were living in places where we didn't have to lock the doors, leave your guns and everything in the house, shotgun what you hunt with, pistol, whatever. Go out of town, wherever, leave your door unlocked. Come back and everything is the same. You can't do that now. They won't let ya.

When you were young, was it a more difficult time in terms of people having to work harder and having to face racial prejudice?

Well, yes. It's always been that way. We worked hard. The black worked hard down there, the white did too. In farming, all of us work about the same, but the white farmer got different treatments than the black farmer. It always has been that we had a harder struggle than the white because they could get paid for some of their cuttin' or their ginnin'. The black people had to wait until the end of the year before they got theirs, so that was tough. That's why I left.

When you were young, was there a difference between spiritual music and gospel music?

Yes. Spirituals is a song like "Swing Low, Sweet Chariot, Comin' to Carry Me On" and gospel music was brought out sometime in the late '30s or '40s, I believe. Songs like "Precious Lord, Take My Hand" by Rev. Dorsey—that was a gospel number. There's a difference between spiritual and gospel.

Some people call Rev. Thomas Dorsey the "Father of Gospel Music." Do you think that's fair?

I know it is! Whoo, ain't no "think"—I know it is. Yeah, he's it. Dr. Dorsey was away on a tour—I don't know whether he was singing the blues then or what, because he was a bluesman too—and his family passed, his [child and] wife. And she was the backbone of him. He didn't know what to do. And that's when he wrote "Precious Lord, Take My Hand." It come off from that, and he been goin' ever since then. He's still livin'—oh yes! He's just layin' there, a sick man, but he's still livin'.

Is he still at Pilgrim Baptist Church in Chicago?

Yes, yes. Still there.[2]

What year did you leave Mississippi?

'35. Got to Chicago, I had $12 in my pocket. Winter time. Nowhere to stay. But I did check up with my wife's uncle, and I had a sister there. I went and stayed with her until I got a job.

Was there a church in Chicago where you played regularly?

You know, I've got to go by there and get a picture of the first church I ever sung at in Chicago, if it's there. I doubt it's there, though. It was just a small storefront church. I sung at Pilgrim Baptist Church, Canaan, Metropolitan, and Shiloh. Lot of churches are still there, but I want to see the first one.

Do you still play in church?

Yes, I play in church. We hardly play any shows in church, because churches don't like to charge, but they like to use the Staple Singers because they can rent a hall and charge at the hall and raise benefits for the church.

I've read that you were one of the first people to bring the guitar into a Methodist ceremony.

I was the first artist with a singing group to take the guitar and go into church, which they didn't allow. And they had faith and believed in Pops Staples and the Staple Singers. You know, we wasn't trying to start something for money or nothing. We were just singing because we love God's word and we love God. We were singing for the praises of God. And the ministers could see that. They let us come in with the guitar, and that started the whole ball

rolling. The Soul Stirrers, Blind Boys, Nightingales, Swan Silvertones, all of them—we would come to Chicago to sing on radio. They got to their songs, and I was on one end of the studio and had a guitar, and that was fascinating to them. The next time around, everybody came to Chicago had guitar. Something new, see? They had sung themselves out, went all over the world, just singing a cappella. And that was a new thing—the guitar was new! Now, they got guitar, bass, drum, everything.

In the beginning, were you playing electric guitar in church?

No. Acoustic.

Was this in Mississippi or Chicago?

Chicago. I started playing blues down in Mississippi. I was playing blues on Saturday night in house parties. Didn't have my heart in it, but I just knew how to play. Weren't enough guitar players around to go to all these parties, so I was hired to play in that style.

[I hand Pops an old photo of Charley Patton.] Were you familiar with this fellow?

[Laughs.] We stayed on the same plantation. Sure enough. How old is this picture—do you know?

That's about 1930.

Mm, mm, mm. Charley Patton used to be on the lower place at Dockery— I was in the upper. Last year I was down in Indianola, Mississippi. We put a tombstone there. That man been dead how long, about fifty years? And they just put on his tombstone. I went down and sung at the ceremony.

Did you see him play when you were young?

Saw him on the upper place, yeah. I didn't know much about it—I was just a boy. And he—whoo! And from there, I seen Howlin' Wolf. Howlin' Wolf was a young man. And Dick Banks—Dick Banks never did make the records. And Bill Holloway, the guitar player. I said, "If I get to be a man, I'm gonna play a guitar." So when I got to be about twelve years, I bought me a guitar and started to play.

Did you buy it from a catalog?

No, I bought it right out of a hardware. A Stella—cost five dollars. One of the best acoustic guitars I ever owned. I bought it in Drew, Mississippi, where I be on the 5th of June this year. They'll name the park after me. We goin' to celebrate there. So I bought that guitar there. Paid five dollars for it. Times was so hard, I bought it on time. Put fifty cents down, and I paid it off.

B. B. King told me that back then, guitarists used a pencil and string to make capos.

Yes! *[Laughs heartily.]* Did you ever see that?

No.

Yeah! That's what we'd use for a capo. Piece of string to tie it down. Yep, that's the way we'd do it, see. [*Pops gets his Stratocaster to demonstrate.*] Take the pencil, put it across like that [*indicates the space between two frets*], take a string right around there [*demonstrates how to wrap a string around both sides of the pencil*], bear down on that tight. Tie the string, you got a capo.

Mr. King also said that worked when you broke a string—you could sometimes tie the string back together and put a pencil capo above the knot.

[Laughs.] See, that was the problem: we weren't able to have strings if you break one. We had to piece it together and put a capo on it and just keep on usin' the string.

Were those Black Diamond strings?

Yeah, Black Diamond.

Those things were like baling wire.

Yeah! Yeah.

When you saw Patton playing, was he by himself or with another guitarist?

Patton be by himself, more or less. And Howlin' Wolf be by himself. I didn't never see no one play with him. But Dick Banks, there was him and another guy, Bill. There was two guitar players.

Would they play at the train station?

Yes! That was good. Stand around, and people would just crowd up and throw money out there.

If a musician had a record out, would he have better luck?

I didn't never experience seeing nobody had a record.

[*I hand Pops a photo of Robert Johnson.*] *Did you ever encounter this musician?*

Mm, mm. Never did. Now, I heard about him a lot. I never did see him, never did see him. Ah, boy. I heard so much of Robert. Big Bill Broonzy, Willie Dixon, Lonnie Johnson—of course I saw them.

I've always admired Son House.

Son House—I saw Son House! Oh, yes. He's dead. I saw Son House in Boston. We played together. Ooh, Son House—he come up not so long ago. Yeah, not so long ago. He came in the '70s.

He was a good slide player.

Yeah. I always wanted to play slide, but never did learn.

Why didn't you?

Didn't take the time. I played it pretty good, but the way they were playing it, you had to tune your guitar into E minor straight, and I never would change it. I played it one way all the time.

When did you get your first electric guitar?

In the '40s.

Who was the first person you saw with an electric guitar? I heard Memphis Minnie was one of the first in Chicago.

I didn't see her. Now, Big Bill—that's about the first one I saw. Yeah.

Is it true he was a kindhearted guy?

Didn't know too much about him. I just know he was good to musicians. I was quite young then too. I had just got married when I met Bill. I wasn't even playing then. I had been playing down in Mississippi, but when I went to Chicago, Big Bill Broonzy and Memphis Slim, they was playin' together, and that started me back to wanting to play guitar.

So you gave up playing for a while?

Yes, I got married, and my wife was having children so fast, I had to get out and get a job. So I got that job. I worked about twelve years before I even picked up a guitar. I'd got rid of all of them. I got the kids, they was on the way, and I got them up. They was about eight years old when I started to go back [to playing guitar]. There was a time I always was active, and they had us both working—my wife and me. We did it ourselves. We worked to make ends meet. She worked at night and I worked in the day. So on my time off, I taught the children to sing. I'd babysit in the day while she worked, and we gathered around, and that's the way we started singing. Right around the house.

What were the first songs you taught your children?

"If I Could Hear My Mother Pray Again" and "Do Not Pass Me By"—those kind of songs. "Swing Low, Sweet Chariot."

You have such a distinctive guitar sound on your early records. I'd like to play you one of your old songs and ask you about it. [We listen to the opening of "If I Could Hear My Mother Pray Again."]

That was one of the first songs we ever played! Isn't that something.

What were you doing with the guitar to give it that sound?

Nothin.' I was just playin.'

What kind of amplifier?

Gibson. [*At this point, Pops picks up his Strat and sings and plays the first verse of the song we've just heard. Even without amplification, that distinctive tremolo sound is there—it turns out he created the effect by gently moving his left hand.*]

That's so beautiful. Let me ask you about something else. [We listen to the first verse of "The Lord's Prayer" from the Freedom Highway *CD.] Who did the vocal arrangement?*

I did. The children were so young, they didn't know how to sing in a key, what key, or nothin.' It's four sounds, so I just took them and . . . [*Pops plays* four descending notes of a major chord on his guitar, one at a time, singing the pitch for each one.]

Each child would take a note?

Yes, yes! That's what I did. I give them a note [*plays an A*]. I said, "Now you keep that. Hold it!" So she sings [*sings an A*]. Each one gets a note. When they all sing together, that makes a chord. That's the way I taught them how to sing. I said, "Now you just keep that sound all the way through." That's the way I taught them—no music or nothin'. I hit the string where they should be—where this one should be and where that one should be. That's the way I taught them how to make that music.

When did you become aware that Mavis had such a great voice?

Mavis was two years before we could get her—like I was hittin' that string—to hold her tune. For about two years, we kept on singing around the house. That's the reason I said, "Never think about going on no road," so we was just singin' for ourselves. After about two years, Pervis and me was singing lead. Mavis was singing contralto, and then Pervis's voice got too heavy for lead. I said, "Mavis, you try it." And right then, when she hit the first song, I said, "That's something." I knew then. One of the guys said, "Staples, man, you sure got a good group"—that was when Pervis and me were singin'. He said, "You did right to leave the other group and start your family." And I said, "Yeah, you think so? You just wait a minute—you ain't heard nothin' yet." Sure enough, about six more months, Mavis was taking off.

If somebody wanted to make a record of Pops Staples's best guitar playing, what songs would have to be on there? Which ones have your best guitar arrangements?

Those, and "Uncloudy Day," "I Been 'Buked and I Been Scorned," and "Swing Low, Sweet Chariot." Some of those songs. That would be some of my old songs, back in those days. I play about the same—I don't change much. But I can't get a amplifier now. They changes up so—instead of going good to better, it seem like that sound I was getting out of the amplifier then, can't get it now.

Did you have a reverb or a tremolo?

It was a tremolo on it, but they don't make the tremolos like they did. It's different things.

Have you tried getting one of the old amps or do you still have yours?

No. I found one, but they wouldn't sell it to me. Down in Los Angeles. Ry had a pretty good one, but Jackson Browne had the best one. Jackson Browne had what I needed. See, that's the one that I wanted to get and put it on the song with Bonnie Raitt ["World in Motion"]. That was a Fender Twin.

I don't know if it was a 10″ or 12″ speaker, but it was a Twin. It had a little foot tremolo [control], and you step on it. On one side [of the effects device] a wire come into the amplifier, and on the other side a wire come to the guitar.

Do you know what kind of tremolo it was? MXR?

It wasn't no MXR. I just can't remember. Whoo! Lord knows, if I had knew that this day was comin', I would have kept all that stuff, but I didn't.

You got rid of your classic gear?

Yeah. I didn't know how valuable it was.

Are there any guitars you've kept through the years?

No. I wish I'd have kept that Stella, and the Les Paul I got in Chicago. I got rid of it—it's worth about three, four thousand dollars now.

Is that what you used with Vee-Jay?

Yes. Les Paul.

What kind of guitar was on the songs we just heard?

Gibson Les Paul.

When you played on the Grammy Awards a couple of years ago, you conjured that old sound.

[*Pops fingerpicks and sings the first verse of "Nobody's Fault but Mine," using his fretting fingers to create a tremolo effect.*]

That's so deep, so Mississippi.

[*Laughs heartily.*] That's the Mississippi sound! Yeah.

Who are the best slide players you've seen?

[*Sighs.*] Ry Cooder in the late days. I didn't pay much attention to them before Ry Cooder and Bonnie Raitt. I wouldn't give one for the other. So there's two of 'em—Ry and Bonnie. I love both of 'em.

When you were growing up in Mississippi, did people use bottlenecks to play slide?

Yes, broken bottlenecks and pocketknives. Yeah, that's what they used.

How would they make slides from bottles?

They'd break that bottleneck off, and somehow they would make it fit their finger, and they'd play with it like that. But the knives, they would lay the guitar down on the lap and play with the knife. But with the bottle they could play with the guitar up.

That song you just played—"Nobody's Fault but Mine"—did you ever hear an old 78 of that song by Blind Willie Johnson?

Blind Willie Johnson. That's where I got it from.

When you were a child, did you ever hear people call blues "devil's music"?

Yes, yes. That's why they didn't want it in the church. Because that's the "devil's music." Not only the blues, the guitar was the "devil's instrument." And the Bible said we should use strings and wind horns and all to make music and praise God, but they took it for devil's music. It's not the instrument. It's what you play on the instrument. You know that.

Rev. Gatemouth Moore told me last summer that the only difference between blues and gospel is that you say "baby" instead of "Jesus."

I've heard that. I've heard that. You got to have the feeling in your heart and the meaning. So many have took the gospel songs and sung with a blues feeling, and took the blues songs and made a gospel-song feeling. I take the blues feeling and do gospel. What I call "gospel" is truth. I sing truth for song. Songs have meaning.

Rev. Dorsey defined gospel music as "good news."

Yeah, it is. It is.

What song did you play at Muddy Waters's funeral?

"Glory, Glory, Hallelujah, Since I Lay My Burden Down." Same thing I sang at Willie Dixon's. I was in London when I sung for him. He passed while I was in London. We made a beautiful tape. He was doing some talking, and I sung on it. Muddy Waters's and his.

When you're looking to get a guitar, how can you tell when you've found a good one?

Well, I've been using a Fender all the time. I been using this one here, that Strat, for about a year now. It's different in the feel of the neck. You can get the same guitar, same color and everything, but it won't play like this guitar. You have to pick by the way it feels to your hand. That's the way I pick mine. Of course, Fender made me a beautiful guitar—I guess it cost, oh, $1,100— and they give it to me. I endorsed it, and they gave it to me. It's beautiful, but I haven't learned how to play it like I have this one [*points to the Strat in his hotel room*]. I got this one. The one Fender made me got pearl all up and down the neck and got my name engraved in it, but I play this one. And they gave me this one for half price.

Do you play as much guitar now as you did twenty years ago?

No. I hardly ever play that much. I play more now since I made this record than I played in five or six years.

How great to be able to make this record.

The Lord has given me the strength and the will and the songs and brought stuff to me to do. I'm doin' very good with it. I got more write-ups with it than with anything, even with the Staple Singers. [*Pulls out a copy of* Jet *magazine and points to an article.*] That's what come out in the *Jet*—that's the Staple Singers' magazine. That *Jet* came out last week. You can't hardly get nothin' in the *Jet*, but they thought enough of me and they think the record is well enough to put me in there.

This article says it took you forty years to go solo!

[*Laughs.*] I didn't want to go solo! I always said when I was a boy, "If I ever get to be a man, I'm gonna make me a record." So I'm just now getting to it, just now getting to it.

Must feel pretty good.

Yeah, it does. It does.

Plus in such a difficult time, it's wonderful to have an uplifting message.

Yeah. I wonder sometime, does it do any good. It must be, because everybody talking about all the destruction in Los Angeles and all this stuff going on. The record seem like it come up just at the right time.

The title says it all—Peace to the Neighborhood.

"Peace to the Neighborhood"—see, that's what I strive for, Jas. Tryin' to bring peace to everybody that's miserable tryin' to make it. You can't pull yourself up by your own bootstrap. You need help sometimes. I was a lucky guy to be able to bring my children up. Through the time that I was comin' up, I had to work for three dollars a week—a whole week, sunup to sundown. Three dollars a week—that's less than you get for an hour's pay now on the minimum wage. But now, I am blessed to bring my kids up and we made a nice living out of it. Because I want to do the right thing. I'm trying my best to help if I can. That's what I'm trying to do. That's my aim and my purpose.

CODA: *Peace in the Neighborhood* earned Pops Staples a Grammy nomination. His follow-up album, *Father Father*, won the 1995 Grammy Award for Best Contemporary Blues Album. In 1999, the Staple Singers were inducted into the Rock and Roll Hall of Fame. Months later, eighty-five-year-old Pops Staples fell in his home in Dalton, Illinois, and suffered a concussion. He passed away on December 19, 2000.

The arrival of rock and roll in the mid-1950s brought a seismic shift in American culture. When a guitar-clutching Elvis Presley shook his hips on national television, and when Chuck Berry's "Maybellene" and Carl Perkins's "Blue Suede Shoes" came blaring through radio speakers, American youth embraced the music as theirs and theirs alone. Unlike the immaculate, uptight pop that came before, early rock and roll was fast, hard, visceral, even dangerous. Critics panned it, parents forbade it, preachers burned records. But kids *loved* it. Rock and roll brought tumultuous changes to fashion, attitudes, even lifestyles. Suddenly, it seemed, playing guitar became just about the coolest thing a young person could do.

Two schools of guitar playing dominated early rock and roll. On one side was Chuck Berry, who showed on single after single how to play a guitar just like ringin' a bell. On the other were the rockabilly cats, who blended white country music with black R&B. At the head of this class were Scotty Moore, Elvis Presley's lead guitarist; James Burton, who played alongside Ricky Nelson; and Carl Perkins, Buddy Holly, and Eddie Cochran, who did their own soloing. Nelson didn't have Elvis's snarl and swagger, and at the time he didn't compose his own songs like Perkins, Holly, and Cochran. But he was an excellent singer and decent rhythm guitarist, and he'd been blessed with movie-star good looks. And unlike his peers, he had the best promotional platform imaginable: a hit TV show.

Originally a 1940s radio show about a real-life mom, pop, and their two sons, *The Adventures of Ozzie and Harriet* made its television debut in 1952, when Ricky was twelve. By April 1957, when he performed his first on-the-air rock-and-roll song—a cover of Fats Domino's "I'm Walkin'"—the show had an estimated 15 million viewers. Within a month, his Verve single of "A Teenager's Romance" / "I'm Walkin'" had reached #4 in the *Billboard* singles chart. After switching to the Imperial label, Nelson brought in James Burton on guitar and rapidly produced hit after hit. Kids eagerly tuned in to each new episode of *Ozzie and Harriet*, hoping for another rock-and-roll performance. No mere teen idol, Ricky Nelson created some of the era's finest rockabilly and pop records.

With the British Invasion and the cancellation of the family show, Nelson hit a commercial dry spell. During the late 1960s he shed his teen-idol image and became one of the first rockers to explore country-rock. Getting booed at an October 1971 rock-and-roll revival at Madison Square Garden inspired him to compose his beloved song "Garden Party." During the next decade, Rick Nelson, as he now called himself, recorded albums for MCA, Capitol, and Epic, and toured up to 250 days a year. When we did our interview on

June 16, 1981, it seemed like I'd known him all of my life—and, in a way, I guess I had.

Who are the best guitarists you've worked with?

Oh, boy. You know, it's so hard to say. I think the two best are probably James Burton, who is really an innovator in guitar playing, and Bobby Neal. But it's so hard to generalize, because they have really different styles.

When James Burton joined your band, how well known was he?

He wasn't well known at all, really. The first time I heard him was in the office at Imperial Records. He came up from the *Louisiana Hayride* with Bob Luman. Actually, Bob Luman was auditioning for Imperial. I was looking for a band at that time. I was sixteen and so was James. I heard this guitar playing at the end of the hall. I thought, "Wow, I love the way he plays."

Your promo material mentioned that you recorded "A Teenager's Romance" after your girlfriend said she liked Elvis.

Yeah, I did that, and the other side was "I'm Walkin'."

Were you interested in rock and roll before then?

Yeah, very much so. I remember the first truly rock-and-roll record that I ever heard was with Carl Perkins. It was "Blue Suede Shoes."

What other influences did you bring with you into the studio?

Well, you couldn't help but be influenced by Elvis a little bit. My main influence was probably Carl Perkins at that time. I really idolized him. I really tried to sound like Carl Perkins. I used a standup bass—you know, a slap bass—at that time. Actually, electric basses came in about '57.

Did Ozzie have much to do with your getting signed to Verve?

My dad? Well, he was involved, because I was just sixteen at that time. And sure, he was very much involved.

Do you remember which musicians you used for the Verve sessions?

Yeah, I remember it was people like Barney Kessel—mainly jazz players. They really didn't understand rock and roll. There was a whole group of people that just never quite made it, like Howard Roberts and people like that. They were really great jazz players, but they never quite made it as far as playing rock and roll goes.

Do you remember how those early sessions were done?

Yeah, I sure do. We had one studio that we recorded in. It was just one room, and we'd all go down there and work out the arrangements right in the studio there. There was no title as a producer, you know. There was no such thing as a producer at that time. They were A&R men, and Jimmie Haskell was the kind of go-between for Imperial and myself, and I remember Jimmie used to hold up chord symbols and stuff because nobody could read in there at all. All of a sudden he'd bring out a big "A," and then all of a sudden a "C," things like that. So that was the extent of reading music.

Was there a natural echo in the room, or was the echo on those records done electronically?

It was a real chamber, upstairs.

What were the recording techniques?

It was just really straight-ahead. And what we used to do is we'd record the drums and bass really out front, on the basic track, if we were gonna lay vocals and things on it. They ended up being about four generations down, because that was when they used to overdub.

Compared to today, what was the turnaround time between the sessions and the product hitting the streets?

Oh, God, it was just so basic and straight-ahead, you know. It was a lot more healthy, I think. We'd record like, say, on a Saturday night, and the record would be out in all the stores like on Tuesday or Wednesday. That week, it would have sold a million records, you know, if I got lucky.

Did you pick the tunes yourself?

Yeah, I did, which was a real luxury.

Did you make suggestions to your guitar players, like to bring in the country influence, or did they bring it along with them?

No, they were all from the South, you know, so it was just a very automatic kind of thing. It's a certain feel. Nowadays they call it rockabilly, I guess, for lack of a label.

Being sixteen, how clear of a vision of the final product did you have?

Very clear, because I tried to emulate Sun Records. It was when Music City was happening, and I used to buy up all of the Sun Records down there. Because I love that sound.

Did you play guitar when you were young?

Yeah, I did.

How old were you?

Let me see—I think I was probably about fourteen.

When you moved from Verve to Imperial, was Joe Maphis your guitarist for a while?

Yeah, he was. On the first album, Joe played all the leads, like "Boppin' the Blues" and "Waitin' in School"—all those things.

How did Joe get involved?

There was a show called *Town Hall Party* with, like, Tex Ritter. Merle Travis was on it, and Joe Maphis. I got to know them because I dated Lorrie Collins at that time. I used to see her. They were called the Collins Kids, and Larry Collins was sort of a protégé of Joe Maphis on *Town Hall Party*. I used to go

*Ricky Nelson,
circa 1981. (Susan
Rothchild; courtesy
Capitol Records)*

down there every Saturday night and just sort of hang out there when I was about fifteen. I got to meet all the people and hear all the stories, and I really liked the way he played.

Who were your backup singers on the early records?

It was the Jordanaires.

Was there a lot of pressure on you being compared to Elvis?

Oh, you know, at that time everybody was compared to Elvis if you stood up and played a guitar. It wasn't really a pressure for me. It was something that I always felt was very flattering.

Being that young, did you have much artistic control over your career?

Yeah, I had complete control over it.

Did you go on many tours?

Yeah, during the summer. Actually, the first thing that I ever played was the Ohio State Fair, to 20,000 people. It's a large step from your bathroom to 20,000 people!

Did you see the 1978 film The Buddy Holly Story?

Yeah, I did.

Was that an accurate portrayal of what it was like back then?

I just met Buddy Holly very briefly. My friends during that time were Gene Vincent and Eddie Cochran and the Everly Brothers, people like that that I used to hang out with. But I never really got to know Buddy Holly. I know they used to go out on the Dick Clark bus tours for three or four months of one-nighters. I was very fortunate at that time to be able to play buildings by myself, so I never really had to do that.

Did you do much jamming with Gene Vincent?

Oh, yeah. A lot.

Was what he played with you the same as what he played in public?

Yeah, pretty much. And we were real good friends.

Compared to today, what was the concert scene like back then?

It was really the very beginnings of rock and roll, and people were getting their clothes torn off. It was very physical.

How did you become involved with the Burnette brothers?

I met Dorsey and Johnny right around the same time I knew Eddie Cochran and Gene Vincent. They had driven out from Tennessee, from Memphis, and they pulled up in the driveway. This is after my first record. They were very persistent. They just opened the trunk, took out their guitars, and started playing. I really did like the songs and the way they sang. They had a whole bunch of what are considered to be rockabilly-type songs right now, and I really liked them. So during that time I ended up with a handful of writers that I could more or less count on for material. Guys like Baker Knight and Dorsey, and subsequently I got to know them very well.[1]

How much freedom did you give James Burton on your records?

Almost complete freedom, unless I heard a specific thing that I wanted him to play. You know what? I was thinking about James, and I remember before there was anything like slinky strings, he was probably the first to come up with something like that. It was when we recorded "Believe What You Say." I remember him coming into the studio and going, "Hey, listen to this!" He'd put banjo strings on his guitar, so he could bend them way up, and that was really the front-runner of slinky strings.

What are your favorite cuts from the late '50s and early '60s?

Oh, boy. I'm not sure. It's so hard to say. You're speaking of mine? I don't know. They all have kind of a different flavor to them—at least I tried to make them different. I think "Lonesome Town" has a special meaning to me. It was probably one of the first records with just a guitar—just an acoustic guitar and a vocal.

Over the years, have you embraced new technology as it's come along?

It's kind of a constant battle for me, because all the magical kinds of things that happen have nothing to do with the technology. If anything, the technology does get in the way of those kind of overtones, the generation-down type thing. Like "Hello Mary Lou" was about eight generations down. So all of a sudden we got to about the seventh or eighth generation, and the cowbell started sounding like another kind of instrument. Really. Those kind of things are very difficult to duplicate.

Do you find it easier to put together an album now?

I kind of have to always—not fight it, but just keep in mind that if the technology part of it is heard on the record, it never quite makes it for me. So in a way, it's a little more difficult for me. Every record company wants me to have a producer, which can be easy if you get the right combination where a producer can come in with really good material and things like that. It can kind of ease the burden and let you record. But if you get a producer that wants to change your image and this and that—you know what I mean.

You self-produced the Garden Party *album.*

Yes.

Did you enjoy doing that?

Yeah, I *really* did, because when I wrote the song, I wrote it in one night. It was a very strange feeling because it was there to be written. I could hear exactly what I wanted it to sound like on a record. And then when I went into the studio, it started sounding that way. It was really exciting.

Would you recount the story of that song?

Oh, yeah. We played at Madison Square Garden. Richard Nader had been after me for about four years to do a rock-and-roll revival. I was really opposed to it. And I don't know—he caught me at a weak moment. I had just formed the Stone Canyon Band and I was writing a lot of material. We were playing colleges and things like that. So musically it was a whole other direction that I was going in. And I just thought, "Well, okay." I'd never played Madison Square Garden, and I started thinking of the reasons why I should do it. I never quite convinced myself, really. I've never been very good at faking it like that, you know. I have to make a complete commitment to whatever I'm doing in order to have it be the least bit successful. What I do, I really have to make a total commitment to it, and not talk myself into it. And that's what happened that night—I felt really out of place being there. It was a learning experience for me. It wasn't a sour grapes thing at all. It was just a reminder to myself that you gotta do what you believe in.

What do you view as the best period of rock and roll?

I think right now. It's wide open. I'm playing all over, not just L.A. and New York. I'm playing all over the country, and people are really willing to accept all kinds of music. For the first time, I don't think it necessarily has to fit into a specific slot as far as people go. Maybe the radio stations and the promotions people have to fit it into a slot to get played.

Who would have thought rock and roll would reach the proportions it has?

Oh, yeah! When I first started, people we're saying, "Well, it's gonna be out in three weeks anyways—it's a fad." Really!

And now it's probably the classical music of the future.

Oh, sure.

What venues do you play these days?

We've been doing a lot of schools, a lot of concerts, and they're really rewarding. Actually, we've been doing a lot of high schools.

That must be fun.

They really are, because all of a sudden we're playing to a whole new group of people that just accept you at face value. It's a real good feeling when they like the old songs. Like, say, "Believe What You Say," which is a very basic three-chord, rock-and-roll song. If anything, punk rock and all that has kind of come around a complete cycle to that, and it's a kind of a music I really understand and really enjoy playing.

Any contemporary rock and roll that you enjoy listening to?

Oh, yeah. Very much. I like Pat Benatar a lot—I think she's great. There are so many bands, it's really difficult. And they all have their own personalities because that's what happens when you get bands together like that, like garage-type bands. They end up having their own sound, which is great. I think it's a very healthy kind of thing.

What do you look for in a sideman in your own band?

It's a very intangible kind of quality they have to have. It's difficult to put it into words, but a certain feeling that either works or doesn't work—especially a drummer. It's so important to have a certain body rhythm. Like two people can play the same tempo and have it be completely different. With the band I have now, I'm really happy with it.

Who's the guitarist in your current band?

A fellow named Bobby Neal.

How did you find him?

Well, when I was with Epic, I went down to Memphis to record an album, and he was on those sessions. I heard him play down there, and I really liked the way he played.

What kind of guitars do you own now?

I have a Martin.

Do you know the model?

Let me see—it's a D-35. I've had it since I was seventeen.

Do you play lead at all?

Not really. I tried a couple of times, you know, and it took a little while to get it on tape [*laughs*], so I leave that up to somebody else.

Do you go on the road much now?

Oh, yeah. Really a lot. 200 days a year, on average.

How do you keep your sanity?

Well, that's a good question! [*Laughs.*]

Do you play your guitar much outside of performing?

You mean at home? Oh, yeah.

Do you use it to play yourself in and out of moods?

Yes, I do. And to write. It's weird—the best songs that I think that I have written have come from times when I haven't been necessarily thinking about writing a song—or thinking about anything specific. It's just maybe a mood or something like that, and something starts to happen.

Have songs ever come to you at odd times?

Not really. It's not like I go to sleep and write a verse on a pillowcase or something. I have done that—I've dreamt that I've written this great song. I'll write down a few words, wake up the next morning, and it's ridiculous. [*Laughs.*] I guess a lot of people have done that. Usually I just feel like playing. Sometimes I'll be walking around not necessarily thinking about anything. I know that's how "Garden Party" started happening. When it started to happen, I wrote the whole song on one piece of paper—I didn't want to move. I was writing on the corners, on the back, and everything.

Any advice for young performers?

All I can think about is that I really enjoy performing a lot and playing and doing what I do. That really has to be a prerequisite. It is for me, anyway. I don't see how you can do a really good job on something where you're just going through the motions. I just thoroughly enjoy what I'm doing.

CODA: After our interview, Rick Nelson continued to tour extensively. In 1984 he participated in a Sun Records reunion with his idol Carl Perkins, among others, which brought him his only Grammy Award. He played his final concert on December 30, 1985, concluding his encore with Buddy Holly's "Rave On." The following day Rick Nelson, Bobby Neal, and four others died in a plane crash. James Burton, who played with Nelson until 1968, went on to become an in-demand studio player and a mainstay in the bands of Elvis Presley and John Denver. To this day, Burton is regarded as the "Master of the Telecaster" and one of rock's all-time greatest soloists.

Carol Kaye in Cupertino, California, December 21, 1982. (Jon Sievert)

f there's ever a bible of women in rock and roll, chapter 1, verse one should read: "In the beginning, there was Carol Kaye." Originally a bebop guitarist, Carol crossed over into rock and roll in 1958, when Elvis Presley, Chuck Berry, Ricky Nelson, the Everly Brothers, and Connie Francis topped the charts. But unlike those who found fame and fortune as headliners, Carol chose to work her magic behind the scenes as a studio musician. A half century later, she remains a vital force in music.

During her heyday in the 1960s, Carol was a charter member of the small group of Los Angeles-based studio musicians who came to be known as the "Wrecking Crew." At various times, this collective's members included first-call guitarists Tommy Tedesco, Barney Kessel, Glen Campbell, and Al Casey; drummers Hal Blaine and Earl Palmer; saxophonist Steve Douglas; and electric bassists Joe Osborn and Max Bennett. Working alongside these session stalwarts, Carol played guitar and/or bass on Top-10 hits by the Beach Boys, Ray Charles, Joe Cocker, Sam Cooke, Bobby Darin, Jackie DeShannon, the Four Tops, Ike & Tina Turner, Jan & Dean, the Monkees, Paul Revere & the Raiders, the Righteous Brothers, Simon & Garfunkel, Sonny & Cher, Barbra Streisand, the Supremes, the Temptations, Stevie Wonder, Frank Zappa, and many others. In the 2008 documentary film *The Wrecking Crew*, Beach Boys leader Brian Wilson offered this assessment of Carol's place in music history: "Carol played on 'Good Vibrations' and 'California Girls,' and she was, like, the star of the show. I mean, she was the greatest bass player in the world, and she was way ahead of her time."[1]

Like other members of the Wrecking Crew, Carol eventually began emphasizing movie and TV dates. Her playing graced such beloved films as *Airport, Butch Cassidy and the Sundance Kid, Guess Who's Coming to Dinner, In the Heat of the Night, The Pawnbroker*, and *Walk, Don't Run*, to name a few. Her television credits include *The Addams Family, The Brady Bunch, Hawaii Five-O, Hogan's Heroes, M*A*S*H, Mission: Impossible*, and other popular series. In 2000, Berklee College of Music named her "the most recorded bassist of all time, with 10,000 sessions spanning four decades."[2] Over the years, Carol has also written and produced some of the best-received instructional books and videos for electric bassists.

I first learned of Carol through other musicians, notably Tommy Tedesco, Barney Kessel, Howard Roberts, and Mitch Holder, who'd all worked with her in the studio and spoke of her with great regard. During our January 1983 telephone interview and later in-person meetings, I found myself captivated by Carol's charm, energy, good humor, and get-it-done attitude.

Do you know of any women who were playing rock guitar or bass before you started playing sessions?

No, no. I knew of rock groups using women singers and all that. See, now, I was playing a lot of guitar in the late '50s. You know, in '56, '57, '58, I was playing a lot of bebop. And I was aware of rock, but to my knowledge I was the only female guitarist around in that area doing the records and all that stuff.

What town were you in?

The south part of Los Angeles. I lived there, and I worked in all the night-clubs. Most of the time, I was the only white person there, let alone being the only woman. There wasn't any discrimination as far as I felt. There were times when I felt like I wasn't playing up to par, and I realized it. I went home and practiced on the certain areas that I needed work on. Then all of a sudden I was very much in-demand in jam sessions, jazz work. Like, I played in Jack Sheldon's band in back of Lenny Bruce. George Shearing asked me to go on the road with him, but I was about eight months pregnant at the time, so I couldn't handle that, but it was a real honor.

When did you get into rock?

In the studios.

Do you remember your first session?

Yeah, very well! 1958, Bumps Blackwell came into the Beverly Caverns there where I was playing with a jazz group. I was working with Billy Higgins and Teddy Edwards. I forget who was on bass, but I used to work a lot with Scotty LaFaro, who passed on in those years. Bumps Blackwell walked in and he asked me if I wanted to do a record date. You know, Hollywood being the way it is, I said [*tentatively*], "Sure." I went down there, and it was a real record date! It was a soul group featuring Sam Cooke. It was Sam's second record that we were working on, and Lou Rawls was a singer on that date—it was his first record date too. Jesse Belvin was the other singer, and there was another older guy by the name of Alexander. It was a soul date, and it was fun. I said, "Yeah, this is kind of fun music." It was like gospel music. So I got into it that way. Then I played for H. B. Barnum a lot—a lot of gigs and a lot of record dates. And then I started to add the guitars then.

Were you playing bass at first?

No, no—guitar.

Who's H. B. Barnum?

H. B. is the guy who made the arrangements for Lou Rawls and for others—an arranger. He put a lot of the town to work. He wrote a lot of hit records, and he did a lot of Motown-type of dates. He didn't work for Motown, but it was that kind of stuff. And we did a lot of hits in those years, the early '60s.

Can you think of any?

Yeah. I played the guitar on all of Phil Spector's dates. In fact, the guitar I used, which was my early, early jazz guitar, was an Epiphone Emperor. Most of the secret of Phil Spector's sound was that they miked that. It was an acoustic guitar and an electric, but they miked it acoustically, and they'd dump a lot of echo on it—like on the Righteous Brothers' "You've Lost That Lovin' Feelin'." I played a lot of acoustic guitar on the Sonny & Cher stuff. The guitar fills that you heard, that was me. One of earlier hits that I played on was "Zip-a-Dee-Doo-Dah," but I played electric guitar on that. That was Bob B. Soxx & the Blue Jeans. Remember that one? In other words, I played on all of Phil Spector's hits, whether it was Ike & Tina Turner, the Righteous Brothers, or the Paris Sisters.

Did you play on "River Deep—Mountain High" by Ike and Tina?

Yeah! Uh-huh. Guitar. I'd have to listen to the record to tell you exactly which part, because he always used two or three guitars. He always used me and Barney Kessel, you know. David Cohen came in about '63, but I started working for Phil about 1960.

What was it like working for Phil Spector? Did he have charts and definite ideas of what he wanted?

Skeleton charts, mostly, but there were some dates—especially at Sonny & Cher dates—where Harold Battiste, a sax player, wrote all those fine arrangements. They were pretty intricate arrangements, in the sense that they were different. Every hit that Sonny & Cher put out was different. The style was different, which I think really, really made them successful. But there was one of their hits where the tune just kind of lay there like a dead dog. It was a one-chord tune, and I was starting to play bass, but I wasn't playing bass on that date. I was playing that acoustic guitar that I was telling you about. I was trying to figure out a bass line, a hook line, to make it happen. And I played a bass line, and Sonny heard it on the mike. He said, "Ooh, I love that bass line!" Now, you've got to realize, when I first met Sonny, he was playing tambourine on a Phil Spector date—and not very good at that! [*Laughs.*] I saw him meet Cher and saw all that go down. Anyway, Sonny heard that line, and he said, "Ooh, give that to the bass player." And that's the bass line to "The Beat Goes On."

Really? You invented that?

Yeah, that's my bass line. So we were called upon to read music and/or make up hook lines. See, the secret of a lot of hit records is in the bass line and the drum licks—but mostly the bass lines. Like later on, when I played bass for Quincy Jones, Quincy would get kind of backlogged with work. He had an awful lot of work, and I played on all of his films in the '60s and the early '70s. I played on *every one* of his movies, and every one of Michel Legrand's movies, and every one of the Hank Mancini movies. To cut a long story short, Quincy would tell us to just jam. He'd bring in a rhythm section and tell us to just jam, and we'd sit there and play funk for a couple of days. You know, when you got so much work, you don't know what's what and you don't care—you just want to get in, get out, and get paid. Find a parking place, and that's it.

So anyway, I went to the movies one time, and I said, "Gee, that stuff is really familiar!" And the name of the movie was *The New Centurions*. And what Quincy did, which is very, very hip—and I didn't feel plagiarized at all, I felt like, "Yeah, that's very hip"—he wrote the horn lines on all the bass notes that I played. So it sounded like it was arranged, but it wasn't. He took those bass fills and the bass licks that I played—because I played a lot of conga-type lines, like off-beat Latin kind of lines for funk—and he took an arrangement on top of the bass lines, so it sounded arranged. And some of the guitar hooks too—he'd take a little bit of that. I'm just saying that to tell you how important those hook lines are to arrangers, see. Like "Wichita Lineman," they took one of my bass licks and milked that for the string part. People are not aware how important the bass is to arranging, and I'm just saying this to make them aware. Because a lot of people love to play bass, and that's why, because you've got a lot of control. It's like the basement of a house.

You were with Phil Spector until when?

Oh, all the time. All of his hits. You know, he wouldn't do anything without me. The last time I worked for him was in '69, and I was a little bit spaced out because my fiancé had just died. Phil was trying to make a comeback at A&M, and I was so spaced out I couldn't play. And so he gave up—it was a flop that night.

So you were on all the famous girl-group records?

Yeah. Everything that Phil did, I'm playing on.

Mostly guitar or bass?

Mostly guitar. Bass toward the latter part of his records. Now, I started with Phil about 1960, and we did almost all the dates at Gold Star [Studios].

Were Phil Spector's sessions different from other producers'?

They were *long*. It would be anywhere from twenty to thirty-five takes. He took his time. He knew what he was looking for. Like, the whole band would sit around. It seemed like Hal Blaine used to have to play drums for about an hour before he could get to the bass and then the guitar—you know, to get the balance just right. And the horn section would play chess. I saw a lot of *Playboy* magazines with the guys! [*Laughs.*]

You were the only female guitarist or bassist at these sessions?

Mm-hmm. The only one.

What were some of your other sessions like—say, with the Beach Boys or Joe Cocker?

Okay, now. The Beach Boys, I played guitar on their early records.

Like "Help Me, Rhonda"?

No, that's bass. That's my first bass record. "Help Me, Rhonda" was the first record I did with them on bass. I kept the strings real high in those days. I mean, the bass was a real physical instrument. I kept them real high, and I used the Fender P-Bass with the Super Reverb amp. And they always miked me. They always miked me. They never took it through the board. You know, I got a pretty good sound. Even on some of the Motown dates—like "Love Child" and "Bernadette," I played bass on—I added more bottom, but they miked me on that stuff too. But the Beach Boys took a lot of takes too. You know, it seemed like Phil Spector kind of set the standard—it was okay to go six hours on one tune, which we did. They used all studio guys, except for Carl [Wilson]. Carl would be in the booth, on twelve-string. He mostly played twelve-string. And he'd sit and play with us, but he'd be in the booth. Lyle Rich played acoustic bass—there was an acoustic bass on there too. But you couldn't hear the acoustic bass except like on "Good Vibrations"—for a while there's two parts there. I played the higher part. [*Sings the line.*]

Did you come up with that line?

No, that's Brian's stuff. Now, Brian Wilson wrote all of his lines. Once in a while I played a fill or something that was mine, but I can't lay claim to any of Brian's bass lines. But the feel—if you listen to "Good Vibrations," that feel is a jazz feel. It's a walking feel [*sings main bass riff*]. That's pure jazz, and Brian was greatly influenced by jazz. He was influenced by the Four Freshmen—you know, they way they sung. Barney Kessel, Howard Roberts, and I were constantly on those dates. We were constantly being amazed by Brian, because he's the one that arranged it all, and he came up with all the ideas and everything. We met the other Beach Boys—they were really nice and all that—but it was Brian's talent, really, that did all that stuff. On the *Pet Sounds* album, I played bass on all except one tune—there's one tune on the *Pet Sounds* album that I didn't play bass on. In fact, that's George Harrison's favorite album, the *Pet Sounds* album. A lot of people like that album. I mean, it's a very creative album.

After you played on the Beach Boys' records, would you then teach them the parts?

No. No, it's just that they copied what we did. Like, they copied the feel and they copied the parts that we came up with, but it was Brian that wrote the parts. I mean, he didn't physically really write them very well. He put stems on the wrong sides of the notes and like that, and we'd have to recopy it in another key and that kind of stuff. We spent time doing that too—in other words, the music wasn't legally very good. We had to sit down and re-write it, but it came from his head. And the parts were fairly simple, so they could go out on the road and cut them, but they couldn't get that real, old studio feel that we got because I was in the clique that was playing on all the hit records. That's all we did—cut a hit from 8:00 A.M. in the morning till 12:00 midnight, every day of the week. I'll tell you some of the people I worked with: Johnny Mathis, Hank Mancini, Pet[ula] Clark, Andy Williams, Sam & Dave.

Did you play on "Soul Man"?

I don't know the names of the records. See, I played on thousands of rec-ords, so I know some of the names of the records I played on. But I can hear stuff and say, "Oh, yeah. I played guitar on that." I can remember the rhyth-mic part I played or the lead part. Remember the Alka-Seltzer ad? [*Sings the familiar riff.*] Well, that was me that played guitar on that. I was the lead guitar of the T-Bones—remember that group?[3] That was me on that. And I played lead guitar on the *Green Acres* show that you're hearing right now, and that was cut about fifteen years ago. And I played guitar on—remember the coffee commercial? [*Sings the Maxwell House riff.*] Okay, the very first ones were me. The electric twelve-string that you heard on the first two or three records by the Tijuana Brass, Herb Alpert's group, that's me. A Wrigley's gum ad was lifted from one of his albums—that's me on twelve-string.[4] I got a lot of money for that ad. I'm just trying to give you a brief picture, because it's really a huge thing to describe all the mountains of work that you do.

What were the hardest rock sessions you tackled?

The ones that weren't very musically satisfying, like The Hondells, be-cause it was so dumb, and you'd be playing that dumb stuff for *hours*. And I like Mike Curb—Mike Curb was a pretty nice guy. I played guitar on all those things. Howard Roberts was also on those dates, and we'd just sit there and space out. It was like, "Oh, God, I should have turned this down." But it was a lot of money. You don't turn down money—I mean, a lot of it, that is. That was hard. Some of the Dick Dale stuff was hard.

Did you play on stuff like his "Misirlou"?

I don't know the names. I'd have to listen. But most of his stuff I did. Let's see—some of the harder stuff. The stuff that took hours, and it didn't need to take hours. Like, Phil Spector set this thing that it's supposed to take six hours to cut a hit record, and he had such a phenomenal success that everybody thought, "Oh, I've got to take six hours," and most of them didn't have to. You know, they were practicing in the studios, just like doctors practice on their patients. They were practicing in the studio how to make a hit record, see? And that's why it took so many hours. Now people pretty well have it down, but I'm not really thrilled with most of the music that's coming out. It seems like the feeling is not there.

Was anyone ever surprised when you, being a woman bass player, showed up on the date?

No, no. I never got that—I guess because I had a pretty good reputation for being a live player in jazz. If you were a successful jazz player, you were *very* respected by all the players.

Did you consider yourself a rocker?

Yeah, yeah. I started to tell you that in my mind it was very hard to make that transition from being a very successful jazz player and an up-and-coming giant in jazz, which doesn't pay any money, to doing studio work, which was really dumb, until I got the idea that, "Hey, it's fun to make a hit record, and this stuff can groove too." Even though it's rock and roll and 8/8, it's got its own groove to it. At that time, when I started playing on all the #1 hit records that were coming out of the West Coast, definitely then I thought, "Yes, I'm a rock guitarist." I didn't feel like I was a rock bassist there for a long time, because I always felt like I was a guitar player that just picked up the bass.

So your early sessions were guitar, and you switched to bass in the mid-1960s.

Yeah, '64.

And from there it was primarily bass.

Yeah, it really shot up. I was about number-three or number-four call on guitar in those studio years, and I was making pretty good money. But then when I switched to bass, I put a lot of bass players out of work because in those years they were using acoustic bass and Danelectro 6-string bass guitar. A lot of people call the Fender bass a bass guitar, but the Danelectro is the "bass guitar," because that's got six strings. They'd use, like, three basses on the date. Well, as soon as I started playing bass, I put the other two bass players out of work, because I played it with the pick and it got a really good sound. And I was the only one in town that was really working my tail off.

Was it always charts and reading, or did they sometimes ask you to come with parts on your own?

Both. It was both. If I couldn't make a Motown date, Gene Page would have a real simple bass part for the other bass player that could make it. But he would write some outrageous bass parts, and I'd sit down there and sight-read them. Quincy Jones would occasionally write some great bass parts, like the *Ironside* theme. And I'm also the one that played the theme of *Mission: Impossible*—Lalo Schifrin. So you had to be able to read all kinds of music, you know, depending upon if it was films or records. But at the same time, there'd be times you'd go on a date and there was no music written, and you'd have to skull-out a part with chords. You write them on a blank piece of paper and come up with a bass line.

Were you ever asked to join groups?

Yeah, yeah. Occasionally. See, most of the groups in the '60s didn't want people to know that they did not record their own music. Okay. But occasionally there'd be a call to go out on the road, but I just couldn't afford to, because I was making so much money and I had my kids. I didn't want to go out on the road.

Did you continue to do rock dates throughout the 1970s?

No, it became more film, but they wanted the rock-type of bass. You know, the rock-funk bass on the film thing. I have to look at some of these credits. [*Carol refers to the quarterly royalty statements that studio musicians received.*] *Valley of the Dolls*, for instance, *The Thomas Crown Affair, On Any Sunday, Walk, Don't Run*, a lot of movies from Universal, which were real murder movies. Oh, remember *In the Heat of the Night?* I'm the fuzz bass player on that. [*Laughs.*]

Did you have to keep up with all of the effects?

Yes. I'm the first one who used effects in the movies—like on the theme of *Airport*, I used that Gibson box that had all the things like the octave doubler and that one that sounded like steam. What's the name of that little Gibson box? Oh, the Maestro. And I'm the first one that used the fuzz tone on a bass in the movies. So yes, I did have to use the effects, but not like they're doing now. Like, I never used a flanger or anything like that.

So in the 1970s it was mainly film.

In the film dates they still wanted the rock thing, but it was kind of like pseudo-rock. It wasn't the real rock that we did on the Phil Spector dates or with Gary Puckett. For instance, I played on Gary Puckett's stuff, and Harry Nilsson.

You also played with Joe Cocker and Stevie Wonder.

Yeah. "I Was Made to Love Her"—there's a few of them I did with Stevie. A lot of that [Motown] stuff was cut on the West Coast, and people don't know that. And then the Joe Cocker was "Feelin' Alright." I liked that—it was a fun record. And then Jerry Vale—a lot of pop stuff. Sam & Dave and Ike & Tina

Turner—I played on their stuff a lot—and a lot of Ray Charles too, but that was like gospel-rock. That wasn't really rock-rock.

When did you become aware of other women playing rock guitar and bass?

Well, not really until about the '70s, when I started to see women play in rock groups live. You know, I've been out of the studios now—well, I *do* do occasional studio work—but I've been out in the public. Because when you're in the studios, that's the only life you know, and it's like being locked up in jail or something. You don't interact with the general public, so you don't know what's going on out there. You're in there cutting all the hit records and they're listening to you and everything, but you don't grow any other way but in your music. See? Now, coming out, I realize the attitudes that women have to develop. But you know something? It's really not that much different than when I got started, because I never thought of myself as a woman. I thought of myself as a guitar player. Now I'm seeing women in groups, and it seems like they've cut out the notion, "Well, I've got to play like a man." You know, that's not it either. You either play or you don't play. And that's the attitude. And the ones that seem to come across the best seem to have that attitude.

It's like if somebody puts you down, you just gotta put the blinders on and keep going. Forget their trips—that's their trip and that's their hang-up. For women in rock nowadays, the ones who are successful are the ones who exploit their own talent and get it across with strength and with conviction. But the ones who are trying to put the men down or they're trying to be cute with the boobs and that kind of stuff—you know, pretty soon they die out. But I've seen a lot of women players that I really like. In fact, the women that were in the group Heart [Nancy and Ann Wilson]—I like those women. They weren't really technically fantastic players, but I like what they did onstage. And the new women's groups coming up, I like the way that they put themselves across without being real cute and coy. In other words, they're taking care of business without saying, "Hey, look at me! I've got the curves too."

CODA: These days, Carol Kaye still plays bass, produces instructional material, gives lessons via Skype, and operates her own website at www.carol-kaye.com. In 2008, she had a starring role in the film documentary *The Wrecking Crew*.

During the pre-Internet era, few musicians had as rapid a rise to fame or as profound an impact as Jimi Hendrix. Issued in mid-1967, the Jimi Hendrix Experience's *Are You Experienced* is arguably the most revolutionary debut album in rock history. The album instantly upped the ante for guitarists on both sides of the Atlantic. While others before had experimented with massive volume, feedback, distortion, whammy, wah-wah, octave doubling, and other sonic effects, Hendrix was the first to harness them all into music so extraordinarily imaginative and enduring. And then there were the album's innovative songwriting, multi-layered arrangements, ping-ponging production, unprecedented approaches to tones, chord voicings, and solos. . . . In short, *Are You Experienced* surprised *everyone*. During his remaining three years in the spotlight, Jimi would further refine and redefine the role of the electric guitar in rock, R&B, and blues settings.

Fast forward to 1983. Synthesizer-saturated pop ruled the airwaves and singles charts, while harder rock and especially blues music seemed to be in a tailspin. Even the most venerable of bluesmen—John Lee Hooker, Muddy Waters, and Johnny Winter among them—had experienced drops in album sales and bookings. Then, like a bolt of lightning, Stevie Ray Vaughan arrived on the scene. The native of Austin, Texas, struck first with his Albert King–inspired licks in David Bowie's "Let's Dance." His subsequent debut album, *Texas Flood*, rapidly made him the most important American blues-rock guitar hero since, well, Jimi Hendrix. For years to come, B. B. King, John Lee Hooker, Buddy Guy, and others would credit Vaughan for revitalizing interest in their music.

Like his hero Jimi Hendrix, Stevie Ray Vaughan was part bluesman, part rock and roller. And Stevie, bless his heart, was always quick to credit the musicians who influenced him. These ranged from lesser-known figures such as Larry Davis, who recorded the original "Texas Flood," to movers and shakers like Chuck Berry, Albert King, Buddy Guy, and Albert Collins. But no influence loomed larger in his repertoire than Jimi Hendrix, many of whose songs he mastered note-for-note. He recorded live and studio versions of "Voodoo Child (Slight Return)," "Little Wing," and "Third Stone from the Sun," and often played Hendrix songs in concert. When I contacted Stevie to ask if he'd be willing to do an interview about Jimi Hendrix, he readily agreed. On February 9, 1989, he called me during a break from sessions for his album *In Step*.

When did you first become aware of Jimi Hendrix?
The first time I ever heard his name was when my brother brought a rec-

ord of his home in the mid-'60s. I guess it was around '67, '68. And Jimmie had found it in a trash bin! Behind it. He was playing a gig at this [television] show in Dallas called *Sump'n Else*, and he found this record. He recognized it because he'd seen a little blurb in a magazine, just a short paragraph about Jimi Hendrix. He knew he was supposed to be something really happening, and he just happened to see this record that had gotten thrown out with a bunch of other stuff, because it didn't fit in with the show perfectly or something, you know. And he brought it home and put it on the record player, and we just about—what can you do? [*Laughs.*] What can you do but say, "*Yeah!*" It really knocked my socks off.

I'm not sure exactly the year, and I'm not sure which song it was. It's kind of a blur, because around the same time my brother Jimmie, he had this knack of figuring out who was really happening. And why! [*Laughs.*] And he would bring home these records. It seemed to me that Jimmie would all of a sudden bring home stuff, and it would be months before you would hear it anywhere else. He would bring home so much of it. He would get into a certain style of music, and he would bring a *lot* of that stuff home about the same time. It just seemed as if for some reason he could just come up with a style and all of a sudden he had all the ifs, ands, and buts around it. All of the things of different people who were in the same school—that went to school together, you know, instead of a different school. He would bring home all these things at the same time, so a lot of the different influences that were on Jimi Hendrix, I heard those things at the same time.

So you were listening to people like Albert King and hearing the relationship.

Albert King and Lonnie Mack and Albert Collins and Muddy. Jimmie would bring home all that stuff at the same time. It seemed as if it was like within a month or two.

Did you sit down and learn to play from that first Hendrix record Jimmie brought home?

Sure! Hey, man, I remember getting my little stereo—it was an Airline with the "satellite speakers." That's what they called them, but they were really these cardboard boxes with a long wire. I would set that up, mike that up. I had a Shure P.A. in my room—this is in my bedroom. For some of my first gigs, I'd go and rent like four Super Reverbs, and I'd have all this set up in my room. [*Laughs.*] Of course, the parents were at work. I would go in there and floorboard it, you know. Dress up as cool as I could and try to learn his stuff. It all went together. I would try to learn his stuff, and I did the same thing with a lot of B. B. King records. I think back and I must have really—if somebody had walked into the room, they probably would have gone, "What are you doing?!" Because I wouldn't stop at one place—I'd go for every bit of it I could find.

You'd go for all the tricks?

I remember doing it a lot with *Axis: Bold as Love*, even though I didn't have the phasing deals, and I'm sure I didn't have a lot of the sounds. But some of them I could find.

Were you playing a Stratocaster?

Well, at different times, different things. Jimi had a Strat, and a lot of times I would use a Telecaster, but I had a little bit different pickups. I'd rebuilt the guitar myself, so there was some blood in it, you know. I would go as far as I could to get as close as I could.

Did you think of Jimi as coming out of the blues tradition?

Some people don't see it. Some people really do see it. See, I don't know whether to call Hendrix a blues player along with a lot of the originals, but he did go and play with a lot of those people. He did do a lot of it during that heyday, before he got famous. It's like he was on the tail end of something.

That whole R&B movement.

Yeah. And a lot of it wasn't even the tail end. A lot of it was the peak of it. He was doing that stuff as it was going on, you know. See, in his music, I hear not just the newer stuff that everybody seems to think was a lot different— and a lot of it is—but to my ears, there's just as much of the old-style warmth.

The blues style.

Yeah! Like "Red House." I hear it in that. I hear it in just the way he approaches things. Even though he was not ashamed at all of doing some things different, I still hear the roots of the old style. I mean, not just roots, but the whole attitude of it.

Jimi's sometimes not that far removed from Muddy Waters.

To me, he's like a Bo Diddley of a different generation. If you were a kid and you heard Bo Diddley for the first time, back when all that was going on, wouldn't you think that was the wildest thing you ever heard?

Yeah, sure.

Okay. [*Laughs.*] I'm not saying that Jimi Hendrix was a Bo Diddley, but in that sense, there's not that much difference. Or Muddy Waters or Chuck Berry. It was that different. He just happened to have those influences as well.

Jimi, who was left-handed, used a right-handed guitar that he flipped over, so his high-E string had a shorter scale length than the low-E string. Could this have affected the way his string bends sounded?

Yeah. I have guitars where the necks are set up that way, and there is a difference. However, to me the bigger difference is the shape of the neck.

I've got a left-handed neck on an old Strat that I have—someone gave me a left-handed neck—and the main thing I notice about it is the neck feels different because it's shaped backwards. I didn't know about it until I put one on there. The neck feels different. The tension of the strings does work well that way. One thing that I noticed that's a lot different is where the wang bar is—if it's on the top or on the bottom. Whether I hold it with the same grip as if it was in the other place or not, it still feels different to me at the top. It seems more approachable or something.

What have you observed about Jimi using a whammy bar while playing blues?

I think he did it cool! I think if somebody else had thought about it first, they would have done it too.

Do you think Jimi was one of the first?

Uh, no. I say that because there's a record that I think Hendrix must have heard this guy and gone, "My God! I need to check this out!" It sounds like something Hendrix would do, except it was recorded in '58. The album is called *Blues in D Natural*—it's a compilation album—and the [catalog] number is 005. The label is Red Lightnin', an English import. The songs are called "Boot Hill" and "I Believe in a Woman." It's by Sly Williams. Go get you a copy and listen to it, and you'll go, "Shit!" [*Laughs.*] I've never heard anybody other than Hendrix get this intensity and play as wild as this guy. He uses a wang bar, and he uses it real radical in places.

Do you know anything about the guy? Where he was from?

From what I've been told, it's Syl Johnson a long time ago. Now, I don't know if it is or not, but that's what I've been told by someone who's real checked-out about their information. What it says under it [the song title] is something to the effect of "Sly Williams, guitar and vocals," and then it says something like, "Bass, drums, and piano and horn, unknown. California? 58–59." It's unbelievable. It's like this guy's teeth are sticking out of the record! [*Laughs.*] It's unbelievable. And ever since I ever heard it, every time I hear it, it seems impossible that Hendrix didn't hear this guy. And some people seem to think that it might be him playing guitar.

I haven't heard of that artist.

I hadn't either. That's the only record I ever heard by this guy.

What made Jimi's blues playing so distinctive from other guitarists?

[*Pause.*] I think a lot of it's his touch and his confidence. I mean, his touch was not just playing-wise, but the way he looked at it, like his perspective. His perspective on everything seemed to be reaching up—not just for more recognition, but more giving. I may be wrong about that, but that's what I

Jimi Hendrix onstage at Woodstock, 1969. (Courtesy MCA Records)

get out of it. And he did that with his touch on the guitar and his sounds and his whole attitude—it was the same kind of thing.

What pickups settings did he tend to go for while playing blues?

Well, I have my own ideas about that, but I tend to not necessarily get that right. [*Laughs.*] The way I play, sometimes I tend to play harder than I need to, therefore I don't get as much out of it.

Tonally, I hear a similarity between your "Texas Flood" and some of Jimi's records.

I'm trying to get as close to a natural, old-style sound as possible, and I think a lot of his tones were that way. He was just reaching for the best tone that he could find. Actually, I kind of think a lot of his tones were just that's the way he heard them, and he didn't have to worry about it—which is something that I do a lot!

You worry?

Yeah, I'm a worrywart! [*Laughs.*] Sure.

That doesn't come across at all onstage.

There's not a whole lot of time to get stuck in it. I know that either I can turn up or I can turn down, so if it's not working right, I usually stomp my foot and turn it up! You know, I have a real hard time with amps, and I'm having a hard time right now with them. They keep dying.

Are you using older ones?

A combination. With this record we're doing now [*In Step*], I brought thirty-two amps with me.

How can you possibly need thirty-two amps?

They keep dying like flies! I brought them for different configurations to see which ones sound the best in the studio, because we haven't been in the studio for a long time. And many times an amp will sound good at home, and when you put it in the studio and you close-mike it, its little quirks stick out a lot more.

You hear all the buzzing and rattle . . .

That you wouldn't necessarily hear in a concert situation. But so far I've ended up having to have everything I brought rebuilt—either rebuilt, or just put it back in the case. And it's real frustrating. However, sometimes an amp when it's dying, it sounds better than it has in a long time—with every last breath, it really wants to live! [*Laughs.*] I think the quality of the amps for guitar and for warm sounds, the quality of the parts themselves, used to be better. Therefore they worked better. And with some of the old effects, when they don't work properly, that's when they sound so good.

You never found one amp that had everything you're looking for?

I bought these Dumble amps—I bought the first one because I was really amazed. After it broke down the first time, it's never sounded the same. I've bought several of them, and every one of them sounds different and is built different, and I keep wanting the same one that I bought in the first place.

A final question about Jimi Hendrix. Right now, he's more popular than he ever was during his career. He's selling more records, getting a lot of coverage in the press, his videos are on TV. Why is this?

He's not putting out more things. It's a good question. A great question. Why might I think so? I think a lot of people need what he had to offer musically—there was a lot of honesty in it. Yeah, there was a lot of drugs and things, but people are looking back because they miss something that's here. A lot of people tend to look somewhere else for something that they want to fix them. His music, though, is wonderful. It's full of emotion. It's full of fire. At different points it's full of different things. It's full of light and heavy things, you know, feelings. By "light feelings" I mean uplifting feelings, and "heavy"—well, you know what "heavy" means! It could mean anything from one day to the next, really. But I think a lot of people miss what his music was doing for them. A lot of new people are coming around to going, "What's this?!" In very few instances has anybody surpassed what he did. And it should be popular! It's a damn shame that he's dead and gone, and now is when people are listening. But, at the same time, I'm glad they're listening!

CODA: Stevie Ray Vaughan remained devoted to Jimi's music for the rest of his life. On August 26, 1990, he gave his last concert with Double Trouble, concluding the set with Jimi's "Voodoo Child (Slight Return)." He then joined Eric Clapton and others for a final encore of "Sweet Home Chicago." Soon afterward, Stevie Ray Vaughan perished in a helicopter crash.

*James Gurley
in San Rafael,
California,
September 30, 1978.
(Jon Sievert)*

R hapsodic, cathartic, and stoned-out, psychedelic music came roaring into existence in the mid-1960s. The style's guitar-centric, anything-goes approach ushered in the era of extended solos, wild effects, ringing eardrums, and an unprecedented merging of influences—from post-war American blues, jazz, folk, and rock to sounds culled from Africa, India, and other parts of the world. "Certainly drugs played a role—that's way up front," remembered Sam Andrew, who helped pioneer the style in San Francisco. "Psychedelic music was not powered by alcohol. In many ways, it was a reaction to the beat era that came right before, which was an era of cynicism and despair and the humor that comes from having given up. The beat movement was a cool jazz thing and very literate and verbal. This all melted into that 'hippie' thing, which was a derogatory term used by the beats for younger people hanging around trying to crash the beat scene, like I was. We were all younger and hopeful and hadn't given up. That sense of possibility had a big influence on psychedelic music."[1]

Barry "The Fish" Melton may have been the first in the San Francisco area to play a psychedelic guitar solo on a commercially released record, Country Joe and The Fish's 1965 EP featuring "Bass Strings" and "Section 43," but he's quick to credit another as the style's creator: "James Gurley is the founder of psychedelic guitar because he was the first guy to play in the *zone*. He never really played straight all that well, but the thing that defines psychedelic guitar—because certainly the chord boxes are the same as folk—is that it gets improvisational and goes out to this place where the beat is assumed. The music is kind of out there in space, and James Gurley was the first man in space! He's the Yuri Gagarin of psychedelic guitar."[2]

The son of a stunt car driver, Gurley grew up in Detroit, where he began his entertainment career as a "human battering ram," which required him to be hurled helmet-first through burning wood. Inspired by folk, blues, and a sense of self-preservation, he switched to performing music in his teens. His cross-country hitchhikes eventually landed him in San Francisco. Moving to the Haight-Ashbury district, Gurley would sometimes spend hours sitting in a closet, listening to his acoustic guitar through an attached stethoscope. He'd never played rock or owned an electric guitar before auditioning for Big Brother and the Holding Company in 1965. Sam Andrew, his co-guitarist in Big Brother, recalled that during the band's earliest phase, he and James often listened to recordings of John Coltrane, Miles Davis, Ornette Coleman, Sun Ra, and South Indian veena and sitar music. "Another musician we listened to a lot was Cecil Taylor," Sam remembered. "We were consciously striving for that, and we would very often play one song an entire set, which is what Cecil would do. Big Brother was such an atypical band. A case could be made that we were the most psychedelic of the early bands, simply because we really hadn't put in a lot of time in clubs."[3]

Janis Joplin, who'd quietly been singing traditional blues songs in coffeehouses, completely transformed her style upon joining Big Brother in 1966. "The moment Janis heard the volume increase, she had it," Sam explained. "It was like she switched a channel that brought out the power. And the music was louder by a quantum leap than what went before. It made everything different. It took away all the rules. And the velocity was something too—it would just shift into overdrive."[4] Weeks after Janis joined, Big Brother rushed into a studio to record their eponymous debut album for the short-lived Mainstream label, to little acclaim. Soon thereafter, though, their mind-blowing performance at the 1967 Monterey Pop Festival brought them worldwide attention. A Columbia Records mega-deal led to the band's landmark *Cheap Thrills* album. Janis's voice was rightfully hailed as a force of nature, but many critics and listeners decried the band's guitar playing as woefully out-of-tune. Fans, though, snapped up copies, and beginning in September 1968, *Cheap Thrills* spent eight weeks at #1 in the *Billboard* album charts.[5] "Piece of My Heart" became the band's highest-charting single, reaching #12. The song has endured as one of the psychedelic era's defining singles and the finest example of James Gurley's unfettered approach to lead guitar.

Big Brother's ride to the top of the charts would be short-lived. After *Cheap Thrills*, Janis Joplin quit the band to pursue a solo career. Big Brother carried on for two more albums—*Be a Brother* and *How Hard It Is*—before disbanding. For a while Gurley performed around San Francisco with a band called Ruby. He then moved to Salt Lake City and finally settled in Palm Desert, California, where he attended the College of the Desert. Five years after Big Brother's breakup, Chet Helms, the band's original organizer, persuaded its original members—Gurley and Andrew, bassist Peter Albin, and drummer Dave Getz—to reunite for the Tribal Stomp concert held in Berkeley, California, on October 1, 1978. Helms invited photographer Jon Sievert and me to the band's rehearsals in San Rafael the day before the show. When Jon and I arrived, we watched as Gurley and Andrew greeted each other for the first time since the band's breakup five years earlier. James readily agreed to do an interview.

Coming from Detroit, how did you end up getting involved with Big Brother?
Through Chet Helms.
How did you run into him?

I was living at the Family Dog—this was before Chet was part of the Family Dog. The Family Dog was started by four other people as a group. Alton Kelley was one, the poster artist in the San Francisco days. They started the Family Dog, and then they gradually dropped out of it—I don't know how it evolved from there, but gradually Chet took hold of it. Through them and through all this interaction, I met him. He said that he was trying to manage a band and was auditioning guitar players. I went and auditioned. I don't know—I don't think they really knew what to make of it at first, because I had been listening to a lot of John Coltrane and stuff before that. When I heard John Coltrane, I thought, "Jesus! If you could play a guitar like that, that would be really far out!" So I was trying to get a grip on something like that, but nobody could understand what I was trying to do, you know. I don't know if I understood. So they auditioned a bunch of guys and chose me.

How did Janis Joplin come in?

We'd been gigging and playing. We were doing a lot of instrumentals—you know, real wild instrumental stuff—and we felt the need to expand more vocally. Peter and Sam both have pretty good, strong voices—pretty nice, deep voices. But we felt we wanted something else. Me and Peter had seen Janis at the Coffee Gallery in San Francisco a couple of years before this. See, we'd just been in there and saw her sing. She was doing a folk thing, a Bessie Smith kind of a thing. I think there's some out—I've heard it on the radio, but I don't know what it is. It's just her playing guitar, and it's real good. As a matter of fact, I think she did that best. It's too bad that she didn't get a chance to do something more like that before she died, because she could really do that with a lot of soul and power. It was really great. I thought that was her best stuff.

What was it like working with Janis?

Oh, she was temperamental. I mean, one day she'd be up, the next day she'd be down. You never knew what to expect. It was crazy days for everybody. That whole period, it just seemed like everything was happening at once. It was just all happening so fast, it was hard to keep track of things. At times she could be great to work with, because she was very intelligent. She was really smart, a very smart woman. Had a lot of understanding about things. But also she could just get real petty and bullshitty about something for seemingly no reason. I guess we all do that. We were all developing, and the band was just breaking out. Everybody's going crazy with all this.

What did you think about the first album, the one on Mainstream?

I listened to it the other day to learn these songs over again, because I couldn't remember them. I thought there was some pretty good energy on a couple of cuts, but I thought it was poorly recorded. I remember it was

119

recorded at a four-track studio in L.A. I think we did it in two days. It was the first time we'd ever been in the studio. It surprised me—the sound of the thing is so trebly. You know, there's no bottom to it. The way they cut it, there's just no bottom to it at all. But *Cheap Thrills*—I like the whole first side of *Cheap Thrills*.

Did you learn to read music somewhere along the line?

I can read, but not sight-read. Like B. B. King says, "My reading is more like spelling." [*Laughs.*] Because I learned by ear first. See, I'm ear-trained. I can learn a song faster by listening to it than I can by trying to read it, although I know what all the notes are and I can read the staff and everything. It's just that I don't have the discipline to sit around long enough to wade through all the books.

When did you first start playing? In Detroit?

Yeah. I was nineteen, I think it was, when I got started.

Did you start on electric guitar?

No. I went into a folkie kind of bag first. Blues—country rural blues. Lead Belly and Brownie McGhee and Lightnin' Hopkins. I loved Lightnin' Hopkins, man. As a matter of fact, I once hitchhiked to Houston. I was coming from Mexico and hitchhiked all the way to Houston to try to find Lightnin' Hopkins. But I couldn't find him, and I didn't have any money. I was backpacking and sleeping under bridges.

Was Lightnin' Hopkins your first major inspiration?

Yeah. He was really my most impressionable. I really wanted to play like him most of anybody. I just loved his raw sound. And John Lee Hooker I liked. There's this one song John Lee does called "Down Child." Oh, God—it'll raise the hair on your head, man. Oooh! I love that. That's like a razor, that song. It's really a fine song. And then from Texas, I hitchhiked to New Orleans. You won't believe this—I'm walking down the street and I get arrested. The paddy wagon comes along, and they throw me in jail—for nothing. I was just walking down the street with my guitar. The paddy wagon was going down the street, and the guy would go [*pointing*], "This guy. This guy. This guy. This guy." And they would just be stuffing them in, man. This was the late '50s, early '60s, and New Orleans seemed like a very brutal, totalitarian kind of police state. So anyways, they got me down to the police station and they were making out the papers and stuff. The guy says, "You play that thing, boy?" I says, "Yes, sir." He said, "Well, whip it out and play that thing." So I played a bunch of Elizabeth Cotten stuff—"Freight Train" and a few things like that. He says, "Damn, boy, you shouldn't spend the weekend in jail." I said, "Well, I don't want to." He said, "What were you gonna do?" I said, "Well, I was gonna leave town right away, sir, if you let me out of here."

He says, "Okay, I'll let you out of here, but don't you be in the county on Monday." "Yes, sir!" Grabbed my guitar and split. I thought, "Wow, that was great—just like Lead Belly."

Sang your way out of the jail.

Yeah! [*Laughs.*] But I got the hell out.

What kind of playing did you do up until 1965?

Mostly acoustic. It was folk stuff and country blues. I never played any rock and roll at all.

After you were listening to country blues music, what styles did you explore next?

After listening to rural blues kind of stuff, I was listening to a lot of classical guitar. I began trying to develop a sort of synthesis, putting different things together. I was playing some classical things on steel-string guitar, which really sounds nice sometimes.

When did you get your first electric?

The first electric was not until I joined this band. I didn't even have an electric when I joined the band. I auditioned with an electric that they had there. I don't even remember what it was or anything—it was real hard to play, I remember. My first electric was a Les Paul Junior—you know, the old flat, big, thick one with the double cutaway. Real nice guitar, man. That was a good one. That one got smashed up. I used that for about a year. I used it on the Mainstream album. On the second album, *Cheap Thrills*, I had to use the Gibson SG; it had two humbucking pickups on it.

Did it have any modifications on it?

No, not at that time. The Gibson Les Paul Junior, it got broken and I put it back together, and then I decided that since so much wood was missing—it really got smashed—that I was just gonna fill it up with woods that didn't match. And then I just painted the whole thing so that you didn't see the wood. I carved it and I did a lot of modifications on that. I installed a little fuzz tone from a box. See, I worked with a guitar maker, Tim Cameron, for about a year at one time—about '64, I think it was. I worked about a year with him, making guitars, learning guitar repair and stuff. And now I do my own repairs—I don't have anybody touch my guitars, hardly, for that stuff. Although if I had a really good acoustic with a split down it, maybe I would defer that to someone.

Did you use the SG on other albums after Cheap Thrills?

Well, on the other ones I played a lot of bass—on *Be a Brother* and *How Hard It Is*.

How Hard It Is *is the last one?*

Yeah, right. The last one.

What kind of effects were you using?

At that time I had a fuzz tone device—I can't remember who made it. I don't think I have it anymore. The Judson or Jason? They make amps too—it started with a J. I also had a Gibson fuzz tone that didn't work out too well.

What kind of amps were you using?

In the *Cheap Thrills* period, since we were on Columbia Records and Fender was a subsidiary of Columbia Records, they sent a whole truckload of stuff. It was just beautiful. Two Dual Showmans apiece, plus a Twin Reverb apiece. I think they gave Dave a set of drums. They gave me and Sam guitars. They gave me a Strat, which later got stolen also. Well, they gave me a Tele first, and I turned that in for a Strat. Then the Strat got stolen.

But you stayed with the SG instead of the Strat.

Yeah. I couldn't get a grip on 'em at first because the pickups aren't as hot as Gibson's. You got a Gibson, you got that nice sound. And I wasn't used to that other kind of drier, less-driving kind of sound, so it was quite a change.

Your leads were a lot different from just about everybody else. What were you trying for?

Like I said, when I joined the band, I'd been listening to a lot of John Coltrane. And I thought if you could play a guitar like he played the sax, it would really be far out. So that's what I was trying to do. Of course, nobody understood it, especially me! [*Laughs.*]

Did you and Sam just naturally fall into which part of the song you were going to do?

Yeah, it came about pretty naturally. At that time I had no grounding in theory or anything at all. In fact, I learned a lot from Sam, because Sam is really well educated in theory and all that stuff. He really taught me a lot of things, because up until that time I was always just playing by ear. I was to the point where I was playing chords, but since I was only playing by myself, a lot of chords, I didn't even know the names of 'em. I just knew where to put my fingers. Then when I got with Sam, since you had to communicate these things on a verbal level a lot of times, it saved time. So then I started learning.

My first musical experience that I can remember, teaching theory and all that stuff, was a music class I had when I was in about fourth or fifth grade, where the teacher was so horrible, man, she just turned you off to music. People like this should be shot. They're on the taxpayer's money, teaching. That woman! For years I wandered around saying, "If this is what learning music is like, I don't want no part of it." And then when I started playing by ear, it wasn't the same thing as learning music, so I was okay. I had a definite aversion to even wanting to learn music theory and all the rest of it, from that early experience in my life. I think that had a lot of effect on me.

When you and Sam started playing together, how did you work out parts?

Our first method would be to just play the thing any way we could. We'd have a general idea of what we wanted to do, and we'd try it each man for himself. Just figure out what you want to do and jam it all together. We'd see what we had, and then we'd sort of take it apart and see what didn't fit. Throw that out. The main thing was to approach it from a feeling standpoint, an emotional standpoint of what we were trying to do, and not get too involved with the nuts and bolts right at first. Get sort of an idea of what is there, and then you can shape it. Clean it up after you get a general mold of what's there. Bring it into focus by leaving one chord out or putting another chord in, or whatever it was that was needed to make the song flow along.

Was there a lot of overdubbing on Cheap Thrills?

Yeah, a lot of overdubbing, and we used studios in New York and L.A.

Did you or Sam play more lead than the other, or was it pretty evenly divided?

It was always pretty close. Peter plays guitar too.

Did Peter play the acoustic guitar on "Turtle Blues"?

Yeah, that's Peter playing that. That was my mahogany Martin, the one that got stolen and thrown out the window and got the neck broke.

Were you living together in the Haight?

No, but we were all very close to each other, just a few blocks apart. Janis was living on Lyon. I lived in Clayton, Sam lived on Fell.

It's estimated that there were 1,500 bands in the San Francisco Bay Area at that time. When did you first realize that Big Brother was starting to happen?

I think Monterey Pop was the breaking point.

What were your impressions of Monterey?

To tell the truth, Jimi Hendrix, man. I'm still . . . [*Shakes head.*]

What did you think when you saw Jimi Hendrix at Monterey?

[*With awe*] Oh, I was blown away. Just totally blown away. I was just . . . oh, my brains were dribbling out my ears. I kid you not, man. I was right in the front row—we were in the performers' section, right up close, and I was just . . . [*Shakes head.*]

Had you expected anything like it?

No. I had no expectations of anything like that—the whole sheer flamboyance. It was almost like a flow from the subconscious mind. I remember a time in New York when he played that club [Generations] with B. B. King. The same week we were there with B. B. King, Martin Luther King got shot.

B. B. King really played his set to him, just really played beautifully. B. B. King played so beautifully and delicately that night for Martin Luther King. He was fantastic. But anyways, Hendrix came in every night that week and jammed. They stayed open all night. After the regular scheduled acts were over, they stayed open all night for jam sessions. And Hendrix came in every night, and he played *everything* under the sun! He played all the Beatles stuff, he played Bach, Beethoven—on the electric guitar. And not only that, he could play the guitar right-handed and left-handed. Either-handed!

You saw him do this?

Yeah! Upside-down. He played Sam's guitar.

Did he flip it over to play it?

Either way! He could play right-handed guitar left-handed, left-handed guitar right-handed, right-handed guitar right-handed, and left-handed guitar left-handed. I could not tell any difference when I was listening to him play—we sat there all night for a whole week, every night, with him playing. And he played all night long.

With B. B.?

Well, B. B. maybe sat in—I don't remember. It was just like a jam session. People would get up, some people would sit down, and then another guy would get up and play.

You know, New York guys who were really hot. Jimi played all the Beatles stuff, all the Stones stuff. It just seemed to go on and on and on, without ever stopping! And he was very good at directing things, when he felt like a change or something, getting everybody tuned to another thing without breaking the flow. He could go through all these different changes. Play "The Star-Spangled Banner," "Three Blind Mice." I mean, it was just incredible! It just came pouring out, a constant flow, a stream of consciousness of music. It was almost everything that you ever heard in your life. It was amazing.

How well did you know Jimi Hendrix as an individual?

He was very sweet and rather more shy and unassuming than you would suppose someone of that flamboyance to be. I mean, offstage you would talk to him, and he was a very gentle cat. Just the sweetest guy. He babysat one of my kids while I went onstage at Winterland one time. There was nobody around, and he said, "Okay, I'll stay back here and take care of the kid," just like that. He'd sit back there and take care of my kid—you know, what a guy. We saw each other a lot. We played quite a bit on the same bill.

How did the first initial rush of success strike you?

It was a thrill of a lifetime, the whole experience.

How'd you find being on the road?

That was hard. It's hard being on the road.

When did you reach your highest point as a band? What was your best moment in terms of the music or overall experience?

'68. I think after Janis announced to us that she was gonna split. I think that really reduced the tensions a lot. There was a lot of tensions between her and us, because she wanted to go more soul and have more horns—back-East stuff. They wanted to make her Barbra Streisand or something.

Did she think you were the wrong backup band?

Right, right. That's the trouble: it was a backup band. See, we were not a backup band. We were a band before she joined the band, we were a band after she left the band, and would still be a band if we wanted to. I think we played a lot better for the last six months we were together there. Well, it wasn't that long—it was maybe three months. It was in the summertime. We were in New York, in August of '68, I think it was, when she said she wanted to split and was gonna stay with it for a few more months. I think we played up until about November of '68. So between that time, those three or four months there, it was real nice because the tension was off, and we played really well, I thought.

Do you feel you got burned?

Yes! In one word, yes. By the managers—the people who managed us—by the lawyers that *we* were paying to do our business.

Did you see a lot of money from Cheap Thrills?

Not to what we could have. Not what you would think. You would think that we'd all be rich, but we're not. Barely middle class—in those days, lower middle class.

What can you do to avoid getting burned?

Know what some of the tricks are. Education. Until you've been burned and gone through all these things, you don't know. We didn't know. They serve you all these papers that got so much of all this legalese that you can't figure out. And you go, "Well, I'm paying these guys to work for me—I'll just trust their judgment." That's one thing they gotta learn: you can't trust 'em.

At the very least, you should have your own attorney and not use the company's lawyers.

Right. Our own lawyer, we feel, was working in collusion with Columbia Records. The lawyer for the band. If you read our contract and said, "Who wrote this for whose benefit?" you would say, "Columbia Records wrote this for their own benefit." It's obvious in every paragraph. Recording costs was one thing—we had to pay all recording costs, plus all production costs. Plus we had to pay for the records to be pressed, the labels to be printed, the photographer to shoot the picture. Out of the royalties! So that's $100,000-$200,000 right there. So they've got a free business, right? We pay for everything—they pay for nothing. We have to pay for it all, we give them the tape—we don't even own it—and they go out and sell it and just reap all the profits.

That album made a lot of money.

Yeah! It was gold. It was #1 for six weeks when it first came out. You can't even hardly trust the guys you got working for you. You've got to watch them like a hawk. You can't assume that just because you're paying them to do the job for you that he's actually going to be doing it for you. He's gonna be doing it for himself. You need to have lawyers to watch your lawyers.

In retrospect, was the experience of being in the band more positive than negative? Did the good outweigh the bad?

For sure.

What do you think is the place of Big Brother in music?

It's hard to assess. Collectively, the whole thing was a movement, if you will.

Would you go so far as to say that period produced a Renaissance of the arts?

More like a Renaissance of spirit. A spirit of goodwill, of good vibes, if you will.

Was there really a "Summer of Love"?

Oh, yeah! There was. Yeah. It was real.

Do you feel like you still have the spirit?

Yeah. Yeah. It's been modified a bit. Subsequently, the world has changed a lot since then. There were a lot of excesses. We did a lot of things then that we wouldn't do now.

A lot of critics are now calling Janis Joplin the best female white blues singer.

In retrospect, I feel too much importance was given to Janis. It also was like the back-East mentality of the record companies and executives there who want you to be slick and commercial, you know. They think in terms of things that have happened. They can't think of what's going to happen or making something happen. We're talking about creation. As much as she made us as a band, we made her as a singer. She had to sing the way that she did in order to sing with us. She had to sing that way. She just didn't have any choice. If she was gonna sing with us, she had to sing that way. We didn't say, "You have to sing like this," but we said, "This is the way we're gonna play. How are you gonna sing?" And she went, "Whoa! Okay. Here's this. [*Imitates Janis*] *Whaaaa!*" It went on from there. She had a lot of power.

What was Janis's role with the other members?

We had a very close relationship. I think success probably spoiled the relationship. I'm sure of it.

Where was Janis heading?

James Gurley and Jas Obrecht interview, September 30, 1978. (Clara Erickson; courtesy Jas Obrecht)

"Mercedes Benz." Yeah, I think she would have got back to her country blues kind of thing. Eventually she would have recorded some, like her early stuff.

What did you think of the speculations that she committed suicide?

Just baloney. Oh, yeah! It was an accident. She sought relief. She was under a lot of strain.

How did you take to fame when it came to you?

I think it went totally to our heads. We became irresponsible in our personal conduct, shall we say. In other words, we drank too much, we used way too many drugs. You know, out too late, partying too much. Too many chicks running around. Which is all great fun—I mean, it was a blast at the time.

Did your musicianship suffer?

Oh, it certainly did! It certainly did. Yeah.

Was studying technique important during your time in Big Brother?

No. We tried to escape the confines of techniques, because you can become so conditioned that you want to try to break through your conditioning. But the point was to break through the conditioning. It wasn't like we didn't practice, but it wasn't from an intellectual kind of approach. It was more energy, more feeling. "How does it feel?" "It feels good—let's do it." "Okay, here we go."

What did you feel back when reviewers started panning your sound?

They were right, in terms of their expectations. They expected entertainers who are supposed to try to be slick and commercial and try to please them with stuff that they already know about. We were coming from a point of view of "Here's something you ain't never heard before. Try this." They're given too much importance, I think. What the hell do critics know?

Like a lot of records I get, I don't like 'em the first time, but they grow on me. Like the Wailers—I really love the Wailers. I've been really heavy into reggae. For the last three years, that's been my main passion, musically. The first time I listened to most Wailers records, I didn't like them. But I'd say, "This is the Wailers. I gotta like it—I liked all the ones before it." See? So then I play it again, and then I play it ten times, and pretty soon I'll be liking it. It has a lot to do with your conditioning. If you're not prepared to hear something, like if you haven't heard Devo—there's a perfect example. I would expect that record to get a lot of panning from critics. It really just comes out of left field. There's some pretty weird stuff. Of course, I'll suppose there will be critics who want to show how elite avant-garde they are and try to pick up on it. It's a whole other kind of thing—they're not just talking ordinary chord changes and stuff. There's weird electronics and stuff that sounds like a factory going on, just all this weird stuff. The first time you hear it, it will make your hair stand on end. But I really like 'em.

What do most people ask you about when they learn you played in Big Brother?

"What was Janis like?" [*Laughs.*] That's number one. "Did she really drink as much as they say?"—that's number two.

What do you think is the heritage of the late 1960s for us today, especially as related to the counterculture?

Well, the heritage, I think, is that there's a lot more individual freedom available to people now than there was before then. You know? We can have all kinds of hairstyles, we can have our hair any length we want. We can wear any kind of moustache, beard, whereas before, you didn't really do that. I remember when I first grew my hair long, it was an outrage. People used to chase us on the streets—it was like scenes from Frankenstein movies—"Get the monster!" with flaming torches, you know. When we first went to Chicago from California, there was nothing like that in Chicago at all, like we were. Some people just didn't know how to react to it at all. A lot of people reacted with hostility and hate and all kinds of things. Before 1965, the world was in black and white. You can see it. Now there's more creative emphasis and a lot more freedoms, I guess. The '60s were a breakthrough for a lot of things.

What do you think of the music today as compared to ten years ago?

Oh, I think there's a lot of great stuff going on. The level of musicianship is much higher than it was ten years ago, that's for sure—especially the guitar playing. There was nobody around ten yours ago who could play like some of the guys around today. It's just amazing, the incredible guitar players that are around now. There's a definite increase in musical consciousness and musicianship as such. This has swung the other way: there's a lot more emphasis on technique. At the same time, I see less individuality among players too. It's like you can't tell one guy from the next. One Eric Clapton lick from the next Eric Clapton lick, you know, a lot of times, which is one of the unique things about Hendrix. You always know it's him. Just the *tone* of his guitar—you just know it's him.

The attack.

The attack, right! It's his signature. It's just him, whereas today there are so many great guitar players from a technical sense, but they lack individuality, I think, so it's hard to tell one from the other. Although there are some who do have a pretty identifiable sound, like Robin Trower. He's pretty good—I like him a lot.

What has psychedelic music contributed to music in the 1970s?

It opened the mind to more involvement in general with music. People are much more involved with it. There are many more people playing nowadays, it seems. There's a hell of a lot more information available in books. The music opened the door to new sounds and fresh, creative ways of going about it—sounds that just were never heard before.

Has the use of drugs by psychedelic bands in the 1960s been overemphasized or underemphasized?

It was a big part! It was a big part. I mean, everybody was involved with drugs.

Did they help the music?

It helped and it hurt, probably. I think it led a lot of people into creative blind alleys. In other ways it led people out of blind alleys.

Did they help you loosen up?

Yeah, that's what I mean. It broke your conditioning so that you were able to step back from what you already knew to try to perceive something that you don't know. Because all these things come from your subconscious—that's the source of your creative endeavor, somehow. Sometimes when I'll be falling asleep, I'll hear something, almost like hear it in the air, and I'll think I left the radio on in the other room. I'll get up to turn it off, and I'll realize it was just in my head. You can just feel it at that moment, like in the Twilight Zone of your mind. An auditory hallucination, maybe. Yeah.

Where does this come from?

From the workings of the subconscious mind. I'm sure the same thing must have happened to Bach—those kinds of feelings where it just becomes so real that it almost becomes physical in a sense.

Did you ever find drugs could help you tap this?

Sometimes, yeah. Other times, I would say no. They'll change your perceptions. But what you're gonna do about it, that still has to do with your personality and how you perceive yourself in the world. The ball is still in your lap, so to speak, although you have these fresh perceptions. I don't think anyone should try to rely on drug experiences in order to be creative or feel that you have to have these things in order to create or play well or whatever. I couldn't have talked about it like this ten years ago because I didn't have this perspective on it that I do now. And it's been assimilated throughout the culture. Like I heard an old lady at the supermarket the other day—something bad happen to her, and she said, "Well, I just have that kind of karma." Just a perfectly straight old lady saying, "I just have that kind of karma," which is an obvious influence from the '60s psychedelic.

How do you view the period from 1965 to 1969 in terms of your whole life?

Probably the most important years of my life, maybe. Yeah. That was an experience that I'll never forget, an experience of such an intensity that it has a long-range effect on my life. I mean, here it is ten years later, and you're talking to us now. Why? Because of what happened then. It's something that's gonna stick with us.

CODA: Following this interview and the 1978 Tribal Stomp concert, it would be another nine years before the original lineup of Big Brother and the Holding Company would reunite. From 1987 through 1996, James Gurley occasionally toured and recorded with the band, but he devoted most of his time to raising his family. In 1999 he fulfilled his goal of recording an album of his own songs. Credited to Saint James, his *Pipe Dreams* featured his son Hongo on drums and percussion. The visionary guitarist did not make it out of his own sixties, dying of a heart attack on December 20, 2009, just two days shy of his seventieth birthday. Sam Andrew, who worked later in life as a music journalist, painter, and sculptor, passed away on February 12, 2015.

The way Bob Weir tells it, the Grateful Dead's long, strange journey began on New Year's Eve, 1963, when he followed the sound of a banjo into a Palo Alto music store. There he met bluegrass veteran Jerry Garcia, five years his senior and awaiting a student. The sixteen-year-old Weir played folk guitar, and the two enjoyed a marathon jam session. They decided to form an acoustic band—Mother McCree's Uptown Jug Champions—with Ron "Pigpen" McKernan, who doubled on harmonica and drums. Inspired by the Beatles, the musicians switched to electric instruments in 1965, changed their name to the Warlocks, and brought in drummer Bill Kreutzmann and bassist Phil Lesh. The Warlocks served as the house band at the first Acid Tests later that year. Soon thereafter, Garcia renamed the lineup the Grateful Dead. "While established bands like the Beatles, Rolling Stones, and Yardbirds went through their psychedelic phases," Weir explained, "the Grateful Dead was born right into the full fray of our psychedelic phase. We began turning up pretty quickly. From the start, it was faster, looser, harder, and hairier. We were going for a ride."[1] According to Weir, by the release of their 1967 debut album, the band had moved past the psychedelic stage.

The Grateful Dead, of course, went on to become the most beloved and enduring of San Francisco's psychedelic bands. For decades they delighted Dead Heads—the most avid and loyal family of fans in rock-and-roll history—with extended concerts highlighted by inspired improvisational jams. Jerry Garcia, the band's figurehead, retained his passion for old-time music, returning to his bluegrass roots with the Grateful Dead, the Jerry Garcia Acoustic Band, Old and in the Way, and Garcia/Grisman, his duo with mandolin virtuoso David Grisman.

In celebration of the Grateful Dead's upcoming twentieth anniversary, I was asked by *Frets*, a magazine devoted to acoustic stringed instruments, to do a Jerry Garcia cover story interview. Jerry and I met mid-afternoon on January 12, 1985, at a friend's home in San Rafael, California. Garcia shuffled slowly into the living room, his black T-shirt sprinkled with white powder. His fingertips were blackened. Minutes into our interview, he nonchalantly pulled out a rock of cocaine, chopped it into lines, and consumed it as we spoke. Jon Sievert, on hand to shoot photos, observed that "Jerry was probably at his absolute nadir at the time of the interview, as witnessed by his bust in Golden Gate Park six days later. In between the interview and the bust, the band and Mountain Girl [Jerry's wife, Carolyn] staged an intervention in which Jerry was told he had to choose between drugs and the band. In the few times I was around Garcia in a private setting, that was the only time I saw him openly snort coke. What I remember most, however, was how articulate he remained when talking about music. As you can tell by listening to the tapes, his enthusiasm never waned."[2] I have to agree. Even though Garcia stated at one point, "I can't remember anything, and my mind is gone," I found him to be bright, articulate, and self-reflective the entire time. He spoke quickly and often locked eyes with me. Settling into a chair, Jerry began the conversation.

JERRY: Have we met before?

Yes, probably at the Tribal Stomp in 1978.

Oh, yeah. I recognize ya. You're familiar.

Do you know about Frets *magazine?*

Yes, I do.

So this is for the cover story on the 20th anniversary of the Grateful Dead.

Say! [*Laughs.*]

What's the appeal, for you, of acoustic music?

What is the appeal? Hmm. First of all, my appeal is just music, you know. And I don't really distinguish. It's not like one kind of music is more appealing to me than others. For me, the acoustic guitar is a different instrument. I don't think I would do it, really, if it weren't for the technological advance of the successful electric-acoustic guitar, like the Takamine that I play onstage. I've never had any luck at all with the acoustic guitar and microphone.

Too much squeal?

Too much everything. Too much boom. It really has to do with the kind of microphones that you use and the kind of guitar. Most acoustic guitars are built to project in a room, just acoustically. And most microphones are designed to hear a small source, like the bell of a horn or a voice, and a guitar is something you hear all over it—I mean, in order for it to really sound like an acoustic guitar where you hold a microphone up to the soundhole. For example, if it's a big guitar, like a D-28, it woofs and booms and does all these things that are nonmusical in nature. There's stuff you don't intend to be heard. They are part of the sound of the guitar, for sure, but they are not what you mean when you're playing. It's the Frankenstein nature of the microphone as an electric ear that makes it so I haven't had much luck with just acoustic guitar. Also, the difference in touch is too radical. The way you have to dig in with an acoustic guitar and a microphone, as opposed to the way you play an electric guitar, if I were to try to do both, my electric guitar chops would go way downhill.

Do you tend to pick up an acoustic much less frequently than an electric?

Well, electric is my instrument. But I like playing acoustic, especially now with this advance, because it means I don't have to radically change my touch so much, but I get the nice qualities of the tone and, you know, the pretty features of an acoustic guitar. But only really because I take that line in and get a nice clear signal that sounds to my ears like an acoustic, so the behavior of the instrument and the idioms that I find myself pulling out of it are what I associate with acoustic guitar. For me, they're very different. It's like they're very different instruments.

Does your way of visualizing the fingerboard or your approach change?

Uh, yeah. Very much so. For me, on the electric guitar I have a holistic approach to the fingerboard. On acoustic guitar, I have a preference for the first position and the open sounds, the open quality. I don't use a capo on acoustic guitar, but I would. But I would never do that on an electric guitar. On electric guitar, I deal with the whole neck as a harmonic medium. I don't see it in patterns or groupings. All those have become continuous for me.

In the last Guitar Player *interview, you spoke about finally making that breakthrough.*

Yeah, I'm through that. Yeah.

What have you found on the other side?

What it is is that there are really endless numbers of overlapping patterns, that's all. That's what it really boils down to. Depending on what half step or whole step, what partial you want to start on, you have all series of fingerings. You can either play them across the fingerboard or up the fingerboard or up the strings or across the fingerboard or any combination thereof, and really that's just a matter of fluidity and a matter of breaking out of position playing. For me, it's become a matter of now I play for a preference in the tone that I get, like playing high notes on low strings. For me, it's much more a matter of what sounds nice—not where I play it, but where the lick sounds. So I can play the same lick in any of, say, three or four positions on the neck—the same lick in the same octave—and the tone is very different depending on the thickness of the strings you're playing on. So that's the kind of stuff. For me, it's a matter of having much more choice over harmonic series, harmonic range, and tonal quality.

Do you know what you're doing in theoretical terms?

Yeah, yeah, yeah. I couldn't not. There was a time when I could get by with not knowing, you know, but not any more, not with the caliber of musicians I play with. Besides, for me it isn't satisfying to not know. It's not satisfying to bluff. I like to know because for one thing, it makes it a lot easier to communicate what you're doing. Just that alone is a good reason to know.

How has your approach to soloing changed?

It keeps on changing, but I don't have an approach. I still basically revolve around the melody. I think I come more from the point of view of the melody and the way it's broken up into phrases as I perceive them. With most solos, I tend to play something that phrases the way the melody does. The phrases may be more dense or have different value and so forth, but they'll occur in the same places in the song as they do in the melody. Basically, most of the time there's some abstraction of the melody in there—at least that's what I'm thinking. I'm not necessarily meaning to communicate that, but that's what my mind does.

When you're onstage, what influences the types of notes you choose?

Anything and everything! [*Laughs.*] Nothing in particular. I don't watch my decision-making process that carefully. But usually the reason I start on a course of action is because I have a kind of a loose plan in mind going into a chorus. I take a chorus as a unit, generally speaking. I have sort of a loose plan there. Or something else that happens elsewhere in the music gets me going, like some rhythmic figure or that kind of stuff—detail.

Can improvisation be learned or is it inherent in someone?

No, I think it can be learned.

What advice would you give someone who had lessons and theoretical knowledge, but wanted to find more freedom on the instrument?

Mostly, the best possible thing, really, is to have somebody else to play with. One other person to play with. If you have one other person who plays the guitar, then you just trade off choruses or you play, like, five choruses against each other. You know what I mean? Like one guy backs up for five choruses or four choruses, and the other guy backs up for four choruses. That's really the best way to do it, I think, to get a handle on it. I don't know. It's not the sort of thing that advice helps. It's really one of the things where time spent is more profitable.

Do you do much practicing?

I don't do as much as I'd like to, but I go in and out of that. I go in and out of it. I'm about to enter into practicing.

Anything in particular you want to work on?

Yeah, there's a whole bunch of stuff. I've got two or three books that I've been wanting to crack for some time, but I haven't made myself go into them. I'm lazy, just like everybody else is. [*Laughs.*] But these are some real nice studies on fourths and some really nice, just melodic humps that are very good. That's why I'm going into a little woodshedding there—there are some things in there that I like.

Do you have favorite books that you've gone over more than once?

No, I rarely go over them more than once. If I take a book and decide I'm going to go over it, I really go over the sucker. I go over it in depth and really do it, and after that, I'm done with it. Then it's an absorption process, you

*Jerry Garcia in
Golden Gate Park,
San Francisco,
September 28, 1975.
(Jon Sievert)*

know. Unless I've really forgotten something—and I haven't gotten to that point yet—I may be losing stuff down at the back end somewhere. But as soon as I get to the point where I look at a book and draw a blank and then open it up and find a bunch of little marks and stuff and realize I've been through this book and I don't remember a thing about it, then I'll start going back. I haven't gotten to that point yet—but soon, I hope! [*Laughs.*]

Do you do much jamming?

Virtually 90 percent of the playing that I do is jamming.

I meant outside of the band.

No, I don't. There's not a situation around that has both a loose enough structure and good-enough-quality musicians where I can get into it and enjoy it. The level of musicianship that I exist at right now, it's not much fun to play unless the people play really well. You know what I mean? There aren't too many situations where you can just jam with somebody.

When do you play your best?

I wish I could tell you that! Because if I could tell you it, it would mean that I knew when I was gonna play my best. It's something I don't know, when I'm gonna play my best. And a lot of times, I can't even judge if it's my best or not, until, say, like, later on I might listen to a tape and say, "Geez, that's the best I've ever heard myself sound." And that happens to me a lot. Almost all the time when I listen to a tape, I can't believe it's me. My own mental image of myself is that I play a lot worse than I actually do. I'm usually surprised when I listen to tapes.

Are you self-critical?

Yeah. Almost to the point of nihilism. [*Laughs.*] If it was left up to me, if I'd never heard anything, I think I would have given up long ago. Yeah, I am self-critical. Yeah.

Do you ever feel like you're in a rut?

All the time. Yeah. Then I do something about it. When I feel like I'm really seriously stale, that's when I start to crack books, because you really need something to move. And there's so much to music, there's no excuse for feeling stale. Nobody is such a great musician that they could be burnt out on all of music, you know. So for me, it's just a matter of going out and putting a little bit of effort into it, and I can almost always find something that I don't know anything about and pick up on it and start a sort of itch-scratch cycle.

Does listening to other musicians or bands ever inspire you?

All the time. Yeah. Yeah. There's nobody playing right now who knocks me out completely. I mean, there's nothing that I hear right now that really makes me want to dash to my guitar. But there's plenty of stuff in the past. You know, if I go looking for stuff, I can find it. But there's nobody really playing right now who kills me. Music right now—everything that I hear right now is pretty derivative sounding.

What's your source? Do you listen to the radio or MTV or . . .

All those things. I'm just a human in the world—you know what I mean? And then I have a huge record collection. And I also have access to music stores, some of which are pretty hip, where the people who run them are music collectors and like that. That's helpful. It's helpful to have somebody's taste. And also, the society that I'm in has a lot of musicians in it, and musicians are always turning you on to music, so there's always input.

What are your views of young guitar players now?

Well, it's a little hard for me to listen. The thing is, they're much more accomplished than they used to be, but that just means that the instrument itself has a much better book than it used to have. The electric guitar has an enormous vocabulary and several different kinds of mediums, all of which have expanded enormously in the last ten, fifteen years. That's all to the good—it just means the instrument has expanded. But young players, even if they're really brilliant technically, there's a thing like a guy like John Lee Hooker or somebody like that who can play two or three notes so authoritatively on a guitar. There's like sixty years of real mean person, right, who can scare the pants off you in one or two notes played with such immense authority and such soulfulness. There's that, and that's a real thing. For me, I'd much rather hear something like that than a lot of facility.

Do you ever listen to people like Eddie Van Halen?

Not seriously, no. Because I can hear what's happening in there. There isn't much there that interests me. It isn't played with enough deliberateness, and it lacks a certain kind of rhythmic elegance that I like music to have, that I like notes to have. There's a lot of notes and stuff, but the notes aren't saying much, you know. They're like little clusters. It's a certain kind of music which I understand on one level, but it isn't attractive to me.

If you could go back in time and question any old musician, does anyone come to mind?

Uh, yeah. I'd still follow around what's his name—the Gypsy guitarist?

Django Reinhardt?

Yeah, Django. I can't remember anything, and my mind is gone. I have all of Django's records—every single one of them. Most of what he plays is even hard to understand, no matter how much I've listened to it, in terms of the actual technical how it's happening. Because I listen to it and I hear when a note is being struck and when a note is being articulated with the left hand somehow. And he does things I don't know how he's doing them. I can't imagine. You know, he's got fingers that are about half a mile long. I mean, I just don't know how he's doing it. And this is with a fucked-up left hand.[3] He's able to cross his fingers over this way [*demonstrates cross-finger techniques*]. He was able to do runs where the middle finger crosses over the index finger. That much I've figured out because there are things he plays that work that way, and he couldn't do them any other way. There's no other way he could do them. And they're lightning fast. His technique is awesome! Even today, nobody has really come to the state that he was playing at. As good as players are, they haven't gotten to where he is. There's a lot of guys that play fast and a lot of guys that play clean, and the guitar has come a long way as far as speed and clarity go, but nobody plays with the whole fullness of expression that Django has. I mean, the combination of incredible speed—all the speed you could possibly want—but also the thing of every note having a specific personality. You'd don't hear it. I really haven't heard it anywhere but with Django.

The other guy I'd like to hear live would be Charlie Christian, who has an incredible mind, an incredible flow of ideas—they're just a relentless flow of ideas that are just *bam*, pouring out. It has this intensity that's really incredible. And he has also a tone that I think is very hip. It sounds very modern to me. His whole playing, to my ear, it sounds very modern. And it's amazing because what people extracted from his playing, the Top-40 stuff in his playing, doesn't have that quality, really. People pick the lamest shit from his playing. But that great *Solo Flight* album, you know—I mean, that improvisation is amazing! You listen to that, and still it sounds incredible, to this day.

He's really the first guy who could cut it with the horns.

Yeah, right. Right, exactly. And could play the way a horn plays, play with that kind of flow of ideas. What horn players have to do is they have to learn chords as arpeggiations. They don't have to think of playing all the notes at once. Well, he's the first guy to play the guitar the way horn players play through changes. He has that sense of where everything goes harmonically.

It's amazing what Charlie Christian accomplished in seventeen months.

Yeah, right. That's the way it is, man. [*Laughs.*] That's the way things are sometimes, you know. Yeah, well, he's a guy I would love to be able to hear. And those are the two guys whose reputations are well-deserved. They're the solid gold of American-derived music, guitar playing.

Where would you put in somebody like Robert Johnson?

Well, he's a primitive genius. And there's others that I like that I feel are in that similar category. Blind Blake. Rev. Gary Davis too, when he was young, but he was always great. I had a personal preference for Mississippi John Hurt—his early records sound so smooth. They're just like magic. And, you know, one or two others whose playing is just extremely beautiful to my ears. I like Chet Atkins.

Are there non-guitarists?

Oh, yeah, sure. Art Tatum is my all-time favorite. Yeah, he's my all-time favorite. He's the guy I put on when I want to feel really small. [*Laughs.*] When I want to feel really insignificant. He's a good guy to play for any musician, you know. He'll make them want to go home and burn their instruments. [*Laughs.*] Art Tatum is absolutely the most incredible musician—what can you say?

What era of Tatum's stuff appeals to you?

Well, all of it is fascinating, and I also haven't heard everything, but I've got the two big sets from Norman Granz, and everything on those is beyond the pale. It's just so incredible, you know. What a mind!

Were you a fan of the bluegrass masters?

[*Tentatively*] Yeah, uh, but bluegrass for me is band music, and I'm a fan of bands more than I am a fan of musicians. The musicians I like sounded best in a certain context—to my ears. So my favorites are certain bands, you know, certain vintage bands. That's the way I think of bluegrass music. I am much more attached to that side of it than I am to individual players, because there are so many good players in bluegrass. But not all bluegrass bands are good.

What are your favorite bands?

I think one of my all-time favorite bands was Bill Monroe's bluegrass band when he had Bill Keith playing banjo and Kenny Baker playing fiddle—I guess that must have been right around '64. '63, '64—somewhere around there. That was a great band. And Del McCoury playing acoustic guitar and singing. That was a great band, really a sensational band.

You saw that band?

Oh, yeah. A bunch of times. And the classic Reno and Smiley band, with Mack Magaha playing fiddle. Also, the original Bill Monroe band with Lester Flatt and Earl Scruggs. Also, the classic Lester Flatt-Earl Scruggs and Foggy Mountain Boys band—that was a great band. I loved Jim & Jesse when they had either Jimmy Buchanan or Vassar [Clements] and the two great banjo players they had at the same time—what's his name? It's been such a long time with banjo players. They had two real great banjo players back in the old days. They both had the same big, square-style sound. They both had rhythmically a real symmetrical style. It's hard to describe, but it's that era, back when Vassar was playing with them or Jimmy Buchanan. Both about the same era. That was also in the early '60s, right around there. They had a couple of really great bands in those moments back there. And also the Stanley Brothers. My favorite singers were the Stanley Brothers. Ralph Stanley was my all-time favorite singer, I think.

What was your banjo style like? Could you describe it?

No. [*Laughs.*] No, I couldn't. I really couldn't describe it. I can't describe it any more than I can describe my guitar playing.

Do you still have a banjo?

Sure, I've got several banjos.

Old-time ones?

Yeah. Great ones.

Ever have a six-string banjo?

No.

Those things sound loud.

I bet they sound like hell! [*Laughs.*] I don't think I could stand a six-string banjo. I don't think I could stand the combination. It'd be too alien for me.

Do you still play banjo?

Uh, once in a while. Once in a very great while. But like I say, I burned out on banjo. I'm a burned-out banjo player. I really am. I went to the end of the rope, you know. It's the band that counts. If I could play in a real great bluegrass band once or twice a week, I would definitely get my chops back together on the banjo.

Were you a five-string man?

Oh, yeah, yeah. Bluegrass banjo—that was it.

Do you think much of the technique transferred over to guitar?

It doesn't transfer.

The right hand?

Not really. Not really. No, to me, again, it's apples and oranges. They really aren't the same instrument. They have strings and a bridge and frets, and that's it, you know. Other than that, they really are very different. Also, I thought there might be some crossover when I took up pedal steel, but they're not the same either. The technique is very, very different. And the concept is also very different. And so when you're dealing with those instruments, it doesn't help to try to take one to another.

What about going from acoustic guitar to electric guitar? Are there songs that you only play on acoustic?

Yeah.

How large is your repertoire?

Well, I don't know. I haven't played through it yet. [*Laughs.*] I know a lot of songs—I know an awful lot of songs because I was into the traditional music scene. I like music! So I've learned a lot of songs in my life. I know a lot of 'em. And I know bits and pieces of a lot of 'em, as well. And there are also a whole lot of songs that I plan on learning. For me, repertoire isn't a static thing. And even when I go on now with John and we do our acoustic thing—John Kahn who plays bass with me—there's always a few songs I think of on the road that I think would be fun to do. And if I don't remember them, I go and find a book somewhere that has them in it or something.

Are you always adding songs?

Oh, yeah. Part of the thing about music is the thing of staying interested, and you have to motivate yourself to some extent.

Do you compose on acoustic guitar? Have you written any Dead songs on acoustic?

I have done that a few times, but more often I tend to compose on the piano. It makes me think differently.

Do you know as much musically on piano as guitar?

No.

Maybe that's why it's easier to compose.

It is, because it just puts me in a different head. Theoretically I know as much, but my hands don't know anything. I don't know the instrument. But I can sit and figure anything out, you know, if I have a little time.

Art Tatum.

[*Laughs.*] Yeah, right. Give me twenty years and another head!

Why have the Grateful Dead more or less limited their acoustic sets?

I don't know. I don't think Weir feels comfortable playing acoustic music. I don't know. I'm not sure exactly why. I personally would like to do it more often. Bob doesn't seem to like to do it very much. So we don't press it. If anybody feels even a little negative about something, we don't do it.

How did the 1980 acoustic Dead sets come about?

I just thought it would be a good idea, so we tried it. It was fun. And also the technology came into place. That was one of the reasons why we didn't do it for so long, because we used to try it with microphones. It really didn't work. But with the technology it's much, much easier now that you have instruments—like I say, the improvements in electro-acoustic instruments have been vast.

Did your audience react as well to acoustic music?

Oh, they have reacted as well, sure. They like it a lot. I like it a lot too. It's a nice way to play. It's a nice way to constitute. I like the combination of drums and electric bass and acoustic guitars. I think it's really a nice sound. There used to be a nice-sounding band with those two good English fingerpickers with Bert Jansch and whatever the fuck his name is—that other guy—in a band called Pentagram that played in the early '60s.

Pentangle, with John Renbourn.

Pentangle. Yeah, John Renbourn and Bert Jansch. And they were great! I mean, they had a nice little jazz drummer, a tasty jazz drummer that played brushes, and an excellent acoustic bass player and a lady that sang in sort of a madrigal voice [Jacqui McShee], an English voice. It was a lovely band. The texture was really nice, and it sounded great onstage. We played a lot of shows with them, and we heard them a lot in certain circumstances, and they sounded beautiful. It had a lot of possibilities, that combination of two acoustic guitars and so on and a standard rhythm section.

Do you miss having a second guitarist when you play in the duo?

No. No. It's just a different thing. For me, the more the merrier. I like playing in a band. But when it's an acoustic thing, it's challenging to play with just two instruments. I like to think of relating to just one other instrument, especially if it isn't another guitar.

What's the appeal of working with John Kahn?

He thinks like me. He's got the same "fuck it" attitude that I have. [*Laughs.*]

Are you as willing to go out on a limb?

Yeah.

Is he good about following you?

Oh, he's real good about following me, and that's the thing about it. He and I have very, very similar—we have the same musical taste, with a slight overlap. It's almost guaranteed. I mean, that's why we've played together for so long—we think like each other.

What are your audiences like with the duo? Mostly Dead Heads?

I imagine they are. I imagine they're from Dead Heads. But the audience is much more sensitive, I would say. We can get down to a whisper, and that place shuts up, man. I mean, nobody hollers nothin'. We can get it down to [*gives a quiet whistle*], where it's really whispering, where the strings are just [*quietly*] ping, ping. Little tiny sounds are coming out, and the place is just [*whistles quietly*]. You can draw them down to absolute silence.

Ooh, that's good.

Yeah, it is. It really is. It's something real special. I don't know how many audiences would do that, but I found that in every case when I go out acoustically with John and I playing, we can do it every time.

What's the difference in pressure between fronting your own acoustic duo versus playing with the Dead? Do you feel there's a lot more weight on your shoulders?

Uhhh. I do, in some cases, but that's just because I have a martyr complex [*laughs*] or something like that. You know, a "poor me" complex here. No, no. Actually, it's great to be able to play at all for anybody under any circumstances and have anybody like it. That's really an incredible thing. And it would be so small-minded of me to complain about any, any part of it. You know what I mean? It would be so chickenshit, you know? Ah, man, how could anybody think differently? To complain about any level of it would be so, ah, so . . . [*Laughs.*]

What do you feel an artist owes his audience?

Everything. Shit. I mean, either he doesn't owe them anything at all . . . I don't know how you even get an audience. Ideally, nobody owes anybody anything. You know what I mean? In other words, everybody gets paid off. The artist gets off playing, and the audience gets off listening, and that's it— that's what it's about. You know, the rest of it is somebody else's story. That's what I think the thing is about. And for me, being in the audience and getting off myself—I've never wanted any more than that. And the times when I'd get off, I love it! There's nothing better. That's where I get it from. The reason I'm onstage is because I've been in the audience.

What is your favorite part of your business? Of everything you do, what do you enjoy the most?

I just love music. All of it—listening to it, playing. I mean, all of it. Everything about it, really. There's really nothing about it that I don't like. Possibly interviews is the worst of it. [*Laughs uproariously.*] Well, that's the most non-musical part, you know what I mean? That's the part that's the strangest. Music is easy. Talking is not so easy. And it's really something you have to learn. You learn how to bullshit, really. [*Laughs.*]

Is there any music you play that doesn't come out onstage?

Yeah. Yeah, sure. There's a lot of music. Yeah, right! I have this kind of a weird kind of music that I play, mostly just to myself, for myself, at times that's just weird.

Can you describe it?

No, I can't really. It's only just something I do when I'm sitting around with a guitar and there's nobody else around. Sometimes I get off into these zones that, to me, are very fascinating for some reason. I've never tried to record it, so I have no idea really what it's like. But I know as far as getting absorbed in something, I can get really absorbed in these things. But I have a feeling that they probably don't sound so great.

Is it more abstract?

Yeah, yeah. I can get really carried away in it. Yeah. It's formless music—music that doesn't have any form. It's not even music that I could play *with* somebody. I think it's that weird. I'll have to try and record it sometime and see what it really sounds like. I've never really objectively gotten away from myself and listened to it. This is not something I do all the time, but once in a while I fall into this zone, you know, when I'm comfortable enough and have a nice-enough instrument and I just feel like playing and I don't have any ideas or anything like that. I drift into a few kinds of areas that I just don't really know what they're like.

This is on electric guitar?

Any kind of guitar.

Is it more like playing solos?

[*Laughs.*] I don't know what it's like. It's just playing, you know. Like I say, it doesn't have any form. Sometimes it's chordal things, sometimes it's progressions, sometimes it's just chords, you know. Sometimes it's kind of weird chord melodies that just have leading tones. Sometimes I play a whole bunch of real dense chord things that have these leading tones, but they aren't songs. It's just music. Sometimes I'll get this idea that has a kind of counter melody of some kind in it, and I'll start stretching it out and fooling around with it, and gradually it'll turn into this whole thing. But it's never stuff that I can repeat or remember, and I don't even know whether it has any musical value or not. It's just stuff I do. You know, it's kind of a free-form music. Sometimes ideas come out of it.

Do you ever get a musical idea or hear a line or some phrase in your mind without an instrument . . .

Yeah!

And then apply it to the instrument?

Oh, absolutely! That's where "Terrapin [Station]"—you know "Terrapin," that Grateful Dead tune?—that's where that came from. Dropped into my head—boom.

Which part?

The end part. The big theme. It not only happened, it came fully orchestrated too. Yeah. I've had melodies drop into my head a lot, but they're usually short. They're usually not that long. That's quite a long melody. And all of it came in—the conversational part of it, the way the instruments answer each other and that. Yeah, that's one of those things. Yeah, that happens to me. Not very often, but it does. And then I do try to apply it. But usually I lose it. Usually I forget it. Usually I get a great idea, and then eengh! By the time I get somewhere where I can either solidify it with an instrument or write it down or something like that, it's gone.

Ever have song ideas come to you at really strange times?

That's the only time they come to me! [*Laughs.*] There's always some music continuum going on, that I can sort of turn it on and off like a radio. But usually it's just mind rot; it's just stuff. Every once in a while a good idea comes through, and I never know when it's gonna be.

Have you heard musical sounds that can't be gotten on traditional instruments?

Not yet. No. Nothing that can't be got. I haven't heard anything that can't be got yet.

What are your limitations as a musician?

Shit, I've got nothing but limitations! I mean, I'm limited by everything. I'm limited by my technique. I'm limited by my background. I'm limited by my education. I'm limited by the things I've heard. I'm limited by all that stuff. I'm limited by being a human being. Yeah. I think in a way that a musician—and particularly a musician with a distinctive style—is, in fact, a product of their limitations. What you're hearing is their limitations, really. I assume that almost everybody plays at the outside edge of their ability, so that's usually what you're hearing—as good as they can do.

How long could you last in a band where when you went onstage, you'd have to duplicate what's on a record?

Not a minute! [*Laughs.*] I don't think I could last very long. I mean, that would be so dull for me. In fact, I don't even think I could do it.

What percent of a Grateful Dead show is improvisation?

Oh, about 80 percent. I mean, almost all of it, really. All the stuff that isn't the words and the melody.

What happens when someone else in the band wants to go off into an improvisational tangent that you might not necessarily be able to follow or want to get into?

You have to make an effort. Then I'll lay out. If it's something that I don't have a handle on, then I'll lay out. If somebody's got something going, rather than wreck it by playing stuff that fucks with it, I'll lay out until I either apprehend it—you know, understand it on some level and can do something to support it—or else I'll just lay out, because that's the best thing to do. And a lot of times I just like to listen to what's going on, because a lot of times there's some beautiful things happening that don't have anything to do with me, and it's nice to be able to just listen. The Grateful Dead can be very fascinating that way. I love to lay out, because sometimes Weir and Brent [Mydland] get into some incredible things. I mean, everybody does, really, so it's nice to just stop: "Wow! What's that?" I like that.

Can you psyche yourself into creative moods?

Uh, I almost always have to. I mean, yeah, they don't come to me. In other words, if I don't sit down and work at stuff, I don't get song ideas. I'm not that creative, really. I'm not real prolific. I write maybe three, four songs a year, if that. And I have to work at 'em. I have to say, "Now I'm gonna work," and sit down and work. It's one of those things where I'll work for a couple of hours and nothing will happen. I won't get anything. I'll stop for a while, pick it up again and work for a couple of hours, nothing will happen. The next day I'll do the same thing, and the next day, and the next day. Maybe three or four, five days into it, I'll get a little idea: "Hey, this is kind of nice." You know, it's like that. Then every once in a while you get a stroke—you get something, "Oh, far out!" But then usually then once I get going, once I've got the first idea, then maybe three, four songs will come out in the next two days. That's the way that works for me, generally speaking.

Were any of the songs you've written particularly frustrating?

Oh, yeah. Some were really frustrating. "Rubin and Cherise" took about three years to write, literally—maybe longer than that. I kept writing and writing versions of it—"Oh, this sucks." Hunter would rewrite the lyrics: "No, that doesn't make it." I'd write a new melody: "No, that isn't it." It's so utterly and totally different from the very first conception of it. That went on forever. It just went on forever.

Did any songs ever happen spontaneously?

Yeah! A whole bunch of 'em. A lot of 'em. I'd have to go through the whole list and say, "Yeah, this one, this one, this one." An awful lot of them have just *boom*—they come out real quick. Because usually we're cooking, Hunter and I, when that happens. The majority of our songs are cooking. It's that first one or two or that really different one occasionally that we had to labor like crazy at or whatever.

Do you give Robert Hunter a chord progression?

We do it all different ways. He gives me lyrics. He gives me a stack of lyrics this big [*holds fingers a couple of inches apart*], and I give him about two melodies. [*Laughs.*] You know, his output is enormous. My output is teeny. But usually what happens is I go over to his house, and we just work on something.

On piano?

Yeah.

Then do you teach it to the other members of the band at a rehearsal, do you give them a cassette . . .

No, I let them guess it! [*Laughs.*]

Onstage, right?

Yeah! No, I like to just teach it to 'em. I just tell them the chords: "Here's the chords." Like that. I like to keep it simple.

Are there any songs you're particularly proud of?

Oh, yeah, there's a bunch of them that I love. I really do love them. There's a lot of them that I'm proud of. I don't know. All of them are songs that I can perform time after time and not get bored with, and that's saying a lot.

That's a good sign.

Yeah, it really is. They live for me. And after I've written them, I don't feel like they're mine anymore—luckily, because I'm self-conscious about my own work if I think about. If they reminded me of myself somehow, I don't think I'd be able to stand to do them over and over again. So it's nice. They don't have any context, in a way, so it's nice. I can perform them over and over again in lots of different moods, with lots of different coloration, and still feel good about 'em.

Are there songs you'll only call out to play when you're in a certain mood?

Geez, that's hard to tell. For me, playing onstage is so subjective, I don't know how I feel about it a lot of the time. It may be that there are, yeah. There are definitely songs that a lot of times I am not in the mood for, so it works that way for sure. Whether it works the other way, I'm not so sure. That is to say that it's possible that if I'm in the right mood, I can play any song. I can feel like doing any song. So I don't know about that part of it. But I know on the negative side of it that there are times when I definitely don't feel like playing a certain song. This is not true with every song, though. There's only a few songs that are sort of mood-triggered or attached in some way to a mood—for me, in that subjective sense. [*At this point photographer Jon Sievert came in and we took a short break.*]

You were talking about composing...

I'll tell ya, I don't think of myself as a composer. I only do that because that's what you do. I learned how to do it. It's a craft. I can do it as a craft. I know about the craft of writing, but I don't think of myself as a composer. I've never been compelled by my own compositions. I don't feel that I'm particularly gifted in that area.

If somebody wanted to hear the essential Jerry Garcia, are there any cuts you'd tell them to listen to?

No, not really. I don't think of myself as being on records. But any half a dozen live concerts of the Grateful Dead or my band would pretty much give them the more or less of it.

Do any concerts stand out?

I don't keep track. No, I don't.

You're not like your fans, huh?

No. For me, it's the next note. It's not the last one.

When you make a mistake onstage, is that your attitude?

Yeah. Oh, yeah. There's no such thing as a mistake.

Do it again, and it's improvisation.

That's right. There's no such thing as a mistake.

Are you satisfied with your accomplishments and your career?

Not at all. No. No, no, no, no, no. I still think of myself as someone trying to learn how to play the guitar. If I learn how to play the guitar, I'll be really happy.

Why do you think you've attracted such a loyal following?

It must be really hungry out there. [*Laughs.*] I blame the general low quality of life, you know.

Yeah?

Well, yeah! I don't know why. To tell you the truth, I don't know why the first person stayed for the first song. It's been a mystery to me, because there was a time when that didn't happen. I played for a long time, and nobody cared about it at all. [*Laughs.*] That was never a criteria, as far as I was concerned. I would keep playing for nobody if that was what was happening. People hanging out and liking it is just another one of those things of just tremendous good luck, I think. Or at least that's how I feel about it. I'm glad it's that way—I'm glad people like it—but I don't know how or I don't know why or what, particularly. It's hard to appreciate from this side of it.

Have you perceived a large change in your audience?

Our audience has changed a lot of times, but our audience is still a Grateful Dead audience. That is to say, the kind of people that they are—I think there's a certain kind of person, maybe, that likes Grateful Dead music. I don't mean that in a narrow kind of way, because it seems to cut across all kinds of lines. I mean, it cuts across all kinds of cultural and social lines, so it's not some easy formula for the Grateful Dead person. Our audience now are people who are sixteen, seventeen years old, eighteen years old now, that weren't born when we were started. That's a sobering thought, you know.

Does the ambience of the concert seem the same?

Oh, yeah. Well, pretty similar, except there are some large differences, but they seem to be basically cultural in a big way in America. On the East Coast, they're more vehement, you know. They're more yaaah! The energy is higher, frankly. But the energy is higher on every level on the East Coast. You know, New York has that thing that only New York has. The West Coast has a thing that only the West Coast has. Those kind of differences, you know. But other than that, the Grateful Dead audience basically is the same kind of people. They get along pretty well with themselves, from coast to coast and all around. They seem to be a pretty good-natured lot. I like 'em. They're good people.

For the work I do, I have to see a lot of heavy metal and jazz and different types of music . . .

Lucky you! [*Laughs.*]

Any bands you'd go out of your way to see?

There are a few, yeah. Let's see—the last band I went to see is Dire Straits. That was the last band I went to see live, a couple of years ago. There are others that I would, but most of the time I'm out working and stuff. So I don't really get a chance. But there are more that I would go to see if I were in a situation where I wasn't working nights so much. I would go out more. But yeah, there's actually a lot of music that I would go to see. It's just the opportunity doesn't present itself that often. That's the problem. Time and space, you know.

Do you ever have trouble with being recognized in public?

I've given up worrying about it, because I'm recognized almost everywhere now. It bothers me sometimes, because there's that thing—you'd like to not have to think about yourself all the time. That's the drag—the thing of constantly being forced to think about yourself all the time. And there are times when you'd like to, uh, . . . I feel some sense of responsibility toward that person too, the public Garcia person, you know. In other words, I don't feel that I have the freedom to get roaring drunk and start fights and scream at people and do all the kinds of stuff that I might do perfectly comfortably if I were just nobody. You know what I mean? [*Laughs.*] I don't like to be obnoxious. There are things you might be able to do in perfect comfort if you felt that you didn't have to answer for it in some way. And I feel some sense of stricture. Although I might not ever do those things, I do feel some sense of restriction down at that end of my personality. And sometimes I have mild fits of resentment about it, but shit, mostly people are very nice to me, and so far I've had no really bad experiences. I've had a few weird experiences and a few close brushes with total weirdness of one sort or another, but nothing that's really freaked me out or made me feel too awful about it.

That'd be a great book title: "Close Brushes with Total Weirdness."

[*Laughs.*]

What's your acoustic guitar?

Takamine. I don't know what model it is, but it's a lot like a D-21 except that it's got a cutaway. A dreadnought with one cutaway.

With slider controls?

Yeah, little slider controls. It's got a high and low cut and boost and a volume, so it's got three sliders as opposed to two. It's right off the shelf—it's a showroom model.

Do you have it set up to approximate an electric?

No, I use significantly heavier strings and also a higher action and all that. I have it set up like an acoustic guitar.

How much preparation do you have to do, playing wise, before you go on tour and onstage?

Well, I like to warm up. Before I go on tour, I like to spend two or three days with John, just warming up my chops on the acoustic guitar. We've done it enough now where it only takes a few days to warm up, chops wise. And then before a show, I'll do more and less as the tour goes on—warming up before a show. There's the long-term warming up, and the short-term warming up.

On acoustic, do you have to make many compensations in terms of technique with your right-hand picking attack?

Yeah, it's a whole different ball of wax, yes. It's very different. I hold my whole hand kind of differently. And just the position of the guitar and the thickness of the guitar and everything means my whole arm and wrist and everything have a whole different attitude. Electric guitar is real thin, so my elbow is close to my body and my wrist is close to the guitar. It's all in here [*demonstrates close-up playing position*]. With an acoustic guitar, it's all out here [*holds arms further away from his body*].

Do you hold the pick the same way?

Pretty much, yeah. But I move it around all the time while I'm playing anyway. I don't have "a" way I hold the pick in an iron grasp. I constantly adjust it. I move it around a lot.

Do you always use the pointy end?

Yes.

A lot of guys lately have been using the rounded shoulder.

Yeah, I know. It's because it makes it seem like you can play faster. But what you pick up in speed you sacrifice in point. I like to have a lot of control over the point of the note, the attack. And when you use the point of the pick, it means that by relaxing or tightening upon the pick itself you get, uh, . . . I use a real thick pick, one with absolutely zero flexibility. It's like a stick. And the point is you get a lot of change in touch and a lot of change in tone and point attack of the note and coloration on that level and harmonic content of the attack by holding on to the pick tighter or looser. That makes a big difference in the tone. And on acoustic guitar, that's one of the ways you can really color your playing.

Can you play a vibrato with your fingers the same way on acoustic?

I do a slightly different kind of vibrato. I don't do the same, because I use heavier strings, for one thing. It's a different thing. But yeah, I don't have any trouble with vibrato on acoustic.

Which fingers do you use?

I tend to draw my vibrato from my whole hand.

Like a violin player rather than B. B. King?

Yeah, yeah. I don't do independent vibratos with my fingers very often. Once in a while I do. More often, I do a vibrato with my wrist.

Do you bend strings much on acoustic?

Yeah, but I don't make an effort to. On an acoustic guitar, I'm more likely to bend a half-step.

Will you back the finger bending with other fingers?

No. Usually it's unsupported.

You must have strong hands.

Yeah, yeah. I always use relatively heavy strings for rock-and-roll guitar and a high action.

Do you play in open tunings on acoustic?

Never. Well, no, I wouldn't say never. There are things I especially do, but I never perform in an open tuning. If I had another guitar that I could tune up in an open tuning and leave it there . . . I hate to retune the guitar onstage. I feel they settle into a tuning, and I don't like to retune them for that reason—because you lose that sense of settling in.

How do you amplify?

I just run it into the board, because usually I travel with the same P.A., the same monitor system. I bring it up through the monitor, so it's plenty loud. Sometimes I use just a little Twin Reverb onstage as a failsafe—just in case something goes wrong, I can still hear the guitar.

Do you have plans for acoustic recordings?

No plans, really, but if something comes up, maybe. Really, the acoustic thing, the thing of performing as an acoustic artist, is something kind of new to me, really. I still see a whole lot. Like, John and I are just starting to get a feeling for it, and we're starting to flash on how many kinds of things we can do. We can do all kinds of different styles of music—we haven't even started to touch on it yet. I'm just doing a few things that are very available. I haven't started to put a whole lot of effort into it. But John and I are starting to think of all different tunes we could do and different styles and all that, so in the future I think there's a lot more happening in that acoustic format. I feel real good about that. John and I both do. It's really a kick to do that.

Is a lot of your acoustic repertoire drawn from traditional tunes?

Yeah, yeah. A lot of it is, because I love those tunes. I just do whatever I love.

Would you feel comfortable playing, say, a reggae song?

I don't think so. I might find some comfortable way to do it, but no, I'm too conscious of style. I associate style with the way it is. I don't like taking a style and doing an inferior version of it. I don't like trying to choke a style down into some package. Reggae is really an ensemble style—I would feel funny about trying to sort of force that down to one instrument or two instruments. It wouldn't work for me.

Can you comment on your plans for the future?

No, except that I have plans for the future! [*Laughs.*] I plan to have a future, yeah! That's as far as I'm gonna go.

That's good enough for me.

Yeah, me too.

Any predictions for the future of rock guitar?

I'm sure it's just going to get more interesting—at least I hope so. Or maybe it won't. It seems as though guitar goes through those things of being like—there was sort of a reductive school of guitar playing that went on there for a while during the '70s. There was kind of an anti-guitar school.

Minimalist.

Right, right. And that was kind of okay, you know. But I'm a guitar player.

It put more of a focus on tone versus notes.

Yeah, that's true. And sometimes it's a good idea to get down from the guitar tree. I also am not that much of a nut about guitar music, just guitar music. I like music music. It's the thing of a guitar as a voice in the music—

that's really the thing. So it's the music that counts to me. I mean, I'll be happy whatever happens, as long as something happens. [*Laughs.*] You have to keep adjusting. I'd rather feel good than bad, you know. So given the choice of worrying about the development of music or being optimistic, I think it's easier to be optimistic.

Are you concerned about what you'll be remembered as?

God, no. I hope people don't remember me beyond what's necessary. Don't hang anybody up by having to remember me too much—that's what I would hope. It's like, remembering is dangerous.

How would you like to be remembered as a musician?

As a pretty okay musician. I don't know. I don't really expect to be remembered—that's way ahead of me. I'm still trying to just get good. If I get good, then I might say I hope people remember how good I am. The idea of being remembered would be embarrassing to me at this point.

You've got a humble attitude.

If you were me you wouldn't think so! [*Laughs.*]

CODA: Jerry Garcia's poor dietary habits and ongoing struggles with drug addiction led to his falling into a diabetic coma in 1986. He recovered and continued to play, but his physical decline continued. On August 9, 1995, the fifty-three-year-old suffered a fatal heart attack during a stay at a rehabilitation clinic. The Grateful Dead formally disbanded soon afterward. Surviving members reunited in various bands over the years, culminating with the 2015 series of concerts billed as "Fare Thee Well: Celebrating 50 Years of the Grateful Dead." The lineup for these shows included longtime members Bob Weir, Phil Lesh, Bill Kreutzmann, and Mickey Hart, and Phish's Trey Anastasio on guitar.

Johnny Winter in the early 1970s. (Courtesy Teddy Slatus Management)

The British blues boom of the 1960s brought rapid fame to groups like the Rolling Stones, Yardbirds, and Animals. As these bands began touring North America and selling millions of albums, the originators who inspired their exploration of the blues—notably Muddy Waters, Howlin' Wolf, and John Lee Hooker—finally began playing to white audiences at home. "That's a funny damn thing," Muddy Waters said. "Had to get somebody from out of another country to let my white kids over here know where we stand. They're crying for bread and got it in their backyard."[1] But by the time the Beatles and other British groups landed in America, several savvy—and soon to be influential—young American guitarists were already studying blues records, just as their counterparts had in England. In Seattle, young Jimi Hendrix copped licks from his dad's Muddy Waters and B. B. King singles. In New York, John Hammond, son of the famed Columbia Records producer, played along to records by Blind Willie McTell, Robert Johnson, and Howlin' Wolf. In Chicago, Mike Bloomfield and other young white musicians made pilgrimages to local clubs to jam with the city's renowned bluesmen.

Among all of the American-born white bluesmen, none had as dramatic an impact during the 1960s as Johnny Winter. He emerged to national prominence in 1968, after a journalist for *Rolling Stone* magazine wrote, "If you can imagine a hundred and thirty pound cross-eyed albino with long fleecy hair playing some of the gutsiest fluid blues guitar you have ever heard, then enter Johnny Winter."[2] Winter's scorching blues-rock playing more than lived up to the hype. The singer/guitarist signed a huge deal with Columbia Records and rapidly became the first American blues-rock guitar hero to headline stadiums. In concert and on record, Johnny proved himself extraordinarily adept with old-time country blues and high-energy blues-rock played bare-fingered or with a slide.

During the ensuing half century Winter remained remarkably true to his roots in the blues, classic rock and roll, and the songs of Bob Dylan and the Rolling Stones. He had many ups and downs, including long periods of inactivity and intense bouts with drug addiction. He also enjoyed many successes; his favorite among these was playing a vital role in resurrecting the career of his idol Muddy Waters during the 1970s and '80s.

Through it all, Johnny Winter remained intensely devoted to the guitar. "I really love playing guitar," he said near the end of his life. "It's the only thing I've ever really been great at!"[3] This type of understatement was typical of Johnny, who, like his fellow Texan Stevie Ray Vaughan, was always quick to praise and credit the musicians who'd inspired him. In truth, Winter excelled at producing, arranging, and performing, and he was exceptionally knowledgeable on the history of Texas and Mississippi blues music and early rock and roll. We spoke many times, and I always found him to be unpretentious, upbeat, and accommodating. At the time of this May 2, 1984, conversation, Johnny had just released *Guitar Slinger*, the best of his albums on Alligator Records. We agreed to focus the interview on the art of slide guitar.

Would you be willing to discuss the art of slide guitar?

Sure! It's kind of hard to explain it, you know, but I'll be glad to try.

On this new record, you used a couple of open tunings.

Yeah. I always use the same two. Usually it's the open E and open A, but on this record I think I used the open-E tuning in G in one case, and the A tuning I use on "Iodine in My Coffee." I'm not sure if that song is in A or not—I think it is. But I use those two basic blues tunings that I picked up from Robert Johnson, mostly—listening to Son House and Robert Johnson records. In fact, when I was learning, I wasn't aware of any books, so I had to learn it by listening to mostly, like I say, to Son House and Robert Johnson records. You just had to figure out what the open strings were by listening to the records, and it was a whole different thing. I later found out that I was right, when people started writing books and stuff. But before they started writing on the back of album covers and telling what that stuff was, they called it bottleneck guitar at first because that's what the guys would usually do—break the neck off of a bottle and use that. It was definitely difficult. That open A, they usually call it open G.

If you have a guitar tuned regular and you're going to go to open A, how would you tune it?

It's like that hillbilly A chord, putting your fingers on the second fret on the second, third, and fourth strings.

So you tune those strings up a whole note.

Right.

When you said you played one of the songs in open E, but in G, do you mean you capoed at the third fret?

No. I just had real light-gauge strings on and just tuned it all the way up to G.

So if you're going to an open E, you leave your guitar tuned regular and then you tune your fifth, fourth, and third strings up.

Yeah. It's usually open E, so usually I just turn the third string up one fret. I just tune it to the regular E chord. Usually if I'm gonna do a song in G, I'll use the open-A tuning. But I had real light gauge strings on my guitar, and if I'd have tuned down and used that tuning, it just wouldn't have had as much balls. So I went ahead and tuned it all the way up. Luckily I didn't break any strings. That was for "It's My Life, Baby."

For a beginner, could you explain the advantages of playing in an open tuning versus standard tuning?

Well, when you're playing with a slide, the advantages are that you've got that chord there. You can just barre the strings and you've got a chord to work with. That's *the* advantage—that you've got an open chord to work with, and you can have that chord ring down in the bass notes while you play the top strings with your fingers—I do some of that. You know, I keep the bass going with my thumb and play lead with my fingers, especially if I'm just playing by myself. That's a big help. The notes are easier to go to. It's easier to go to blues notes in those two tunings than it is if you're just tuning to standard tuning. Duane Allman was about the best slide man at playing with a regular tuning. You just don't get too many chords, especially if you don't use your little finger [for the slide]. That's pretty important. I started out using my ring finger because it really feels weird playing with a slide on your little finger, but a guy from the Denver Folklore Society—I think his name was Dave—he was a blues freak, and he got me my first National guitar for about a hundred and fifty bucks, and he really helped me a whole lot, man. He just forced me to use that little finger. He said, "Man, you're gonna be unhappy later on down the line if you don't change." It's hard to do at first.

So you were playing on your ring finger, like Duane did?

Yeah, yeah. That's what feels natural at first, but when you do that, you really can't play chords. You can fret with those three fingers if you put the slide on your little finger. You can do a lot of fretwork with those three fingers. If you put the slide on the middle, it pretty much screws you up. You can't do much chord work that way. So I have the slide halfway up my little finger, not all the way on it, but halfway up to where I can still bend that little finger.

What kind of slide do you use now?

I've had the same slide forever. This same guy took me to a plumbing supply place and I had to buy a twelve-foot-long piece of conduit pipe, and then I had the guy there cut it into pieces for me. I think they are about an inch and a half, pretty close to two inches, long. I gave the rest of them away years ago. I've had the same one. I should have buffed it down immediately, but I didn't. It started out like a garbage can color, not shiny at all. It changed from that to a kind of a black shiny color, and then that finish wore off and now it's kind of bright silver. I did that just playing guitar. I should have just buffed it down as soon as I got it because it sounds much clearer now. At first, it wasn't slick at all, so it didn't really sound good. It's got to be nice and smooth to get a good tone. But before that, man, I'd use my wristwatch, I'd use knives, I'd use lipstick covers, I'd use a test tube. And this piece of conduit pipe is without a doubt the best. I've never had a store-bought slide that was small enough to fit just halfway up my little finger. I went to the plumbing supply place and tried different pieces of pipe until I found one that fit me perfect.

Is it heavy?

No, it's not really heavy, but it's not super light.

Do you know what it's made of?

I sure don't, man. It's not copper. It's shiny. It's just some kind of metal. It's fairly thick. It's not super heavy like some of those store-bought slides I've seen that are really heavy. I really don't know the thickness. It's kind of right in the middle, though. It's perfect for me. It's not real heavy and it's not real light. But it should be right for you. If it's too heavy, you're not gonna really be able to feel how hard to press down. If you press down too hard, of course, you're gonna hit the frets. And if you don't press down hard enough, you're not gonna get a nice tone. And just knowing how hard to press down was the hardest part, for me, in getting that nice tone. At first the harmonics when you slide up there would be as loud as the tone I was trying to get. I was really bad at first.

How did you get better?

Practicing. Just kept on playing, man. That's the way I did everything. I just played with all the records first. Then, after I got down what the people were doing on the records, I started putting my own stuff to it.

What were your favorite slide cuts? What would be essential for a young player to check out?

It's good to start with someone like Son House, because Son played real simple. Robert Johnson, without a doubt, though, is the best of those Delta guys. He's so far above everybody else that it was scary. Robert Johnson, without a doubt. Either one of those Columbia Robert Johnson albums— the first one and *King of the Delta Blues Singers*. That stuff is just great. That's really where I learned most of my first stuff. Well, actually the first slide I heard was Muddy Waters. It was off this album *The Best of Muddy Waters*, on Chess. And I didn't know what it was. I remember hearing it for the first time, and at first I thought it was a steel guitar. And then I could tell for sure there was one cut on there that was just one guy playing, and he would fret the guitar sometimes and sometimes he would use the slide. I didn't know what it was for a long time. I just kept buying albums, and I'd hear somebody else. I don't really remember how I finally found out what it was—I think probably from some album liner notes. But as soon as I found out what was going on, I started experimenting with different things and trying to get the right tuning. First I was trying slide without tuning my guitar different at all, and I knew that wasn't right. And then you just got to where you could hear it by listening over and over. You could hear this must be tuned to this chord, and I would just tune my guitar where I thought was right and then I would play along with it. I started being able to copy what was on the record, so then I figured, "Well, this must be right." That's the way I learned it. Later on, after the Muddy Waters stuff, I found the Son House album on Columbia, right when he had been rediscovered and he'd just put this album out. I think it was *The Legendary Son House*. It was definitely on Columbia. It was right when he first got rediscovered.

Are we talking about the early 1960s?

Early '60s, mid-'60s. Yeah, about the same time I got the Robert Johnson albums. And those albums really took me a long way, man. That was the kind of stuff I was really into. I'd heard Earl Hooker on a couple of 45s, and I could tell he was doing something different, but at that point I hadn't heard that much of Earl Hooker, and I was really interested in the more primitive stuff—you know, the Robert Johnson and the Son House.

Is there much difference between playing acoustic slide versus electric?

Yeah, yeah. In fact, just playing acoustic guitar versus electric is harder for me, because I never did much acoustic playing. I just always played electric guitar. Even if I was sitting around the house, I would just play my electric with no amp. The only thing that made me want to play acoustic guitar was when I heard the National, because that was such a rough, different sound. It reminded me of a garbage can with a wire across it or something. It had a real nasty sound. Most acoustic things are nice and mellow and pretty, and I just didn't really want that. But when I heard that first National guitar, I knew there was something different. And then when I saw one, I was determined to get one of those.

With that nickel-plated body?

Yeah! That was the whole thing for me, the National guitar and getting that sound. And it's a hard guitar to play. For me, it doesn't balance quite right, and I really have to get used to it. I can't just switch from my electric and pick up my National and play on it very well. I have to sit down for an hour or two and mess with it.

Do you ever play slide with your guitar held flat on your lap?

Never have. I mean, I tried it a couple of times, and it just didn't feel right at all to me. Yeah, I do remember buying a steel [lap steel guitar] at one point, and just seeing if that worked. And it just felt full awkward to me. And every time I ever set down with anybody's steel guitar, I just can't do anything. It just feels totally, totally wrong for me. I remember taking piano lessons when I was a little kid, and it felt the same way. If I'd have practiced forever, I don't think I would have ever been a good piano player. It just didn't feel right. Immediately, the guitar just felt like it was part of me. You'd see T-Bone Walker play with the guitar turned up that way. He would just play normally, with a strap around the guitar, but he'd have the guitar turned up like that [strings facing the ceiling] and he kind of played down on it. But he still fretted with his hand around the guitar—he didn't go from the top. I really just didn't ever feel comfortable doing that.

What's your favorite electric guitar for slide?

Well, my favorite guitar for everything was the [Gibson] Firebird.

Do you change the guitar's action for slide?

Yeah, I usually have it up a little bit higher. I have my action pretty high normally, so I can just tune up one of my regular guitars and play slide on it. But I couldn't play slide with action the way most people have theirs. But usually I have one guitar with the action set up just a little bit higher so I can still fret it—I don't have it high enough to where I can't fret it. But it will make it a little bit easier.

Do you raise it at the bridge?

Yeah, yeah. Always. I never have done anything at the nut. I've never had a higher nut or anything like that.

If you're going to be playing slide, will you leave the older strings on the guitar?

No, not usually. I usually change strings when they start sounding dead. I like a pretty bright sound. But when you first change strings, it's pretty bad, you know. When they're brand new, you get a whole lot of that surface noise. So it really helps to play on it for a few hours. If you change strings and go right out and play a job, you're going to have a whole lot more noise than you want.

What string gauges do you use for slide?

I have been using the same gauges for everything—.009, .011, .016, .024, .032, .042. But for the last couple of months . . . I got that Lazer guitar, and the strings on it were heavier. I tuned it down to D, because I think it started with a .010, and then .013, .018, .026, .036, .046, I believe is what he had on there. It felt good but it was a little harder to play, so I tuned it down to D. A lot of the things on the record are in D, just tuned down to a regular open tuning, but starting with D instead of E. I really like that, so I've been doing that a lot lately, just playing the Lazer guitar tuned down to D. Jimi used to go E-flat a lot, and D, boy, you hit that bass string and it sounds so nice. I don't know—it's just been sounding so good that I might keep doing it. "Boot Hill" is in D, just regular tuning. That's kind of an example. And "Lights Out" and "Don't Take Advantage of Me"—I'll play those when I got my guitar tuned down to D and I'm playing that Lazer.

So every string is tuned down a whole step from open E.

Right.

Is that Lazer a full-scale guitar?

Yeah. In fact, it goes a little further. If it's tuned to E, you can hit two octaves—it goes all the way up to high E.

Do you wear a thumbpick when you play slide?

Yeah, I always use a thumbpick. Even when I play mandolin, I play it with a thumbpick.

Do you use the fingers of your right hand too?

Yeah. I use the first two fingers.

For slide?

Yeah. For everything.

How do you keep the other strings from ringing out? Do you damp any-where?

Sometimes I want 'em to ring, but if I don't, then I always use the heel of my right hand to dampen the strings. Yeah, I've always done that. In fact, the first Fender guitar I ever got, it had that tailpiece on it, and I hated that. I thought, "Man, am I the only guy that needs that thing off?" The first thing I did when I got a Strat was take that tailpiece off because I can't play without being able to dampen the strings down there. But definitely playing slide, you also have to be able to use your left hand to deaden some strings, and that's a whole different technique. You know, you're using that slide and not fretting, so sometimes if you don't want but one string to ring, you really have to work it out so you can use some of those other fingers to deaden some of the strings.

In other words, if you're doing an Elmore James slide up to the twelfth fret on two or three of the strings, your index finger or your index and middle fin-gers would be laying across the strings below the slide.

Yeah. Usually. Yeah.

When do you not dampen?

Sometimes you just want the whole thing to ring. That's the whole advan-tage of having the open chord.

As far as amps go, what do you prefer for playing slide?

I been using the Music Man amps for a long time, but the Music Man amps that I have aren't new. They were from when Leo Fender was with Music Man. But on the record, I used a MESA/Boogie. And I had never used a MESA/Boogie before, and I really loved it. It was just an excellent-sounding amp. Most of the album we cut with a MESA/Boogie, and I'm really happy with it. I really like that MESA/Boogie. I'd been hearing about them for years, and it's the first time I actually cut with one of them. But, man, it just sounded great.

What pickups do you prefer for slide?

Usually I almost always use the pickup by the neck. And that's one of the strange things about getting used to these Lazer guitars, because I've never really liked using that treble pickup very much. But somehow it sounds pretty damn good. I've gotten used to it. It's got enough balls to where I like it okay. But usually I tend to almost always use the lower pickup. Muddy loved that real trebly Telecaster sound. He got a *great* sound using the treble pickup. Somehow I have so much treble on my amp anyway that sometimes I use that pickup and there's just too much. There's so much treble you can hardly find the notes. It's just a little too much treble. But with the Lazer guitar, I played "Iodine in My Coffee," and it doesn't have a bass pickup. It only has the pickup by the bridge, but it's not quite as close to the bridge as most guitars. It's got a switch—you can push down on the bass/treble control, and it goes from a one-coil pickup to two coils, and that makes a lot of difference. I really like that because it gives it more body. It's two completely different tones, though.

Did Muddy Waters ever say anything to you about playing slide?

Not really. He just said, "Keep doing it—sure sounds good to me!" By the time that I'd met Muddy, I had pretty much absorbed what Muddy did to where if I wanted to, I could play note-for-note what he was going to play. It's kind of too bad—it would have made it a lot easier for me. But there wasn't anybody that played slide that I had a chance to ask about it, until I met this guy Dave from Denver. Nobody had ever showed me anything.

Did Muddy usually go for single lines instead of chords?

Yeah, almost always, because he had a very, very short slide. You couldn't get but about two strings with it—at the very most. That's all he could get with that slide.

Did he play with it on his little finger?

You know, I can't remember if Muddy played with it on his little finger or on his ring finger. That's unbelievable. That's really unbelievable. [*Asks his wife.*] Yeah, his little finger.

Did he damp?

You know, I really never watched Muddy that much. But just listening, yeah, he did to a certain extent. Yeah.

Did you ever get a chance to play with Duane Allman?

Oh, yeah. Oh, yeah. We played together a lot. In fact, I just got a tape last week when I was out on the road. I just got a tape of me sitting in with the Allman Brothers at the Hollywood Bowl back in '70 or '71. Way back there. I hadn't heard it since we did it. We were doing all those festivals together, and Duane and I played a whole lot together.

How would you characterize the differences between your slide styles?

Oh, there wasn't anything similar. I mean, there was nothing similar, nothing at all. Duane's style is so totally a whole different thing. Even the sound is different. He never played open chords. He never did anything in open tuning, so it was usually one or two strings at a time.[4] And he did a lot of damping on both sides—with both hands. It was very, very original, man. I mean, Duane, it was almost like he just did everything totally his own way. He didn't seem to get that style from anybody else. I mean, Earl Hooker was about his only influence as I could see. It was a little Earl Hooker, but he had a real individual style. In those days, when you thought of slide, you thought of open tunings. Nobody played slide in regular tunings.

Have you ever recorded any slide songs in regular tunings?

Never ever. I hardly ever do it. Once in a while on gigs I'll try it, but I'm not really too good at it.

Are there differences in your approaches when you're playing in E or A?

Not a whole lot. They're pretty much the same—you add an extra string there in the A. The A tuning is the same things as the E tuning, with an extra string on top. The high string.

So the same patterns basically work for both.

And it took me a while to figure it out. It sure seemed fairly easy to go from one to the other, and I realized why—it was exactly the same thing, except for the top string.

You just move the patterns over a string, basically.

That's right.

Do you have any advice for beginners?

Boy, it's so hard. I remember just being really frustrated because things just didn't sound right. I guess just don't get discouraged, because slide really sounds terrible at first. You just don't ever think you're gonna get it right. But you keep on practicing and getting that tone right, just knowing how. You just got to feel it—just exactly how hard to push down to keep from hitting the fret, but hard enough to get a nice tone. It's mainly just keep on practicing and get your tone down. For me, that was the hardest thing—getting a decent tone. And, of course, you got to get used to the totally different tuning. But for me, it wasn't near as hard as I thought it was going to be. It just kind of fell into place. Like any style of guitar, it takes a lot of practice.

There's sure a lot you can do with it too.

Yeah! I've heard people say it's confining, and it is, because you can't go to as many different chords as you can in regular tuning, but it's a whole different thing. It's just great for blues. It seems like it was just made for blues. All the notes are right there, the blues notes. You can get right to them.

It's sure great to play when you're by yourself.

Yeah. It really is. It's got such a nice, lonesome sound that just sustains forever. It does have a real beautiful, totally different sound. I really couldn't believe it the first time that I ever heard Muddy's stuff. That was the first slide that I heard, and it's so unique, so original-sounding. I've heard how it supposedly started, but it doesn't sound like Hawaiian music to me.

It started with Hawaiian music?

Supposedly.

I heard it started with the diddley bow.

Oh, I've heard that, of course. That's definitely one of the main things. I mean, even I played one of those. Every kid from down South at one time does that—puts the wire up on the barn door.

With a couple of spools under it.

Yeah. Just nail it up there. I remember we had a shelf that was hanging up, supported by a wire, and you could tune it by just pulling down on the shelf and you could use a slide. The shelf was just supported by a piece of wire. That was the first time I ever messed with one. I was noticing that you could get to where it made a note. You could put a little tension on the shelf and play tunes with it like that. That was the first time I did anything like that. But I've always heard stories that somehow Hawaiian music was supposed to have influenced slide. But, to me, what makes the most sense was so many people had rotten guitars with bowed necks. I think that probably the guitars' neck got so bad you couldn't fret 'em. It was just a lot easier to play slide.

It's hard for me to imagine that someone like Robert Johnson would have been exposed to Hawaiian guitarists.

Me too. That's just hard for me to believe. But that's what I always heard—that somehow, someway, the Hawaiian music and steel guitar got to Mississippi and they had heard it over there and took the idea. But to me, that never quite made sense. I mean, how did those people in Mississippi ever hear Hawaiian music?

And if they heard it, would they want to play it?

Yeah, exactly! Yeah! [*Laughs.*] To me, it makes a lot more sense that they had cheap guitars with the neck all bowed, and it's just a lot easier to slide something up and down it. But that's just all theory—I never read that anyplace.

Hey, thanks, Johnny.

It's been great talking to you. A lot of people have been asking me, "How come nobody seems to be playing slide anymore?" It does seem like there's a lot less people playing slide now. I think that's just because there's less blues, and slide is such a blues-oriented thing, or bottleneck—whatever you want to call it. You don't hear as many people playing slide, and not many people learning it. So I'm hoping this record will change that around.

CODA: Johnny Winter enjoyed a flurry of activity during the final years of life. He was the subject of a 2010 biography by Mary Lou Sullivan, *Raisin' Cain: The Wild and Raucous Story of Johnny Winter*. He appeared at that year's prestigious Crossroads Guitar Festival and oversaw the release of the *Johnny Winter Live through the '80s* DVD. In 2011 he put out the *Roots* CD on Megaforce/Sony, and then journeyed to Tokyo to film the *Live from Japan* DVD. Johnny's final studio recording, 2014's *Step Back*, featured guest performances by Eric Clapton, Billy Gibbons, Ben Harper, Brian Setzer, Leslie West, and others. He gave his last performance, at the Cahors Blues Festival in France, two days before his death on July 16, 2014.

Gregg Allman plays the Oakland Coliseum, October 24, 1975. (Jon Sievert)

During an extraordinarily fertile five-year period, Duane Allman evolved from a teenager struggling to find his sound to a top-flight session player and the founder of the band that bears his family name. He set new standards for bottlenecked slide guitar, paying homage to its blues roots and casting it in previously unexplored directions. Decades after Duane's death, the majesty and influence of his best work—several of the Muscle Shoals sessions, the Allman Brothers Band's *At Fillmore East* and *Eat a Peach* albums, Derek & the Dominos' *Layla and Other Assorted Love Songs*—remains undiminished.

Jerry Wexler, Vice President of Atlantic Records while Duane worked as a session man at Fame Studios in Muscle Shoals, offered this assessment: "Duane was a complete guitar player, he could give you whatever you needed, he could do everything. Play rhythm, lead, blues, slide, bossa-nova, with a jazz feeling, beautiful light acoustic—and on slide he got *the* touch. A lot of slide players sound sour. To get clear intonation with the right overtones—that's the mark of genius. Duane is one of the greatest guitar players I ever knew. He was one of the very few who could hold his own with the best of the black blues players. And there are very few—you can count them on the fingers of one hand—if you've got three fingers missing."[1]

With the founding of the Allman Brothers Band in 1969, Duane became the figurehead of what came to be known as "the Southern sound." He and his brother Gregg carried their deep-felt love for Southern blues and R&B to rock audiences, just as Johnny Winter and British bands such as the Yardbirds and Rolling Stones had earlier in the decade. Playing side by side, Duane and co-guitarist Dickey Betts popularized the use of twin lead guitars playing in harmony and doing counterpoint lines in a rock setting, as heard in the Fillmore East version of "In Memory of Elizabeth Reed," which ranks among the greatest live performances in rock guitar history.

For most of his life, Duane Allman was inseparable from his younger brother Gregg. Raised by their widowed mother in Nashville and Daytona Beach, they learned music together and played side-by-side in bands. They spent their journeymen days in the Daytona Beach-based Houserockers and then toured as the Allman Joys. In 1967 the brothers moved to Los Angeles to form the Hour Glass. They finally hit their stride in 1969, with the formation of the Allman Brothers Band. In less than three years, Duane was gone, killed in an October 1971 motorcycle crash. Ten years later, assembling material for an as-yet-unwritten Duane Allman biography, I interviewed many of his bandmates, friends, and peers. The most poignant, with Gregg, took place on July 6, 1981. Gregg began the conversation.

GREGG: I think that's really nice, man, that you want to write about Duane.
Can you fill in the early years for me?
Okay. Alrighty.
Duane was a year older than you?
A year and eighteen days.
Were you the only two kids?
That was it.
Your father died when you were young?
Ah, yes. He died in '49. I was two and Duane was three.
Is your mother still alive?
Yes, she is.
Did anyone in your family play music?
My father sang, but not professionally. He sang pretty well.
Did you have instruments around the house when you were young?
No. No, we didn't. When we started school, we both wanted to get into the band. We went to military school, and we both wanted to play trumpet, and we lost interest in it. My mother always called it her folly, because back then $200 for a trumpet, you know, that was quite a bit.
You were raised by your mom?
That's right.
Did she work while you were kids?
Yes, she did. That's why we had to go off to military school.
You began playing guitar before Duane?
Right.
How did you get started with that?
We moved from Nashville in 1957—I guess I was eleven years old, about to turn twelve. No, wait a minute—I may have been younger than that. Anyway, we moved away from Nashville and moved to Daytona Beach, Florida. But every summer we would go back and visit my grandmother and stay there for the summer. We really missed Nashville because we grew up there, you know. She lived in this housing project, and there was this guy across the street. And he had an old Belltone guitar, which later, I think, turned into Silvertone—I'm not sure. One hot summer day he was sitting on the porch, and I walked over there and asked him if I could pick it up. He said sure. The strings were about an inch and a half off the neck—one of those bleeders, you know. So I just got really enchanted with this. By this time, this is like 1959.

So when I got back home, I thought, "Well, I'm gonna get me one of those guitars." I didn't know which end of it to play, but there was something about it that just really intrigued me. Because he'd sit there and he'd play "Wildwood Flower" and "Long Black Veil"—I think that's the only two songs he knew. He knew very little, a real country dude. Jimmy Bain—that was his name. So I got me a paper route and worked on it from March of '60 until about the end of school, right when school let out. Cleared all of $21, something like that—they got me on the office payment: "Yeah, we pay at the office," right? You know how that goes. So I rode my bicycle over to Sears. There was a Silvertone there that I wanted. It was $21.95. And the guy wouldn't trust me for the ninety-five cents, so I had to go home and borrow it from my mother. I rode back over the next day and bought it and started playing it and playing it. I got one of those Mel Bay books, and I didn't eat or sleep. I didn't do nothing but play that guitar. I just was crazy about it. I learned how to make a barre chord, and that really started it.

Was that an acoustic?

Right. This friend of mine turned me on to some Jimmy Reed albums and taught me that lick. So then my brother, he says, "What do we have here?" So I taught him what I knew, and he picked it up real quick. I mean, he was real sharp. So he quit school.

How old was Duane then?

Well, I started playing when I was twelve years old. I jumped a little time on you there. It's been a while. I started playing when I was twelve, and I got my first electric guitar that November. November 10, 1960. It was a Fender Musicmaster. It was really easy to play. By then I'd met other guys that had guitars that had been playing longer. It was just like more and more. I really got turned on to Chuck Berry and Jerry Lee Lewis and Little Richard, Presley—you know, the whole rock-and-roll thing. And then I met this black cat named Floyd [Miles]. By this time Duane, he had to have one. So to keep us from fighting, mom got him one, right? It was a Les Paul Junior, one of the old ones. It was solid, a real thin body, one of those purple ones. Just one black pickup on the back [near the bridge]. So we started playing together, and we really became friends at that time.

Were you like typical brothers before then?

Oh, yeah. Fight every day.

What did Duane want to be when he was little?

Uh, that's a good question. I'm not sure. He didn't like school, but he loved to read. He was always reading something. He read books like *Papillon*, [Tolkien's] *The Lord of the Rings* trilogy. He read all kind of stuff, just anything. He liked real adventurous stories and fiction—stuff like that.

Was he a good kid?

No, he was a rascal. He was a rascal. So we put a band together. Well, first we joined a band that was already together. It was called the Houserockers and the Untils. The rhythm section, the band, was the Houserockers, and the three black singers up front were the Untils.

Were both of you playing guitar?

They only needed one guitar player, so we switched off every other night. This was like the summertime of 1963. I was like a junior in high school, something like that. Anyway, one of those black singers was Floyd, and I watched him because I really dug his singing. See, in the beginning, the first band that we put together ourselves was called the Shufflers. I played lead guitar and Duane sang. And then after he quit school, he'd stay home and, man, he learned it fast.

He played all the time?

All the time.

Did he cop off of records or make it up himself?

Both.

Do you remember his favorite solos or players?

B. B. King—he loved B. B. King! Over the years he loved everybody from Chuck Berry to Kenny Burrell. I mean, you name it. He dug everybody. Back then, Johnny "Guitar" Watson—he liked him. He got into that real old blues stuff, loved Robert Johnson. He just loved any kind of guitar playing.

He never had lessons?

No. The only lessons he had was us sitting around the house, trial and error. And then he had a friend named Jim Shepley. I think Shepley was a couple of years older than him and had started a couple of years before. He's the one that turned us on to Jimmy Reed records. He had a bunch of these hot licks down. I thought, "Man, this guy is something else!" So he sat with him all the time. Before he quit school, they'd both skip school and shoot pool and play guitar. He learned a whole lot from Shepley, and that was probably his best friend back then.

Is Jim Shepley still around?

Yeah, he sure is. I hope he reads this. I think he lives in New Haven. He was in a band with Bob Greenlee, who used to be with Root Boy Slim and the Sex Change Band. I'm not sure if Shepley was in that band or not, but I know Greenlee was. And usually where Greenlee was, Shepley was. But I don't think he's doing much at all now. It's been years. I remember at one of the first few gigs that the Allman Brothers played, we played in New Haven, and sure enough, Shepley and Greenlee were both there. Duane was just—you could have knocked him over with a feather, man. It was great!

Was Greenlee another guy who played with Duane when he was young?

Right, he played in the Houserockers.

What were your other early professional experiences and bands leading into Hour Glass?

Well, after I got out of high school in '65, we had a band called the All-man Joys.

Did you do much touring?

Touring? I don't know if you could call it that. We did what they called the "chitlin circuit"—you know, Mobile, Alabama, at the Stork Club. We worked like seven nights a week, six sets a night, forty-five minutes a set. It was four of us, and we made $444 a week.

Was it unusual for a white band to be playing the chitlin circuit?

Oh, no. "Chitlin circuit"—that means just the clubs and beer joints.

Did the Allman Joys record?

We recorded one song, one 45. We recorded it at Bradley's Barn in Nashville, which is now burned down. It was "Spoonful" by Willie Dixon.

Did you sing it?

I sure did. And it was a terrible recording.

What happened after the Allman Joys?

Let me see. One of them got drafted, one chose to go his own way, and so Duane and I met up with Johnny Sandlin and Paul Hornsby and Pete Carr. They had a band called Five Minutes. We formed a band, and we called it the Allman Joys for a while. And then we thought, "Well, that's wrong," so for a very short time we called it the Allman-Act. And Bill McEuen came through St. Louis, where we were playing. Johnny McEuen of the Nitty Gritty Dirt Band is his older brother. They took us to L.A., and they came up with the name Hour Glass.

How do you view your period in L.A.?

That period with the Hour Glass? It was pretty scary, you know, because I'd never been past the Mississippi. I'd been to New York once. I don't know. It just seemed like it was forever away. We didn't play much. For some reason, there was no clubs or anything around there to play in. I mean, there was, but . . . Our first gig was with the Doors at—well, it's the Aquarius Theater now, but at that time it was the Hullabaloo club. And that scared me to death! I could barely sing. My knees were knocking together, because there must have been two thousand people in that place. The whole thing just kind of turned sour. Both albums came out, and they'd hand us a washtub full of demos and say, "Pick out your new album." All this time now, I was songwriting. I did get a few on those two albums. I don't know if you've heard those albums or not.

The ones with "Out of the Night" and "Power of Love."

Yeah, right.

They're still selling them.

Yeah, yeah. That's what I hear. In the beginning, when we were in St. Louis and they made us a proposition, I said, "No, let's don't go." Duane said, "Yeah! Let's go! Let's go! Let's do it." So we went. I guess we were there for, oh, part of '66, '67, '68—for about two and a half years. And Duane just finally said, "Man, I've had it with this bullshit. I'm leavin'. We can take the band and go on back home where we belong—right down South." We owed Liberty Records about $40,000. They said, "Well, we'll let y'all go, but we'll put a lawsuit on you. But we won't do it if he stays"—pointing to me, right?— "to work with our studio band." So I stayed. And the rest of them, they really didn't like it. They were all cussin' me on the way out the door. They thought I wanted to stay out there, which I did not. So there was no lawsuit, and I cut two records with them. They're with a twenty-piece orchestra. I hope you've never heard those.

No, I haven't.

Please, don't. Anyway, so I stayed out there another eleven months, and that's the longest I'd ever been away from my brother. That's when I wrote "[It's Not My] Cross to Bear." I was staying with this chick, and she was really running me around. I wrote "Black Hearted Woman" while I was out there. So anyway, one Sunday morning my brother called me on the phone, and he said he had this band together—had two lead-guitar players. I thought, "Boy, that's weird." He said, "And two drummers," and I said, "That's real weird!" "And a bass player." And he said, "But everybody is pretty much into their axe, and nobody as yet has written much, and they don't really like to sing. So why don't you come on down here and round this thing up and send it somewhere." Which is probably the finest compliment he ever gave me in my life. I said, "Let me hang up this phone, man. I got to get going." I beat feet over there as fast as I could to Jacksonville. And that was the Allman Brothers' start. It was March 26, 1969.

The difference in sound between the Hour Glass and the Allman Brothers is just amazing.

Yeah, it is. I mean, it's been a long time since I've heard any of that Hour Glass stuff, but when I hear it I can't believe it.

In between this time, was Duane playing in Muscle Shoals?

Right. He was just on the staff down there at Rick Hall's.

Did he ever mention what his favorite studio projects were?

He liked to play with Wilson Pickett—I know that. And he loved playing with Aretha, and he loved King Curtis. They was real tight. And he loved the Herbie Mann. He liked all of them. I think *Layla* was probably his favorite.

Did he have much to say about working with Eric Clapton?

Oh, yeah. Yeah. I was there when it all happened. Our whole band was there. See, we were playing in town, and Clapton came out to the gig.

Was Duane nervous?

Scared him to death! He came and sit right down in front, right on the grass. Of course, Clapton, every time you see him he looks different. I didn't notice him until toward the end, and I got shaky myself. Tommy Dowd was with him, and Duane asked Tommy if it'd be alright if he came and watched part of the session. And Clapton said, "Watch? Hell, come on and play!"

Were you there while they were recording the song "Layla"?

I was there for part of the first of it, and then I had to go back up to Macon. I came back down at the end of it. At one point of it, toward the end, we all got in there—both bands—and did a real long jam. We got it on tape. It's like a medley of blues songs.

It sounds to me that Clapton pushed Duane into playing beyond what he was doing before then.

You know, Duane liked that. He always said, "I like somebody onstage kicking me in the ass, so I'll do better," which I like myself.

It sounds like a lot of parts on "Layla" are Duane's rather than Eric Clapton's.

You got it right. On that song itself, he's got twelve tracks on there.

In something like "Why Does Love Got to Be So Sad?" sometimes it's hard to tell them apart, and then all of a sudden Duane's "Joy to the World" lick comes in.

Oh, yeah!

When you got the Allman Brothers Band together, some of the press proclaimed Duane the father of the band. Is this accurate?

That's real accurate.

How much musical direction did he provide?

He had to do with a lot of the spontaneity of the whole thing. He was like the mothership, right? He had this real magic about him that would lock us all in, and we'd all take off. Yeah, he really had that quality about him.

How much time did the band spend playing together before the first album?

Oh, we used to play every day. Every day. Because for the first album, they said, "Y'all got two weeks. Get in there and do it, and get out." Yeah, we cut that album in two weeks.

What was the first big break for the Brothers?

When it got together! [*Laughs.*] He [Duane] always felt, and I learned from him, that if you lay down a sound, if it's a hit in your heart, it's a hit. I don't care how many it sells or how many like it or whatever—play what you

Duane Allman,
late 1960s.
(Photo by
Twiggs Lyndon)

want to play and stick to your guns. That's how we got out of playing Top-40 stuff, and that's probably what started me to writing songs. He was really that way about it. He did his thing, you know, and if you like it, fine. And if you don't, fine.

Did Duane take stardom easily?

Um. [*Long pause.*] Well, the real heavy stardom. . . . Let me see. He was pretty shy about that sort of thing. No, he didn't. He was just one of the gang, man. The same dude that hung around with Shepley and shot pool. He thought about it the same way I do—you're just another person.

What do you think were the best representations of Duane's live and studio sounds with the Allman Brothers?

The best things he did? Wow, man, I like 'em all. He did some incredible things on—it wasn't studio—"Mountain Jam." "Don't Keep Me Wonderin'"—there's some good slide on that. Let me see. "Revival." Things like "Leave My Blues at Home." I know what! "Dreams." He did one hell of a job on the solo on that. Yeah.

Sometimes in his solos—like on that Boz Scaggs album and at the end of "Layla"—he did that really high part that almost sounds like birds.

That's what it was supposed to be! He put the bottle way up there by the top pickup.

Did he have any unusual recording methods?

He changed a lot. Like down in Muscle Shoals, he'd take a [Fender] Princeton amp and turn it on full blast, you know, and cover it with baffles. He was always working with Fuzz Faces and everything like that, and then he threw all that crap away and got the right amps for the right sort of thing. Like when he started working with Marshalls, he found out that the 100-watt was not it, so he used 50-watt cabinets.

Did he play really loud?

Yeah.

Was he usually standing up when he played?

Oh, yeah. Oh, yeah.

What was the difference between what he was playing on records and what he did by himself?

He did a lot of country blues when he was by himself, on a steel-bodied National or a Dobro, something like that. A lot of time he'd go into the bathroom, you know, with the tiles. I've got a picture of him leaning against the sink, and you can see the toilet there and the toilet paper roll. He's sitting there with a Les Paul. I can hear it, you know. [*Laughs.*] It's a great picture! I've got one and Dickey's got one.[2]

What were Duane's favorite guitars?

Well, for a long time, he played a Telecaster with a Stratocaster neck. This is during the Hour Glass. In the Allman Joys he played a 335 [Gibson ES-335]. Then he got a Les Paul, and he loved that Les Paul, and an old SG that he played slide on.

Did he play much slide on the Les Paul?

No, not at all.

Just on the SG?

Right. Wait—I might be wrong about that. A couple of times, he might have. Dickey could probably tell you more about that.[3]

Where are Duane's guitars now?

I've got some of 'em. Dickey's got some of 'em.

There's a story that Twiggs Lyndon traded you a car for one of Duane's Les Pauls?

Yeah, I traded it to him for a car. See, the guitars I play have to have a wide neck on them. That particular Les Paul had a narrow neck on it, plus it was a 1939 Hypercoupe, plus it's Twiggs. I mean, you know, Twiggs and Duane were real close. I guess you heard about Twiggs.[4] His mama has it now. And my brother had an old Gibson, 1929 J-200, an oval hole and with an arch-top—I've got that one.

What happened to his National?

The one that's on Dickey Betts's cover? Dickey's got it in his living room.

Toward the end of his life, who were Duane's best friends?

John Hammond. All of us, of course. He hung out with us a lot. King Curtis, until he got killed. Johnny Sandlin.

I recently interviewed John Hammond about Duane, and he had some beautiful stories to tell.

He's a beautiful man.

Was Duane hard to work with?

Not at all.

I know if I had to be in a band with my brother . . .

No, it wasn't brothers then. I mean, it wasn't brothers as you would think "brothers." He really respected what I did, and I respected what he did. He'd lean right against the organ. One thing he did, he hardly ever looked down at his guitar when he played slide. How he did it, I don't know. He just knew where he was goin,' I guess, and he'd look back at me and make me sing harder. And I loved it. But every time I walk up on the stage, I still feel like he's standing right there next to me.

The spiritual connection is still strong.

Very. There's not a day goes by I don't think of brother Duane.

What was Duane like outside of being in the band and outside of music?

He was pretty quiet. Homebody. He liked to bass fish. He wasn't very much a sportsman at all.

Did he play a lot in his spare time?

Oh, yeah. Yeah. He'd listen to music all the time. Any time you'd walked into his house, you'd hear music playing.

Did he have a big record collection?

Oh, yeah.

Did Duane ever say what he wanted his legacy to be?

No, he never talked much about dying.

How do you now view the period of the band when Duane was in it?

Very happy days. We didn't have much money. Well, Duane had a substantial amount from sessions, but nobody was rich. But we didn't care because we were playing our music, and we'd come up with a new song. You know, when a new song is born in rehearsal—that's why I like rehearsals just as much as I do recording, just as much as I do playing live. Because when a new song hatches out and it works and clicks, man, it's like Christmas time.

Do you have any favorite memories of Duane?

Yeah, he was one hell of a cat.

Anything else you want to cover, Gregg?

[*Long pause.*] Only that I think his music will live on a long, long time, and I'll support it as long as I'm around. And I loved him.

CODA: Following Duane's death on October 29, 1971, the Allman Brothers enlisted Dan Toler to fill in on slide guitar. The group disbanded in 1982 and reformed with great success in 1989, with superlative slider Warren Haynes stepping in to recreate Duane's parts and carry the band in new directions. During the late 1990s Derek Trucks, son of one of the band's original drummers, joined the lineup and more than held his own on slide guitar. In 2015, the Allman Brothers announced that they'd given their final concerts. Since then, Gregg Allman has toured under his own name.

Carlos Santana at the Oakland Coliseum, July 4, 1977. (Jon Sievert)

With its fiery blend of rock, electric blues, and African- and Latin-influenced polyrhythms, the band Santana burst onto the San Francisco scene in the late 1960s. They rapidly achieved worldwide recognition, thanks to a stellar performance of "Soul Sacrifice" at the Woodstock festival. As seen in the *Woodstock* film, the band's namesake closed his eyes, dug deep into the frets of his guitar, and laid bare his very heart and soul to the audience. Through the years and changing musical lineups, Carlos Santana has repeated this ritual countless times.

For Santana, playing guitar is akin to praying. He views music as a means to a greater purpose—to lift the downtrodden, free the oppressed, enlighten the ignorant, and most of all, to celebrate life. In conversation and onstage he often brings up his musical and spiritual influences, who range from Bob Marley, John Coltrane, Miles Davis, and Jimi Hendrix to Martin Luther King and Mother Teresa. He obsesses about tone, which he considers the single most essential facet of a musician's personality. As he mentions during our interview, "The tone, first of all, is your face. So why do you want to look like somebody else?"

A few days before our meeting, Carlos had sent me a cassette of "Blues for Salvador," an instrumental he'd just recorded in honor of his son Salvador. We agreed to meet mid-afternoon in the main room of the Record Plant in Sausalito, California, on October 28, 1986. Moments after I arrived, Carlos came bounding into the room, a big smile on his face. He stopped to do a quick roll on a conga drum, lit a couple of incense sticks, sat cross-legged amid his guitars on a carpeted platform, and immediately began the conversation.

CARLOS: Remember when we used to go see a band in the '60s? You'd see like Wes Montgomery play at the Matador from 9:00 to 12:00 or 1:00, and then you follow him. After the club, he goes to another funky club on the other side of town, and he'll play there till six o'clock in the morning. Well, that's the kind of feeling that I'm trying to get lately on certain ballads. And it's funny, because four o'clock in the morning is four o'clock in the morning. What are you going to do if it's eight o'clock at night, and you have to capture that after-the-party feeling? It's challenging, but on the other hand it's really beautiful because playing with Chester Thompson makes it more like church. Like somebody from the Grateful Dead said to me, "When music starts playing you, you don't play music no more." You know, music plays you, which makes a lot of sense. The music starts playing itself to you instead of you trying to make it happen.

Can you tell me about recording "Blues for Salvador"?

Yeah. I used a Paul Reed Smith, the early one, the very first one that he gave me before all these changes that they have gone through. That's straight to a Marshall, and they probably put some kind of Lexicon to give it . . . You know, they always take the natural sound of the guitar, for some reasons, through the board. It's hard for anything to sound the way we hear it. That's why they haven't invented microphones to capture Tony Williams's sound or my sound or T-Bone Walker's sound, people like that. Guitars players like myself, I don't use batteries on my guitar. Some people use preamps and they use a lot of pedals to sustain and stuff. That's like having an automatic car. I like stick shift. Automatic means that you gain all this great sounds, but you sound like everybody else immediately. The only way you tell who they are is by their chops, not by their tone anymore. The people who I like still for their tone are B. B. King and Otis Rush, because they're back to play-ing with Twin Reverbs, just naked. The emotion creates all of the things that the gadgets are supposed to create for you, but they sound very generic. So anyway, when they record in here, we usually have the same problem—until now, with Jim Gaines. He knows how to record my guitar. I'll give you an example: if you blow a balloon three times [*pretends to blow into a balloon three times*], the third time it'll explode. And when it pops, you hear ghost overtones. That's what stimulates us to create. When they take those things out to the board—it happens a lot on TV—unless you have a good engineer, that's the first thing they take from you. Call it the "ghost sound," the "spirit sound." So they leave you really dry. The way to put it back is to open up things on it, to give it that room sound.

Do you do that through devices?

Sometimes he does, through a Lexicon, and sometimes he uses an extra microphone away from the amplifier. Because like I said, there's ghosts and notes.

Are you seeking the ghost tones?

Yeah! Without that, man, I might as well be doing gardening or doing something else.

The ghost tones, then, are the harmonic overtones that give it sustain?

Yeah. Uh-huh. The ear picks up a lot of things. To me, when the sound is right, everything rejoices in life. Whether it's a blues or up-tempo, whatever, when everything is right it's amazing. When some music is right, it all fits—Brazilian, shuffle—everything fits when the groove is right and the tone is perfect. So mainly as a musician, that's the thing that I always used to fight for. Now not as much, because with Jim Gaines, like I said, he knows how to capture that. But a lot of time you spend most of the time with engineers or producers getting your tone, because they don't know how to.

Can you get your tone from most guitars, or does it take a special instrument?

I can just about get it from any guitar, but some guitars when I go jamming—I jam a lot, man, I really go out there and jam with a lot of different people—a lot of times with a guitar, as soon as I put my finger on it, the guitar will say to me, "Who are you and why are you playing me this way? Oh, God!" [*Smiles.*] So you know you're going to have to approach it differently. With my guitar, it's like, "Where do you want to go?" Amplifiers—unless they're old Twins or straight Marshalls or old Boogies—I can't use the new stuff because they all sound like Saran Wrap on your teeth or on your ears. It sounds very, very harsh. Even the new amplifiers that Boogie makes or a lot of people make today, they sound edgy, like transistors. It's like something on your teeth, man. It's just weird. With the old sound, you have an elegant tone already to begin with. The old amplifiers. Anything tube that's old, like pre-'75, because after '75 they started getting weird. That's when you really get, like I said, all the other tones that make you hear the song completely.

Tone must be very inspiring to you.

Yeah. The tone, first of all, is your face. So why do you want to look like somebody else? That's how people know you—by the tone. "Oh, that's so-and-so" [*snaps fingers*], just by the tone. If you play one note, they know who you are. So that's the most important thing people have to work on a lot of times—getting their own individual tone.

You are one of the few guitar players in the world where you can hear one or two notes of a song, and you know instantly who it is. Why do you think that is?

It's an accumulation of a lot of things, man. My love for John Coltrane and his tone. My love for B. B. and his tone, or Aretha. All the things that my father passed on to me. My father is a musician. He taught me everything I know on the guitar, as far as, like, the technical chords and stuff like that. His father before was a musician, and my grand-grandfather was a musician. The main thing is the cry. I always talk about the cry—not whining, but when you cry. Sometimes if you go to a funeral, you know, and maybe the guy wasn't such a good guy, but people still want to say something nice about him. Well, the tone in the music that I'm trying to write now is music for people to learn to let go gently and quietly and enhance the beauty that, let's say, Jaco Pastorius had, for example. That's what I remember. I have a natural ability now, thank God, man, for forgetting all the other stuff that I don't need to know about—the *National Enquirer* stuff. That stuff I immediately erase out of my mind, so all I remember is the great times that I had with Jaco Pastorius when we did get to jam and we did spend some time together. That's what I'm trying to do with the tone now. It is that cry, the cry of exalting the elements in humanity.

I wonder if that's what Jimi meant by "Cry of Love."

Yeah. Like I was saying, sometimes you can laugh so much that you start to cry. Sometimes you can cry so much you start to laugh. *That's* pure emotion. Pure emotion. That's the foundation for my music, first of all. Some people's foundation for their music is they learn all about the great composers and stuff like that. They base on stuff like that. And it's fine, as long as we all get to the ocean and get wet together. It's cool. The approach is not important as much as getting there. Getting to a place where, like, Aretha or Patti LaBelle, when they sing, they do a certain note and their eyes roll back to their ears and they take you with them wherever they go. *That's* the goal for me in music and in writing songs now. It's half what can we do to create, whether it's fast, slow, reggae, or African or Western—whatever it is—that you can get imbued and you can get the listener intoxicated and imbued with it. That's really the goal.

There is a whole crop of guitar players now who are just studying the technical part of it to death. They are almost like technical gunslingers.

Mm-hmm.

What advice would you give them about getting more emotion in their playing?

The main advice that I can give is all that stuff, they're toys and they're approaches. Nothing hits the listener in his heart of hearts faster than sincerity. I'll take sincerity over soulfulness *anytime*. If you're sincere, whether you're playing fast or slow, the people will pick it up. If you're just running the changes and running chord, scales, and all that kind of stuff . . . It's like Sugar Ray [Leonard], man. Sugar Ray can hit you with fifty blows really fast. But Marvin Gaye, if he just hits you once, you're gonna go down. So it's the same thing. When somebody hits you with a bunch of blows really, really fast, they're not going to have the same impact as just one solid punch from Michael Tyson. Like he says, everybody has a strategy until they get hit. And it's the same thing when you jam with somebody, man. If you put certain fast musicians with, let's say, Otis Rush, these cats can run the length and breadth of the guitar—the neck, all the notes in between and everything, with blinding speed. But when Otis Rush puts his finger on that guitar and hits you with one note and milks totally the cow, nobody stands a chance against Otis Rush. I've seen him just put away just about everybody in a nightclub in Chicago, because of the *tone*. The tone is more important to me than anything else, because the tone will disarm the listener to let go of whatever is in your mind and you embrace what's happening. And then your soul identifies with it, and then you either laugh or you cry. It's like opening the door to people's ears to their purest emotions. And that's a very, very important thing to do. Because that's what people try to do when they go to church.

How much of your tone is in your hands?

Uh, I would say about 25 percent. Another 35 percent comes from my legs, my guts. When I play a solo, my throat hurts after I finish. My calves hurt. This is *projecting*—it's not volume, see? People don't know the difference between being loud and learning how to project. A lot of musicians play from their fingers on out, so they ain't gonna reach you. But when a person uses his calves, like Jimi—check out Jimi sometime—and here [*taps stomach*] and here [*taps heart*] and they put that thing on that note, man, your hair stands up and you feel this tingle down your spine. This is not a fantasy thing. This is for real. If you put your whole being into it—your vitals, your body, your mind, your heart, and your soul—into that note, people will react to it.

What commonly gets in the way of doing that?

Your mind. Self-doubt. Self-insecurity. Those are the things that block pure creativity. It's just self-deception, ego, stuff like that. Ego, to me, is like a dog or a horse. Make him work for you, don't you work for them. They're supposed to work for you.

Is your spirit more present in your music at certain times?

Yeah.

Are there times you have a better connection?

Yeah. That's when I feel like I took an inner shower, let's say, and an outer shower. I'll give you an example. When I came back from this last tour, I heard within two or three weeks about Jaco. And I went to the Pacific Ocean here in Bolinas, and I jumped in the ocean enough to get wet. It was really cold, you know. And then I cast, as they say, my troubles in the deep blue sea. Some people meditate. And meditation is to let go of *everything*—exaltation and when somebody puts you down. Let go of everything. It's like emptying your pockets. Once you feel that you've been forgiven for whatever things that we do as monkeys or whatever, and you throw everything into the ocean, when you come back . . . you know, imagination is a real world. In fact, Einstein said imagination is infinitely more important than knowledge. So if we imagine, we enter into this world and the Lord forgives us and we're clean, then you're not blocking that flow creativity, that spirit creativity. Self-doubt—"Maybe I did this wrong, and I'm not worthy"—everybody goes through this kind of thing. But if you realize that you've been forgiven for things that you haven't even done yet, you're like a quarterback—stay in the pocket. Then within two or three days of staying in that rhythm, your playing becomes like a telephone, like a monitor. You're just monitoring what can come out through you. In other words, you become like a purer channel for something else. And I think the most beautiful music is when it goes beyond the musicians who played it and speaks for a generation—like Jimi Hendrix, for example. Or Martin Luther King or John Coltrane. Certain people, they don't play for just them[selves] and their immediate family. They play for a whole generation. So that means that those people took a lot of time to become a cleaner vessel.

Don't you think you've done that?

Sometimes it happens. It's an everyday struggle of putting your mind and all the things that your mind brings, putting them on a leash. Make them work for you. You know, sometimes we forget that everything is run by grace. The Golden Gate hanging and sustaining, the planes flying, the note sustaining. When people have pedals and sustain with the pedals, they're not using God's grace.

They are using some company's electronic circuit.

Exactly! And there's good parts of it, but the bad part is that you're always gonna sound like somebody else.

How do you make a note sustain, in a physical sense? What are the elements going into that?

First of all, you find a spot between you and the amplifier where you both feel that umbilical cord. When you hit the note, you immediately [*snaps fingers*] feel like a laser, an umbilical cord between yourself and the speakers.

You hear it catch?

Yeah, you hear it catch. And once it catches, just like a train, it's locked [*mimics train car couplers coming together*]. Then it's easier. See, a lot of people don't realize that when Jimi Hendrix used to play out loud, it is like driving a real, real high-performance car. If you don't know what you're doing, man, you're gonna be off the road. [*Laughs.*] So you have to be prepared for that. You have to practice with that intensity of playing, because Jimi Hendrix, as he said before he left, he played loud, but his sound was never shrill. Even today, a lot of people with all this knowledge that they have, there's a Saran Wrap shrill on your ears. And that eliminates a lot of the good that you're doing. It's like blocking it. Where if you roll a lot of the highs down and put on a lot more bass, then you still sustain, but you don't have that piercing thing that kills dogs—dog range.

When you're going to put a vibrato on a note, what fingers do you use?

Mainly my first and my third. I call them the emotion-expression fingers.

This finger [*indicates his left-hand index finger*] and this one [*indicates left-hand ring finger*]. Those are the expression fingers.

Those are the ones bends come from then?

Yeah. This is the one [*holds up index finger*] that you can use to tickle it, and this is the one [*holds up ring finger*] that you can use to put total emotion.

And the middle and little fingers?

The middle finger is to help you with the chords or to go up and down if you want to play horn-like chops or piano-player type of chops. Django Reinhardt only had three fingers. But my expression fingers are this one and this one. [*Points to his index and ring fingers.*]

You use a giant, triangular pick that very few people use. Why is that?

I don't know. I just formed that habit in Tijuana of playing with the big ones like that. I can turn 'em any way I want to, and even if I make a mistake, it just keeps rotating. When you have a little one [a standard pick], you've only got one way to pick 'em. I would be stuck. This way, gives me that continuous, like a fingerpicking, kind of thing.

Do you hold the pick and use your other right-hand fingers as well?

No. Not usually. Once in a while I just don't play with a pick at all, but if I want to play fast, I have to use the pick. I'm not really fast, like Jeff Beck and a lot of people are fast just without any pick at all. I use the pick for the downstroke-upstroke things, like Charlie Christian sometimes.

When you're working on getting a guitar tone, do you know what you want in terms of pickups? Do you know that you want, say, alnico with 250 winds, or is it more a case of telling someone that you need the tone "warmer"? How far are you into the physical mechanics of the guitar?

I'm pretty far into it. I don't know how to do a lot of things to them, but I do know that I go through a lot of pickups now. And the ones that I'm married to, I'm married to. Because under any weather, any condition, any hall, any bar, or any anyplace, the sucker will sustain and it's gonna sing the song.

What kind of pickups work best for you?

The old humbucking pickups, especially when they dipped them in wax and they do certain things to them.

The old Gibson PAFs?

Patent applied for? Yeah, yeah. And even those are hard to find now. My last three guitars from Paul Reed Smith, I have gone through a lot of pickups because pickups are your voice. The worst pickup for me is a pickup that gives you that out-of-phase. Unless it's a Stratocaster, I can't use out-of-phase. I like Stratocasters when you put it in between.

In the second and fourth positions on the pickup selector switch?

Yeah, either one. But in Stratocasters they sound good, a single-coil pickup. A double-coil pickup, out of phase, I can't use it. It immediately cuts. It's like playing with half a man, half a tone. I need the whole tone on the treble and on the bass to be able to sustain. "Out of phase" means half. And I can't use half. [*Laughs.*] I've got to have it all the way.

Have you ever played with a scalloped fingerboard?

No. What's that?

Where they curve the fingerboard between the frets.

Oh, yeah. I practiced one time with John McLaughlin's guitar. He had one of the first ones that they made in Kalamazoo for him. It was hard for me to stay in tune. It's hard for me to stay in tune, period. But with that it was even harder. It's like learning how to walk correctly on a tightrope.

Are you hard on strings?

Yeah, but I don't break 'em as much as I used to. Sometimes I can go for about a month, two months, without breaking a string.

Do you keep strings on for as long as . . .

No. We change them every week, every two weeks at the most.

What are the best gauges for you? Do you use a heavier string to sustain more?

Only at home I use the heavier string. That's to get my chops up. On the road, I mainly use .008s or .009s, depending on the guitar. .008s on the Strat and .009s on the regular ones. .009, .011, .014, .024, .036, .042—something like that.

I notice that one of your Paul Reed Smiths has a whammy bar on it. I don't associate you with using a whammy too much.

Sometimes I'll play with it. It's like finger painting for me. It's not something that I go wild with; it doesn't fascinate me. But when I do do it, I try to get to it where you start, like, finger painting with the notes, like on a super boogie kind of thing, up shuffles, is when you can play it. Especially when you're playing up-tempo [*snaps fingers three times*], it's easier to use the whammy, because then you start being like surfer, making your own waves. But I usually just depend on bending the note. Like sometimes you can bend the note a certain way, in and out like this [*demonstrates bending a note with three fingers*], it gives you that kind of whammy sound.

Have you found anything special to help you stay in tune?

Yeah. When I change strings, I pull all the strings four or five times, count to seven, really stretch them almost to the point of breaking, and let 'em go. By the third time, it'll stay in tune. They behave. They really give, even if you give them the whammy and everything. Say [*counts slowly to seven*]. You let it go. By the fourth time it will stay in tune. Of course, it also helps when you put lead on [apply pencil graphite to the grooves of the nut]—all that kind of stuff. But if you don't have time, just pull the strings as much as you can—at least four times. By the third time, they know who the boss is. [*Laughs*]

Do you use effects devices?

Yeah. I use mainly a wah-wah, a chorus onstage, and lately I've been using a lot of the octave divider to get that low thing.

Do you know what kind it is?

It's either a DOD or an Ibanez—something like that. The wah is either a Cry Baby or right now I've been using a Morley—it's a volume/wah-wah at the same time, but I took the volume out because a couple of times I hit it by mistake. [*Laughs.*] I usually use it as a wah-wah.

Do you have a favorite guitar and favorite amp from your whole career?

Right now it has to be the Paul Reed Smith and the twelve-inch-speaker Boogie, the old ones.

Do you know the model number?

No. But if I want to play at home and get the sweetest, most beautiful tone, it's still the old Fenders [amps] and the old Strat guitars or Les Pauls, right through anything old that's Fender, the real old stuff. Even those separate Reverbs that they have—that stuff is the best. In fact, the best sound that I've heard lately, man, on a guitar player was on Eric Johnson. He had Marshalls and Fender Bassman tops and one Echoplex—I forget what else he had. And he had the most beautiful tone all the way around. It's very, very masculine and very round and warm and dark. It's really beautiful. I can't stand shrill. I know with Jimi . . . I was watching a video of him talking about that, how a lot of musicians play loud because he plays loud, but he doesn't have that shrill sound. And Eric Johnson doesn't have that, man.

What do you think of Eric's playing?

I think it's great, man. You know, he's somebody that should be playing with either Joe Zawinul or Miles Davis or people like that, along with other musicians like Bill Connors. Those guys, they should be given a shot sometimes to be playing with those great musicians. They have a lot of diverse techniques. Plus he [Eric Johnson] has a beautiful soul also. He knows a lot of techniques, a lot of musical expressions, which are all languages, and he understands that language. I'd like to record with him someday, man, because he is very pure. You can tell what people have in their eyes—knowledge or expectations, this or that, or resentment, or just the beauty of things. It's okay. I've got my tone and my vision, and that's enough. The Lord will provide the rest. And he has that beauty, man. Even though he's from Texas, he doesn't have the gunslinger mentality—you know, "I'm gonna kick your butt with my gun." We played, we jammed, and we both complemented, which is what musicians are supposed to do.

See, this is a thing that a lot of people don't talk about. The first rule of music is to complement and enhance life. That's the first rule of music, whether it's in the bar or the church or a strip joint—wherever it is. In the Himalayas. The first duty of music is to enhance and complement life. And once people approach it like that, then there's order. Musicians are musicians, and you have your businessmen to take care of you. But you have to develop that trust. And you also have to be not naive. You have to know that there's a lot of people out there who are like leeches. They live out of musicians. They work you, they get a juicy contract, and then ten years from now you realize that they stole you blindly. You know, all these things people need to know, like when to trust and when to say, "Hey, man, I can't work with you because I don't trust you. You're dishonest." All that stuff is part of music. You play two hours, three hours. But whatever happens when you're not onstage is gonna effect you when you come onstage. So all that order is important.

You mentioned seeing something in people's eyes. What did you see in Jimi's eyes?

Jimi Hendrix? I saw him two or three times in person. The first time I really was with him was in the studio. He was overdubbing "Room Full of Mirrors," and this was a real, real shocker to me, because he started recording. He said, "Okay, roll it!" He started playing incredible, but within fifteen, twenty seconds into the song, he just went out. We were in the console [room] looking at him, and he was facing the opposite way because he didn't like anybody watching him play or whatever. And then all of a sudden the music that was coming out of the speakers was way beyond the song, like he was freaking out, having a gigantic battle somewhere in the sky with somebody. And it just didn't make any sense with the song anymore. So the roadies looked at each other, the producer looked at him, and he said, "Go get him." So they went and got him. And I'm not making it up. When they separated him from the amplifier and the guitar, it was like having an epileptic attack. Yeah! That's what I observed. "Do I have to go through these changes just to play my guitar?" I was just a kid, you know. When they separated him, his eyes were red, he was almost foaming through the mouth, he was *gone.*

What do you think it was?

Well, to me, it was a combination of the lifestyle—staying up all night, chicks, this and that, all that kind of stuff. It was a combination of all the intensity that he felt. The rock-style life, there is no discipline. You take *everything* on the menu. The wise person says, "Well, I think I'll have that," but a rock lifestyle at that time was everything all the time. So who's to say what brought that on on the physical plane—was it exhaustion or too much drugs or too much everything. But I know one thing, man—it drained me when I saw it. It was like watching somebody have an epileptic attack, and you can't help them. So it made me realize that Jim Morrison was gone, Janis Joplin was gone, Jimi was gone. Then you realize that, like John McLaughlin, I need to know about the discipline. And now I know that out of discipline comes freedom. Because now you have it in your pocket—punctuality, where you've already meditated at five o'clock in the morning, from like '72 to '82. If things get too crazy with the record or the companies or the world or the Iranians, whatever it is, you can click a switch where you go into your own sanctuary and play music that is stronger than the news.

Are there any musicians that you wished you could have jammed with?

My deepest regret, man, until I die, is gonna be not playing with Bola Sete. I didn't find out until not too long ago that he really liked my music, he wanted to play with me, and like an idiot, I never made it a point to give him the time. People like him, Gabor Szabo. I did jam with Gabor Szabo, but especially with Bola Sete. He is a person who could play like T-Bone Walker—on his back and between his legs—and at the same time go right into Segovia. I think because basically he was black, he didn't get too much attention as much as when Segovia passed. Because Bola Sete was right up there with him, in a sense that he was *way* ahead of his time in the stuff that he played.

What struck you about Bola's music?

What struck me, again, is the elegance. I see in him the same elegance as Duke Ellington, the fire of Hendrix. Again, he's sustaining with this overtone on a natural acoustic guitar. And most of all, I guess, like John Coltrane he had that tone and that way of putting notes together that it was more than mortal music. You know, mortal music deals with "my baby left me" or "I can't pay the rent" or whatever. But when somebody plays and it tells you that inside we have something—roaring lions, cosmic lions, and that we're elegant and beautiful inside—it enhances the beauty side of humanity, you know. He did it to a supreme extent.

With your upcoming Anthology *project, are you searching through your own music for those tracks which are closest to that?*

Yeah.

What's your criteria?

Sincerity, again, as much as possible. I have gone through accommodating a lot of producers and record companies and stuff like that. And finally all of us have come to an agreement that the only thing we need to accommodate from now on is the *moment*. The moment in the song, the sincerity of the song. I have experience now not to accommodate plastic producers with their plastic attachés and their plastic ideas for me. So now it's easy for me just to concentrate on, "If I was going to a Santana concert, what do I want?" I want joy. I want a lot of vitality. I want the spirit of when a pastor tells you something really precious at church, that applies to your life and it's not condemning you or making you feel like you should apologize for being a human being, but rather exalting the beautiful things in reality—that's mainly what it is. It's exalting, whether in a cry or in a party atmosphere, but exalting humanity and exalting the spirit of humanity. That's enough, man, because anything else will be the crust. This is the real pure water.

Have you a lot of unreleased material?

I have a *lot* of unreleased material. Tons. But a lot of it, I have to go in and really work with it. The one that I'm working right now is the easiest one, the one that gives me joy—once you have joy and inspiration and stimulation, it's gonna be done in no time. It's the the ones where you go, "Ooh, I have to change this so drastically . . ."

Listening back through these tapes, have you noticed change in your style?

Yeah, I can tell when I played with John McLaughlin for about three years. You tend to sound like that, even though you don't want to. You know, we're all products of our environment. A lot of times, I guess like Jeff Beck says, I can't stand my playing and I need to take a break from my tone and everything. A lot of times, I can't believe that it's coming out of my fingers. But I see the development, like from when I was playing with Alice Coltrane or Herbie [Hancock]. I still pick up the guitar, to this day, late at night, and it feels like the first time I'm putting my fingers on the frets. Some people might say, "Well, that's kind of being torturous on yourself," but I like approaching the music like that, from a naive [standpoint]. And I'm not saying ignorance is bliss. I was reading this interview with Keith Jarrett where he said that he was learning to play trumpet for a while—Keith Jarrett was—and the first week or two weeks, he sounded like Miles. Then he started sounding really polished, and he didn't like it anymore. In other words, there's a certain beauty in learning and playing like Miles Davis told John McLaughlin: "Play like you don't know how to play." Just like on [Miles Davis's] *Jack Johnson* and stuff like that. And you can see after a while what he means. It's like, "Don't play what you know. Make new mistakes."

Take chances.

Take chances. Go for what you don't know. Make it brutally honest. Make something out of it if you make a mistake. That appeals to me a lot, because then every time you do pick up the guitar, when you do get to the goodies, ooh, you rejoice. Because if you get to the goodies really, really quick in music, you're playing something that you already conceived. There's joy in rediscovering is what I'm saying.

If your children wanted to play guitar, what path would you set them on?

Ah, I would give them heavy doses of four people, first of all. John Lee Hooker, Muddy Waters, Jimmy Reed, and . . . Even before B. B., I would probably say Jimmy Reed, John Lee Hooker, Lightnin' Hopkins, and Muddy Waters. I would just give him heavy doses of that for about two, three years. Once I feel that he's got that foundation, then I'll say, "Muddy Waters is the Miles Davis of Chicago, and Little Walter is the John Coltrane." And then you have to go through Little Walter. Eventually, by the time my son be listening to something like "A Love Supreme" by John Coltrane, he will have understood the order all the way from Wes Montgomery to Charlie Christian to Django Reinhardt. I want him to understand that order, because I don't want my son to be fooled by fool's gold. There's a lot of fool's gold out there for kids.

Flash.

A lot of flash. Guys who have the right poses for the right strokes on the guitar, but again, that stuff don't cut it when you really know how to play and you put the note where it's supposed to be. All that other stuff is appearance. So I'm gonna teach my son not to fake anything, but get to, I guess as they say, "earn."

Is it important that he knows the vocabulary of music in terms of music theory?

Yeah. I'm gonna make sure that he learns that on piano in due time. That he learns the old way of reading music—do, re, mi, fa, so, la, si, do. I want to teach him that. Now, it's gonna be hard, because there's not that many teachers who teach that nowadays. They teach C, F, G, and all that kind of stuff. But that's how I think and feel. I still think in Spanish. So when I worked with Joe Zawinul on the Weather Report album, whatever he showed me, I wrote it the way I write—do, re, mi, fa, so, la, si, do kind of thing.

You'd write, like, "Do, so, fa . . ."?

Yeah, like that. And that's how I hear my line, whether it's blues or whatever it is. I hear those notes. And if I want to record with, let's say, Herbie or McCoy [Tyner], that's how I have to write the melodies or chord changes that are given me, and then I'll know.

So that teaches you what to eliminate. What not to play.

Yeah. Yeah. And it gives you a point of reference where the melody is, when it falls, and all that kind of stuff. I want to teach him that way, because if you teach your children the right vocabulary, he's on his way of really speaking the universal language, not just cowboy music or this kind of music. The universal language is something that's deeper than the surface. That way if you do play cowboy music, even the Japanese will be doing the hillbilly dance.

Do you always know what key you're in or what chords you're playing over?

No. A lot of times I force myself just to go for what I feel rather than landing at the root note. You know, if you approach everything from the root note, there's no mystery for what you're gonna play, because intuitively, you're gonna go to the same thing. It's like practicing tennis and doing the same mistake or the same thing that works for you. A lot of the times I force myself, even when I'm playing "Black Magic Woman," I force myself to feel like I don't know how to play it.

Will you put your hand somewhere different to start the solo? Is it like that?

Sometimes. Most of the time it's a matter of where you gonna hit the note from—your stomach, your heart, legs—you know, where you gonna tighten up? What muscle are you gonna use? I guess the main thing is to always approach things in a new way. If you have a swimming pool, don't always jump the same way and get wet the same way in it. Have different ways of jumping in it. Surprise yourself.

Can a song recreate an experience? Can you relive an event as you're playing?

We did the twenty-year reunion last year with the original, original band, '70s band. And yeah, it took me right back, man. The chemistry of that band is intact. We can play right now and it's like we never split. I got together with Gregg Rolie and Neal Schon, and basically we had a ball. They were writing a lot of tunes, and I only got one or two. They got, like, twenty-something. But I still don't know if we're gonna get together. We would have to rehearse for like five days before I could get married again to that band and say, "Let's do it for six months." You know, a lot of bands, they stay together for convenience. One of the exceptions to the rule is the Grateful Dead. Obviously, to this day they make new music. But a lot of bands, they do it for convenience. Musically they have exhausted. So with me, it's not a convenience thing. Wayne Shorter says, "If I feel there's any dead songs in there, I'd rather avoid it," even though monetarily it might be really good for you, because a lot of people want to see it again. It's like Lynyrd Skynyrd right now or Deep Purple—a lot of people want to come and see that. If the music would be so drastically new and enticing, I might change my mind and do it. Right now, everything is on hold until we rehearse sometime.

Is the Anthology *album celebrating an anniversary for you?*

Yeah. We started in '67. For three years, we were playing around the Bay Area. We used to headline the Fillmore West without any records. So by the time the first album came out, we knew that material—we had played it, and the second one too. Sometimes it doesn't seem that long; other times it feels like an eternity, especially when I see the boxes of cassettes for what we did.

Do you tape your gigs?

Yeah. I've been taping it now steadily since '73, but there's a lot of music out there that I don't have from the band still. That's when I feel like "Ohhhhh, I'm forty years and I'm beginning to feel the bones," when you see all the concerts and all the notes that you played. But if I don't see it, then I feel like I'm just starting. I'm starting to understand another set of order. The other set of order that I'm talking about is the John Coltrane order, the Charlie Parker order, the Art Tatum order, Aretha order. There's another kind of order in music. It's the stuff the real musicians understand, not weekend musicians or people who ten years from now they're gonna be doing something else. [Some] musicians, whether it's in front of Macys or in Madison Square Garden eight nights in a row, are twenty-four-hour musicians. And then sometimes you have to go through some sell-outs. Tomorrow they're going to be doing the same thing. So I'm talking about musicians who are *lasting.* There's music for them. And that's the music I'm just *beginning* to understand. And that's what Herbie and Wayne and Miles, that's what they sought. They're so precious.

Can those precious musicians be in any style? You often cite bebop guys, jazz players. Can you find it in country or blues or rock?

Yeah, it's the same order. People who excel above and beyond whatever genre they're in. Like, for example, Willie Nelson has no problem hanging around with Miles Davis. They hang around together sometimes. I guess I'm talking about what they say, "The cream always rises to the top." Whether it's blues or bebop or funk, whatever, the criteria is if it's sincere. The first time I heard Merle Haggard sing, he really blew my mind. He has a voice like diamond, clear cut—cuts through everything. I'm learning, man, that I'm not a kid anymore. I used to be a kid, even it seems like five years ago I still had a kid mentality. Because I'm from America, man, and America doesn't want to grow up. So they program you to all this kind of stuff. I'll give you an example: *La Bamba.* Look at how big *La Bamba* was. So it seems that the '50s was a juvenile delinquent kind of era, *Rebel Without a Cause,* and America is still there. But we're not alone. The whole world's feeling it, man, and I'm grateful for Miles and Wayne Shorter and Michael Jackson and Luther Van-dross, Anita Baker—certain people who are 1987. Because that's what fascinates me right now—'87. And I want to learn that order. And I'm learning it slowly but surely. Since I'm not a kid anymore, I understand more the importance of Bola Sete or Joe Pass or people like that. Where before, their music used to sound to me too respectable. They were songs like my father would want to play, but I didn't want to play. I wanted to play more raunchy or something. Now it's not so subdued anymore. It's just as powerful as Van Halen when you see Joe Pass or somebody doing his thing.

What's the greatest reward in your line of work?

The greatest reward is when people say like in that movie *Round Midnight.* There's a part where this guy tells Dexter Gordon, "Your music—when I was in the army, the way you played those three notes changed my life." When people come and tell me that—and they do. Every so often, they come and say, "Man, I was ready to check out. I put the gun to my head, and I heard this song. It made me cry, it made me want to try it again. It made me feel better." So it's not me. It's a spirit through me that wants to exalt itself and say, "Don't take that out. Don't take that exit. Don't treasure frustration. Don't treasure depression. This is an impostor. You don't make friends with him. You're more than that. Don't focus on the negative things in life. Accentuate the positive." Otherwise, you become darkness. Light up a candle. That's the tone, that's the story that I want to do through my music as much as possible. That is the best rewarding, man. Because platinum, all that kind of stuff, it collects dust, and after a while you don't even know where you stored it. You know, there's Super Bowls and platinum albums, and all that kind of stuff. When you have children, all that stuff doesn't mean that much anymore. What means something is to be able to—not like a minister or priest preach, but in a way that you can tell a story and put wings on people's hearts. If people hear that with music, that's enough.

CODA: "Blues for Salvador" won the 1988 Grammy Award for Best Pop Instrumental Performance. Since then, Carlos Santana has continued to make guitar-intensive records. He attained his biggest commercial success with 1999's *Supernatural*, which reached #1 on the *Billboard* charts, as did two of its singles, "Smooth" and "Maria Maria." In 2000 the album and singles brought Santana another eight Grammy Awards. Carlos published his autobiographical *The Universal Tone: Bringing My Story to Light* (Little, Brown and Company) in 2014. At last count, he has played on more than ninety albums.

W hile many of his peers from the 1960s have faded into music history or been relegated to oldies circuits, Neil Young continues to push the boundaries of rock guitar. In his seventies, he still ranks among rock's most cathartic electric guitarists, conjuring fire and brimstone worthy of players old enough to be his grandchildren. Few players have explored feedback and distortion so deeply, and fewer still have had as profound an impact on young players. On his landmark 1969 solo album *Everybody Knows This Is Nowhere*, for instance, Young showed a generation mystified by Jimi Hendrix that guitarists could keep it simple and still kick ass. Many struggling guitarists strummed their first chords to Young classics such as "Down by the River," with its powerful yet easy-on-the-fingers Em-A7 vamp, and copped their first solos from "Down by the River" and "Cinnamon Girl," with its famous "one-note" solo. Neil's pentatonic solo on Crosby, Stills, Nash & Young's "Ohio" provided another rite-of-passage for beginning guitarists.

And then there's Neil Young's acoustic side. After his celebrated tenure in Buffalo Springfield and first two solo albums, Neil performed his debut acoustic tour in 1970. The following year, he recast "The Loner," "Cinnamon Girl," and "Down by the River" as an acoustic medley on Crosby, Stills, Nash & Young's live *4 Way Street* album. Young released his first acoustic-oriented album, *Harvest*, in 1972, reaching #1 on the *Billboard* charts with "Heart of Gold." Since then, he has continued to move between heavy rock, often accompanied by his band Crazy Horse, and lighter acoustic music.

Never content to rest on his laurels, Young has also made commercially risky forays into unexpected territory, such as the vocoder-shaped *Trans*, synthesizer-laden *Landing on Water*, countrified *Old Ways*, early-rock-and-roll-tinged *Everybody's Rockin'*, and horn-driven *This Note's for You*. In the process, he has emerged as one of rock's preeminent songwriters, with a catalog of songs comparable to those of Bob Dylan, Tom Petty, Bruce Springsteen, and Hank Williams.

When we met at a restaurant in California's Santa Cruz mountains on November 11, 1991, Neil had recently completed his eardrum-busting *Weld* tour, which featured Sonic Youth as the opening act. Typical for Neil, rather than continue with the distortion-drenched explorations of *Weld*, he was in the process of creating *Harvest Moon*, the folk-country follow-up to *Harvest*. Elliot Roberts, Neil's longtime manager, sat at a nearby table.

Are you hard on guitars?
No. I don't have any guitars that are broken because of me playing them. I

treat them pretty gently, actually. I don't think I have to break a guitar to get a violent sound out of it.

Do you have a favorite guitar that you've written a lot of songs on?

Not really. Usually cheap guitars that I buy that are no good are the ones that I write on. Like I got an Epiphone in New Zealand, like a Japanese Epiphone or something. It's terrible, but it's got a particular sound to it. And it's not a good sound, but it is *that* sound. And it's unique. So I always like to get a new guitar—or a new old guitar—because I know that if I find a guitar that I like, or if somebody gives me a guitar, that I'm going to get a song or two out of it—at least. Because every guitar comes to you with all this information, all these feelings and everything from everybody else who's had it. Something always comes out. The way it sounds makes you play certain chords that you wouldn't because you'd never had that guitar. So then you're into another thing. If you're lucky, you get a song out of it.

Is the Epiphone you were talking about a round-hole acoustic?

Yeah, just a cheap one.

Do you keep it where you do your writing?

It's probably lying on the floor of my bedroom. It's a terrible guitar—the action sucks, the neck's all bent. [*Laughs.*] And it doesn't stay in tune—you have to keep tuning it all the time. But I write a lot on it.

What songs have you written on it?

Several of the songs of *American Dream* I wrote on it. I've written a few. I don't know exactly which ones. A few unreleased songs were written on it. I might have written "Fuckin' Up" on it. I can't remember. But I do write a lot on it. And then I've got good guitars too, you know. And they're fun too. Generally fun to record with and write on. I got a lot of guitars—a whole bunch of them. A lot of electrics and a lot of acoustics. A lot of Martins and Gretschs, old Explorers, Flying Vs, White Falcons. [Guitar tech] Larry Cragg has more than I have. Larry's got really a lot.

Maybe I should talk to him about your guitars.

Oh, yeah! Or my amplifier. My amplifier is an interesting world unto itself.

You said that singular. That's one amp?

Well, the amplifier is like a conglomerate. It has several different wings and controls. But I've got a thing on my amp—no one else has this. It's unique unto itself, completely original, and I'm very happy with it. It sits on top of my Fender Deluxe, which is the brain of the whole thing. The Fender Deluxe is where the sound starts. It goes through that preamp. That's where everything emanates—it comes from there. So I plug into that. But on top of the Deluxe, coming down on top of all of the controls, are machined, power-driven potentiometers. They come right down onto the pole and they're locked in. And then there are digital controls for those, where you turn them and preset them to different places. And then that's all programmable into four different presets. Each preset has a button. On a Fender Deluxe, there's a tone and two volumes. The volume on the channel you're not using will affect the volume of the channel you are using, even though you're not plugged into it—the drain on the power amp. So there's all these different settings that I have for different sounds. And I preset them all by turning the digital controls, and they turn the motors, and the motor turns the real knob and it changes. And then I lock that preset number and everything's locked in. And then when I assign it a button and hit that button, all the knobs turn on the amp and go to that. I have four sets of those. So there's no interruption of the sound. I don't have to put my guitar sound through something. There's no volume-pedal loss. There's no split-signal loss from the original sound.

Where did you get this device?

I had it made. I got an engineering company to build it for me.

That's a new one.

And the whole thing, it's very deep. And I have an effects rack, but it's not a rack, it's a box full of effects, because they're all so old. Echoplex, analog delay, Mu-Tron octave divider. Are you into these things?

Yeah!

Okay. And a Boss flanger from 1969 or something, this big purple thing with all the knobs. So those are all connected through these hard switches that are all platinum or precious metal, NASA-quality contacts that I use with relays to throw them. And I have routing that goes around the whole thing. I go into my big red switch [box], which is about the size of a table. I could jump on it. Those old Boss things, I can't use those [on the floor] because I get too into it. [*Laughs.*] I get way too into it. "Oh, I'm sorry!" You know, you see the little Boss thing, pieces of it all over the floor, wires hanging out. Well, there's this guy named Coke Johnson, this producer, worked with Prince. I was working with him on an album three or four years ago, and he put all this stuff out for me. Said, "Try this! This is how he got his guitar sound." I said, "Great. What's this and that?" And he said, "Great, fine." So I started playing live and everything, and I jumped on it and it *broke* into all these pieces. [*Laughs.*]

Has new technology impacted you much? Could you have recorded Weld *with equipment you had back in the 1960s?*

Well, I couldn't have done *Weld* without the Wizard that I've got on top that turns all the knobs on the amp. That's how I get the guitar sounds to change subtly. You can turn one knob two turns—it goes up to 12. The Deluxe goes up to 12, by the way, not 11. 12! Awesome. But anyway, you can back it down to 10 1/2 from 12, and all of a sudden it's chunky sounding on the attack. With everything floored, if you back down the volume 1 1/2 to 10 1/2 instead of 12, the chunk comes back. If you have it up in 12, it just saturates completely and opens up after the attack. But if you back it down, it'll catch the attack by just changing that one thing that much. So I've got one button for one and one for the other and two other settings. So having that ability to change the treble, back the treble down here and there, and change and bring up the channel I'm not even using so the overload thing won't come in while turning up the other channel—those things are all things that I couldn't have done. But that's where technology is. But not in the sound, only in the control of the sound.

What's the source of your feedback? Is it amp gain, devices . . .

Volume. Pure volume. I do not use the amp gain. I don't use a distorted effect at all. Just the Fender Deluxe.

Do you take that amp on the road with you?

Mm-hmm. Oh, yeah. I couldn't go without it. Wouldn't be able to go.

Does that amp go way back in your career?

Back to 1967.

Do you have spares?

There is no spare. I've got ten spares, but none of them sound like it. There's nothing like it. They're all different. All Fender amps are different, the old ones. The way they were made. They've got different metals, different amounts of metal in the windings, and all these things. The transformers are all different powers. Everything used to be loose, you know. The specifications were within a certain thing, so every combination of specs was different. You know, they were within specs, but still a combination. One thing affects another, and they're all different. So every amp is a completely . . . but for some reason mine, the one I got at Saul Bettman's Music on Larchmont in L.A., back in 1967, I bought it for like fifty bucks. Took it home, plugged it in with this Gretsch guitar. Immediately the entire room started to vibrate. The guitar started vibrating. I just went, "Holy shit!" I turned it down, and it kept doing it. Turned it halfway down before it stopped feeding back.

But I do a lot of things to make the sound sound more distorted. By introducing an octave divider *before* the amp, instead of after it, in conjunction with the analog delay, which is before the octave divider—the routing of these things is real important. What hits first and then gets hit by something else. So I have a line of six effects, and I can bypass it completely, or I can dip in and grab one without going through the one in front of it. Or I can use all six of them or any combination that I want to use. And I set them up in an order so that they would affect each other a certain way, and that's how I get my sound.

Does someone operate this offstage for you?

No. I have this footswitch—I don't know if you've ever seen it. It's a big red box. There's no one else operating it.

Are these analog effects devices?

Mm-hmm.

Are you impacted by digital effects—the new do-it-all boxes?

I have a digital echo that I use because it has a particular sound. It's a gated echo sound. When I tried it out at the Guitar Center in Hollywood, I was in there and the salesman was demoing all these sounds you could get with it, you know. Sounded like a Phil Collins record, and then it sounded like another kind of record, sort of like the background of what's the girl from New York? A couple of years ago she was some competition for Madonna at some time—flowery dresses. Cyndi Lauper. Her guitar player had a certain sound that had a certain thing happening. So he was demonstrating all this to me. So then I took it out and I said, "Well, let me try it for a minute." So I took the thing and I hooked it up, turned everything all the way up, except for the mix. And then I started playing the guitar really staccato, and I turned the mix up. Got *whomp, whomp, whomp, whomp, whomp,* like this gigantic popcorn machine kind of exploding kind of a sound. So I liked that sound. So I use it as an effect. When I've gone just about as far as I can go, then I stick that on it and just hit harmonics and choke them, and it just splats out all this ridiculous noise all over everything. That's a good sound. But I don't use it in a real sense to get a sound that it was meant to get.

What analog devices do you use the most?

I use an Echoplex—an original tube Echoplex.

Like Jimi had?

Probably, if that's what he had. He probably had one. An MXR analog delay. Mu-Tron octave divider. A Boss flanger, a huge thing. A Fender reverb unit with springs.

One of the old tweed-colored ones?

Yeah. Well, they weren't tweed. They were white Tolex. With new springs, more springs. Springs are separate. The springs are on the stage. They stand on a microphone stand. The stand goes on the floor of the building, on cement. It goes extended up to the bottom of the stage. The spring stands on top of the microphone stand and the wire comes through a hole in the stage, completely separate, and comes up through. You can't use it if you don't do that, because if you jump on the stage the springs rattle, so it has to be isolated from the surface of anything that's vibrating.

If you can't do that, do you have something you can substitute?

No. We do it. We just do that. We just put a hole in the stage or whatever. There's always a way to do it. And if it can't be done like that, we'll move it father away. But it can't be very far away because of the length of the wire. You can't have it go to the spring and come back on a long wire—you'll lose the fidelity, all of the high end, and that's where reverb lives. So the magic is gone. You've got to keep it close, keep it really short. So I do that.

What do you look for in a guitar when you're thinking about acquiring one?

Well, there's many different reasons to buy guitars. I'll buy a guitar mainly to remember something by. If I'm in a place where I'm doing something, I've generally forgotten to bring my guitar with me or something. And so if I'm in a place and I'm enjoying it, I will go to a music store and buy a guitar. Try to find an old guitar in that area, buy that, keep that. That will always remind me of when I was there. And the way it sounds is the way I sounded when I was there, playing it.

Does the instrument have a big impact on the way you phrase or the melodies you might play?

Yes, if I'm writing. They're all different. Every one is different. I got a D-18 that I really like that I've written a lot of songs on that I got out of Elliot's office. And I always think of Eliot's office whenever I play it, because that's where I got it. And that was years ago. He used to have a guitar around, when people played guitars a lot. He used to have one in the office, so if one of the singers or writers or something came in, they could have a guitar to play. So I stole that one immediately.

ELLIOT ROBERTS: I've always wondered whatever happened to that guitar! I've never, ever known.

NEIL: There are other reasons to buy guitars. You can buy them because they're classics, if you're collecting. I collect them, so I'll buy, like, an Explorer or a Flying V or a black Falcon or a white Falcon, just because that's what it is. But I've got those now, so I don't need those anymore. And material things are becoming less and less relevant to me, so I'm not continuing to collect guitars.

Do you have any instruments so rare that you don't play them?

No, nothing like that. I've got Hank Williams's guitar, but I play it all the time.

Did he have an old Martin?

A D-28. I bought it from Tut Taylor. Rusty Kershaw was at my ranch a couple of weeks ago, and we made some recordings with him. It was [Ben] Keith, Rusty Kershaw and myself, really funky swamp stuff. And we got to a certain point where we'd recorded five or six things, and then I brought out Hank Williams's guitar and said, "Why don't you play it on this one?" It's always great when you have someone who understands what this is that they're holding. The musicians from that era that understand who Hank Williams was and the effect that he's had on all of us are sort of awestruck by being in the presence of anything they can touch. And to actually play an instrument that he played elevates it to another level. So it's wonderful thing to have a guitar for that reason. Bob Dylan used my bus a couple of years ago for a tour, so I put Hank Williams's guitar on the bus so that he would have this guitar on the bus. The only thing I said is that it stay on the bus. So he took good care of it. A lot of people who should have played it have played it. I'm careful about it. But I use it all the time—it's not on the wall in a museum. It's still in use.

Do you have other celebrity-owned guitars?

I don't think so.

Do you have your guitars from Buffalo Springfield?

Yeah, I still have every guitar that I ever played. The only one that I played that I don't have Stills has, because I traded him for something else. I also have a Gretsch that Jim Messina had that's *like* the one I played in Buffalo Springfield.

Have you played Fenders much?

I've got a Broadcaster and a Telecaster and an Esquire and a couple of Stratocasters. But I don't play them that much.

I read somewhere that one of the main ingredients of your sound was one particular pickup.

Well, there's a very lively Firebird pickup on my Les Paul, the treble side. But it wasn't always there. The Les Paul that I played on *Everybody Knows This Is Nowhere*, when I did that record, it didn't have that pickup. That pickup was a wound pickup, and it got a bad hum in it. I took it to a music store to get it rewound or get them to see if they could do anything with it to make it so it didn't hum. I went back to get it and the store was closed and everything was gone, so I never got it back. So I had to replace the pickup. So there have been two or three pickups in place of the original pickup. Now the one that's there is a Firebird. I guess it would be the pickup that I used on all the things I played on my black guitar since 1973.

What's the appeal of having a Bigsby vibrato arm, which virtually no one uses anymore?

Well, it works. It's expressive. The wang bars they have now are not expressive. They're too tight. You can go way down and come way back up and do these metal licks and stay in tune. Big deal—you stay in tune. Great. You already were in tune. It's not a big benefit to stay in tune. I go out of tune every song because the thing just doesn't stay in tune. But then if you keep moving, you never know whether you're in tune—it's like having hand-controlled flanging. If you have a tape repeating on it—if you have an Echoplex—and you use just ever so slightly the Bigsby, then your sound is going up and down like that [*wavers hand up and down*] but the echo is behind it, so the echo is always following behind it, so it's just like you really have two guitars that are not only two different attacks, but you have one that's in a different pitch than the other, which is a huge sound. It's like active flanging—manual.

We hear that on Weld.

Yeah.

Have you tried the Floyd Rose locking whammy?

No. The Bigsby is worn into my hand, and I can't do anything else. It has to be a Bigsby. Lonnie Mack—have you seen his Flying V with the bar on the back that holds the Bigsby? What's that Rhino record he has, something about his V? *Attack of the Killer V.*

Is that Rhino or Alligator?

Alligator.

The new N.M.E. *has a picture of you captioned "The Grizzled Godfather of Gargantuan Feedback."*

[*Long pause.*] I don't know what to say.

I saw a video of you sticking the headstock of your guitar into a toilet bowl during a song off of Ragged Glory.

Mm-hmm. That's just Hollywood shit. Video. None of that's real. It's a cinematic trick. But it was a nice toilet. The toilet was a good visual expression for my sound. I want people to know that's where I get my . . . I had the neck down in there.

Everyone has heard stories of, like, Jimmy Page recording parts in a bathroom, putting the mike twelve feet away. Have you ever tried strange approaches like that?

Mm-hmm. I'll try anything. That sounds like a good idea, if it's the right bathroom with the right kind of tile or whatever. He must have just liked the sound in there. It was very live, obviously. They got a big sound doing that, for sure.

Listening to Weld, *I was thinking that there aren't that many players from the 1960s who are still capable of getting out there and thrashing the way you did on the album.*

Well, that's nice. I think I took that as far as I'm gonna take it, though. I don't know if there's any reason to continue with that thrashing about.

The punk attitude?

*Neil Young
in Woodside,
California,
October 30, 1991.
(Jay Blakesberg)*

No, it's just rock and roll. But it's real rock and roll—that's just all it is. Not punk or anything. I think that rock and roll *is* punk. Punk and rock and roll are all the same thing. Or what it degenerated from is what rock and roll is now. It's not rock and roll. It's pop. It's fabricated for the masses. An imitation, a shoddy semblance of what it was. There are still people that play rock and roll, but they call this other music "rock and roll." It's Perry Como music compared to real rock and roll. Remember when real rock and roll started? There was real rock and roll, and then that other music that your parents listened to and everything? It's like rock and roll now is the music that our parents listened to. It's like gone.

We are the parents.

Yeah, we are the parents and that's it. That's okay. But that's what it is.

Who would you point to as a modern rock-and-roll band?

[*Long pause.*] Well, you know, obviously I like Sonic Youth. They are definitely modern rock and roll. In my eyes. I'm just one guy with an opinion—that's the problem with these interviews, because it tends to take things and put them out of perspective. You know, like everyone should be able to say on the same page what they think. So when you're there, I always tend to think when I make these statements, I go, "Wait a minute."

But the good thing is that some people who are into you but have never listened to Sonic Youth might read that you like them.

They make some beautiful music! Have you heard "Expressway to Your Skull"? That's a beautiful song. That's an unbelievable melody! It's so beautiful. It's classic. It's unbelievably magnificent. And to hear it live, especially—it's awesome. They have several songs of that quality. So they're a great band. I think U2 is a good rock-and-roll band. I don't know what their new record sounds like, I haven't heard it, but their old records sound like a good rock-and-roll band—pretty straightforward, playing-in-the-house recording.

If you could go back in time and meet any musicians living or dead, who would be among the first ones you'd want to encounter?

[*Long pause.*] Hound Dog Taylor. I'd like to meet Hound Dog Taylor. And Lead Belly. I would have liked to have met Robert Johnson. And I also would have liked to have met Chopin and Beethoven—all in one place.

Yeah, right. Try getting Robert to pick up the check!

Yeah, who's gonna pick up the check?

Robert Johnson—it would have been incomprehensible to him that he would have a million-seller record in the 1980s and 1990s.

I don't think Beethoven knew that he was going to be selling as well.

Johnson pulled together all the threads of the music of that time. He was like a human jukebox, it seems.

Mm-hmm. Of course, we've got John Lee Hooker still. He's pretty outrageous. But I go back. I like to go back. You know, there are people still here on the planet or who I knew when they were on the planet that I wouldn't mention when answering your question because I did meet them already.

Who are the best guitarists you've encountered? The ones who left the biggest impression with you?

Well, for the acoustic guitar, Bert Jansch is the best acoustic guitar player and my favorite. And for the electric guitar it would be Jimi Hendrix.

I understand you met with Jimi.

Mm-hmm. Long time ago. Wasn't really very memorable. I did meet him a few times. Stills knew him better than I did.

Why does he endure so much?

He's so good. He was at one with his instrument. No one else had brought the electric guitar to that level. No one else has since. He was like handstands above everybody else, just completely gone. So liquid, and taking feedback and developing these beautiful things. For the guitar freak that I am, he's maxed out. But as much of a great guitar player as *he* is, or was, Bert Jansch is the same thing for acoustic guitar.

Are there any Jansch records that you like especially well?

The first ones. The very first record that he made [1965's *Bert Jansch*, on Transatlantic Records]. Great record!

The one with "Angie" on it?

I think it was on it. And then he remade that record, different versions of the same songs, for someone else. But I don't know. I got this record—it came from England when I heard it. And I was particularly impressed by a song called "Needle of Death." It's a really outrageous song, beautiful song. And this guy was just so good. I don't know what he's doing now. And then years later, I wrote "Ambulance Blues" for the *On the Beach* album in 1974 or '3—somewhere around there. And I picked up the melody from his record, the guitar part, *exactly*, without realizing that I had completely copped the whole thing. And then years later, someone mentioned it to me and I went back and heard him playing it, and sure enough, it's almost a note-for-note cop of his thing. I mean, I wrote whole new lyrics on top, but it's his thing. And he was great! I listened to myself play and I listened to him play it, and I played it terrible.

Have you ever met him?

I think I did meet him once. When I went to England in the early '70s, I really wanted to meet him. So I went and got together with Pentangle. You know, I had a big limo and everything because I didn't know where I was going. I just knew the address and we had a limo, and I went over there.

They kind of had an attitude about me, that I was a pop superstar. I kind of got that feeling. But I don't understand it. But on the other hand, I do understand it. So . . .

I heard this interview tape that Warner Brothers shopped around, where you were talking about recording Ragged Glory. *You talked about cutting live in the studio as being a photograph versus painting a picture. Have you settled into that way of thinking?*

That's been the way I've been for a long time. That's what I like to do because it's faster. Let other people take the songs and make records of them. If someone wants to record my songs, they can record them. They can make records of them. I just want to sing them and play them and record the event of that happening the best I can with the moment that I did it, where I felt the best about it, and then move on.

Have you ever written a song on acoustic that transformed into a heavy rock song? Was any of the stuff on Weld *done acoustically first?*

"Out of the Blue" was written on acoustic.

Where was that written?

In my living room.

Did it come quickly?

Mm-hmm.

What inspired it?

I don't remember. I guess Elvis died, and I was thinking about that. It was just a year after that, I guess, when I wrote it. That was one of them.

I thought it may have been about the passing of Sid Vicious.

No.

Did you go to see punk bands in the 1970s?

No. Never saw them. Just heard about them, saw them on TV. I saw the effect that they had on people. Read stories of what they did.

In this age of guys going to college to learn to play guitar, learning every scale . . .

Paints a pretty dim picture of the future, doesn't it?

Learning all these scales and sight-reading and all that. What would you want musicians to learn from someone like you?

Well, first of all, it doesn't matter if you can play a scale. It doesn't matter if your technique is good. If you have the *feel*, if you have feelings that you want to get out through music, that's what matters. If you have the ability to express yourself and you feel good when you do it, then that's why you should do it. The technical side of it is a complete boring drag, as far as I'm concerned. I can't play fast. I don't play fast. I don't even know the scales. I really don't. A lot of the notes that I go for are notes that I know aren't there.

They're just not there, so you can hit any note. I'm just on another level as far as all that goes. I appreciate these guys who play great. I'm impressed by these metal bands, those scale guys. I'm impressed—like I go, "Gee! That's really something. That guy can really . . ." It's okay. These guys are good guys, and you've got what's his name—the local guy here.

Joe Satriani?

Satriani. I mean, these guys are geniuses. And Eddie Van Halen. They're genius guitar players. They're unbelievable musicians of the highest caliber I can't relate to. One note is enough.

"Cinnamon Girl"—the one-note solo.

Oh, yeah. Two strings, though. Same note on two strings, and the wang bar. See, the wang bar made every one sound different. They're all different. To me, it's like when people say "one-note solo," I listen to it, and every one sounds different to me. They really do. It sounds like it's all different in that one place. You're going in farther and seeing all the differences, but if you get back, it's all one. So I think that every note is different on "Cinnamon Girl."

That song has remained remarkably true to the original version—at least the version I heard on Weld *this morning.*

Yeah, yeah. It is. I think it is. We tried to do our best, put a little of "Norwegian Wood" on the end of it that one time. That was the only night we did that, where it was "Norwegian Wood."

What do you look for in a solo when you're going over different takes of a song to put on the record? What's your criteria?

Elevation. You can feel it. That's all I'm looking for. You can tell I don't care about bad notes, right? I don't care about that.

You've always been more about feel than technique or perfection.

Yeah. I listen for the whole band on my solos. You can call it a solo because that's a good way to describe it, but really what it is is an instrumental. The whole band is playing. I mean, Billy Talbot is a massive bass player. He only plays two or three notes. [*Laughs.*] People are still trying to figure out whether it's because he only knows three or four notes or if those are the notes he wants to play. But when he hits a note, that note speaks for itself. It's a big motherfuckin' note. It's big! Even the soft one is big.

What's the appeal of working with Frank Sampedro?

Frank uses the biggest strings of any guitar player I have ever seen. Frank is even probably more of a crude player than I am, because his lead isn't as developed as mine is. You know, he plays rhythm, but his strings are *so* big— a .055 on the bottom, big wound third, .012 on the E string. I mean, we're talking *big strings*. They're as big as you can get.

Baling wire.

Yeah! And he hits a note, and it's a big note. If I hit a note, it's like here today, gone, where's it going, what's happening? He hits a note or if Billy hits a note, *that's* where Crazy Horse is. Without Crazy Horse playing so big, I sound just normal. But they make it possible, they supply the big, so I can float and move around. And I sound huge playing with them, because the big is them.

Do you think jamming is becoming a lost art?

I don't know. I haven't seen any jams lately. You see all these concerts— what's happening?

It's like hearing the record.

Yeah, I know. It's disgusting, isn't it? Welcome to the '90s.

You once referenced jamming as being akin to an orgasm.

Well, yeah! I think it is. That's why a lot of my instrumentals are too short. [*Laughs uproariously.*]

On record you sometimes have a wild vibrato. Sometimes I think that what Buddy Guy is to blues, you are to rock.

You mean on my guitar vibrato?

Now I realize some of it must be the Bigsby.

It's all the Bigsby. I don't use tremolo. Every once in a while I use a Magna-tone stereo vibrato effect, and I have used on certain recordings a vibrato effect. But during my playing all the time, when you hear what you hear— that's the Bigsby.

When you do a manual vibrato with your left hand or bend strings, which fingers do you use?

This one [*holds up ring finger*]. And sometimes this one [*holds up middle finger*].

Will you back up a bend with the other fingers?

Uh, no. I don't have to. My strings are too little—I don't have to do that.

What are the strings?

I don't know. They're sort of like Slinkies. They're GTRs. I think on the last tour Larry made them even better than GTRs. I don't know what he did—he said, "Try this."

Can you play in any style that might surprise people who are only familiar with you through the records? Have you ever played bottleneck blues . . .

No. I can't play a bottleneck. Never have. No. What I play is what you hear.

Do you ever feel your playing is reaching a new level?

I thought it reached a new level on *Arc* and on *Weld*.

Arc *could be seen as a daring thing to do.*

I don't think so. I think it's the logical extension of rock and roll the way it is today if you want to go the other way—past Sonic Youth. Just off, over there. It's always been there. Feedback has always been there. It's always been a temptation to go that way. It's like jazz—it's the jazz of rock, without a beat.

Coltrane with feedback.

Yeah. Maybe Coltrane is a big influence on me. I love a lot of his things. "Equinox" and "My Favorite Things" are two of my favorites, with McCoy Tyner. Those are my favorite of his music.

What are the records you couldn't live without?

That I couldn't live without? See, I don't listen to records. I don't listen to anyone. I only listen to what's going on that other people put on, because I don't want to make the decision of what to listen to. I really don't listen. I listen to what's going on in the world, what people like, because I hear it coming out of the car radio or I hear it coming out of a jukebox. If I walk up to a jukebox I'll play things. I like to listen to B. B. King or Ray Charles things, old country things. But it's mostly just for rehabilitation purposes or something.

What would you most like to change about what we call rock in the 1990s?

The format that it's produced in.

Could you explain that?

Digital. CDs.

You don't like them?

I hate them.

Why?

I'll tell you this. I told someone else this earlier—let's see if I get it right. Digital is a disaster. It's like this is the darkest age of musical sound since sound was captured. When they started capturing it on the records a long time ago—the 78s—that was pretty shaky. And then they got it a little better. From that point on right up to the beginning of digital, everything that was done is better than digital. And digital is a huge rip-off. And it's completely premature. All of the music that has been recorded in the '80s and '90s through digital means, *any way* that it has gone digital will be looked back on in another ten or fifteen years as what a shame that all this music was recorded this way. We'll never get to hear it the way it really was.

You don't think it captures the sound accurately?

It doesn't at all. It's a complete farce. It's *completely* wrong. I mean, digital has to be taken three or four levels higher. Sampling rates have to quadruple—at least! It has to go *way* out the window to get to where analog was. Digital music has a very limited therapeutic effect, if any, whereas real music has incredible effect with calming the nerves, everything. Any therapeutic application of sound has to be analog, or it won't get results. You cannot use it the other way. You can search around—it's not there. The sound isn't there.

I can use this window as an illustration. [*Points to a nearby plate-glass window in the restaurant.*] When you look out here through the glass, imagine that that's sound out there. Okay? And then look out there through the screens. [*Points to a screen-covered area of window.*] See the little square holes in the screen? Okay. So when you look through there, you'll see that inside those screen holes if you get right up on it, there's all kinds of different colors and everything coming through. Well, that has to be averaged out to one thing for digital. That's all you get—the dominant one.

A 1 or a zero.

Yeah. That's it. Now, take a step back farther, and this is what real digital is. Whatever the dominant color is here, if you were back at the other end of the restaurant and this whole wall was made out of windows like this, that would be like a digital picture of music. So what you see through this whole window here is reduced to the dominant shade. So in music, on the bottom you have this low frequency moving back and forth and everything, so things move real slowly. So it may be just a big dark picture of this big rumbling thing. But when you get in the high end, it's the cosmos. It's a universe of possibilities. The echo, the air—all of those things. And you take a million possibilities for sound and reduce it to the dominant one and make them all that. And they've got the sampling enough now so that when you first start listening, "Hey, that's music." But your brain and your heart are *starved*. They're starved for a challenge. There's no challenge. There's no possibilities! There's no imagination. You're hearing a simulated music. You're not hearing real music. It's not doing what . . . you know, your brain is capable of taking on an incredible amount of information. And the beauty of music is it's like water washing over you. But digital is like ice cubes washing over you. They're not the same!

What do you think when you hear Everybody Knows This Is Nowhere *or* Decade *on CD?*

Well, I think it's not as good as the original. That's why they gotta be remastered every time there's an improvement—from the analog originals. And the improvement is not going to be great for a long time, because the technology is just not there for that kind of a sampling rate. It's a real shame, because music is just not being captured. It's being made—people are still making great music, especially the acoustic musicians that are still playing real music and performing it. It's even more important, what I'm talking

about, to a musician like myself that it not be digital. I've been making records for twenty-six years, working in the studio, writing songs, listening to music. And I'm telling you that from the early '80s up till now and probably for another ten, fifteen years, is the *darkest* time for recording music—ever. We'll come out the other end of it and it will be okay. We'll look back on this period now and go, "Well, that was the digital age, and we can't really hear it." That's what people will say—mark my words. Another thirty years, another twenty years from now, they'll be looking back on it, going, "Wow. I wonder what it really sounded like? They were so carried away that they didn't really record it. They just made digital records of it."

What would you like to hear happen with guitar playing in the future?

I would just like to hear a guitar. See, I don't like to listen to the CDs or records anymore because they're all made digitally. So I'll listen to it a little bit, but it doesn't give me the joy that the earlier recordings did. Not because of the music, but because of the recording, the type of recording. So I would like to hear guitars again on record with the warmth, the highs, the lows, the air, the electricity, the vibrancy of something that's real instead of a duplication of the dominant factors. It's an insult. It's an insult to the brain, to the heart, to the feelings, to have to listen to this and think that it's music.

You must admit that there's a certain emptiness in the air. When you listen to it, you think it might be today's music just isn't as heartfelt as yesterday's, or the '60s or '70s and way beyond in the past. You think, "What happened to music? Businessmen came in and took over and they ruined it." That's the excuse everybody makes. But the real reason is technical. It's not that people don't have souls anymore. All these bands have got *huge* souls. They can't wait to play. They just don't know why they can't sound as good as some things that they used to hear. And now they've never heard it because it's all digital. They go out and buy it and it's a digital copy of the original. They've never even heard the original. So they don't know what to compare it to. It sounds like a record now, because it's digital, and that's the way records sound. They don't realize they don't have to sound sterile. They don't have to sound one-dimensional. It's a big, big concern. It's a massive concern. All the creativity of this whole decade and probably the next decade and definitely the last decade is all sacrificed to this technology.

Are you keeping your music on analog for that reason?

I can't. No, I'm digital. Once you go digital, you're digital. So there's no sense in keeping any analog track of it. It's too complicated to record both things. It's too complicated. I'd have to make every record twice. I'd have to mix it, overdub, the whole thing. You can't do it. It's much easier to work in digital because of the control factor. I go DDD—everything is DDD, because that's the medium I'm given. It's got to come out on CD. They want a digital copy to make analog cassettes off of. It's wrong. It's dead wrong.

If a child you were close to told you that he or she wanted to become a professional guitar player, what course of learning would you suggest?

Start playing.

Do you think it's important to know the names of your chords?

Oh, yeah. They'll learn that eventually. Play with other people. Learn a few chords and start playing with somebody else who's maybe a little better than you are. Don't learn from a book any more than you have to. Learn from other people. That's what music's all about. Pick up things from other people, put them back together yourself. Use them to write new songs. Use them to make new sounds, new chord changes, new time changes. Just create. Just keep creating. Even if it's all shit, just keep creating. Pretty soon you'll be great.

Are there any things you would have done differently in your career as a musician?

No. No. I've learned that even if you wanted to do it better, you could not. Even if you wanted to improve on something. When you go back in and improve one area, you lose everything else that was great about it. There's no way. You can't go back.

How would you like to be remembered?

Oh, I don't care. Whatever happens. Everybody will have their own opinion. I don't want to tell anybody what to think.

Do you think you owe something to your audience?

My life. Without my audience, who would I be playing for? Just myself. What a lonely job that would be. So I owe a lot to my audience. I'm not beholden to it, actually have to send them something. [*Laughs.*] Maybe another record—if they like it.

I heard that your next record will be an acoustic guitar record.

It's acoustic with a band. The Stray Gators, the band I did *Harvest* with—Kenny Buttrey, Tim Drummond, Ben Keith, Spooner Oldham on piano instead of Jack Nitzsche.

It must bring quite a lot of life to your music to be working with different bands.

Oh, I love it. That's what keeps me going. Keep stirring the pot. Put myself in a different situation. I don't ever try to tie myself in to one group of people, because it stifles the music.

CODA: Since our 1991 interview, Neil Young has released thirty albums under his own name and appeared on three others with Crosby, Stills, Nash & Young. His song "Angry World" won the 2011 Grammy Award for Best Rock Song. The same year, Young, who has always retained his Canadian citizenship, won his country's Juno Awards for Artist of the Year and Adult Alternative Album of the Year for *Le Noise*. He's been inducted into the Rock and Roll Hall of Fame as both a solo artist and as a member of Buffalo Springfield.

Eddie Van Halen at the Oakland Coliseum, July 23, 1978. (Jon Sievert)

With the 1978 release of his band's self-titled debut album, Eddie Van Halen pushed the boundaries of rock guitar. His sheer speed, unusual note choices, fiery tone, and fearless approach to whammy and effects inspired guitarists across the musical spectrum. His impact was especially felt among crotch-rock guitarists in big-name rock bands, who saw their dreams of becoming "the next Jimi Hendrix" blown away in the 1:42 it took to listen to "Eruption," the instrumental that introduced Eddie's soon-to-be-much-imitated finger-tapping technique. While others had done it before, Van Halen was the first major-league rocker to make it a stylistic cornerstone. Within months, it seemed, it was difficult to walk into a music store or listen to a garage band without hearing someone doing a rough approximation of Eddie's tapping technique. But as much as his technique and wild energy, it was Eddie's personality—his sense of humor—that made his playing so appealing.

Concurrent with the album's release, I'd just become an editor at *Guitar Player*, at the time America's only guitar magazine. When a review copy of *Van Halen* arrived, Editor-in-Chief Don Menn called several of us over to his stereo and dropped the needle onto "Eruption." "Is that a guitar?" Don asked. At that time, the technique was so unusual we weren't even sure if it was played on a guitar or keyboard. Adding to the mystery was the fact that the cover depicted Eddie holding what appeared to be a Stratocaster, but the guitar on the record sounded unlike any Fender we'd ever heard.

Weeks later on July 23, 1978, I attended a Day on the Green concert in Oakland, California. AC/DC and Van Halen were opening for Pat Travers, Foreigner, and Aerosmith. I was there to interview Travers, who, it turned out, was too distracted to do an interview. Stressed about coming back to the magazine empty-handed, I began shooting basketball at a small court Bill Graham had set up backstage. A lean, muscular young man about my age wandered over and said, "Hey, man, can I shoot with you?" I agreed.

After a spirited game of one-on-one, he asked me, "What band are you in?"

"I'm not in a band."

"Well, what are ya doin' here?"

"I'm an editor from *Guitar Player* magazine. I came here to interview Pat Travers, but he blew me off."

"Pat Travers *blew you off*? I can't fucking believe that! Why don't you interview me? Nobody has ever wanted to interview me."

"Who are you?"

"Edward Van Halen."

We sat down at courtside, I flipped on my tape recorder, and Eddie Van Halen gave what he has since referred to as "my first major interview." Here it is.

You've just been nominated for Best Rock Guitarist in the Guitar Player *Readers Poll.*

Are you kidding? [*Laughs.*] That's a trip!

Tell me about your guitar.

My guitar? Which one? I got like three of them that are kind of tripped out. The first one is a copy of a Strat. It's not a Fender. It's a company called Charvel—they advertise in your magazine all the time. You know, I bought a body from them and a neck. A body for fifty bucks and a neck for eighty, slapped them together, put an old Gibson pickup in it, and it's my main guitar. Painted it up, you know, with stripes and stuff. I guess that's my thing.

Did you keep the original frets?

Well, I usually do all that stuff myself. I put my own frets in.

What kind do you use?

Just large Gibson ones—the high ones.

What are the electronics?

One volume knob and one pickup [*laughs*]—that's all there is to it. No fancy tone knobs over here! I see so many people that have these space-age guitars, you know, with all the phase switches and equalizers in their guitar and treble boosters, you know. When we were in Japan, some company wanted me to endorse their stuff. They hand me this guitar that's got like twenty knobs on it—I couldn't figure out how to work the thing! [*Laughs.*] I said, "Shit, give me mine. One knob." That's all it is. It's simple and it sounds cool.

What about your other two guitars?

Okay, the other one is just an Ibanez which I slightly rearranged with a saw. It's the one I use on "You Really Got Me." I just cut a piece out of it, painted it up. It's kind of like a cross between a [Flying] V and an Explorer. After we do this, I'll show 'em to ya. They're really tripped out. My other one I just put together over the couple days we had off. Yesterday I went down to Charvel's, they gave me a body, and I just slapped a Danelectro neck on it, put an old Gibson pickup in it.

Do you do all the work yourself?

Yeah. Sure.

What kind of strings are you using?

Uh, Fenders. I don't know the number—I think XL 150. The high E is a

.009, the low one is a .040 or .042—something like that. It's a standard rock thing.

And picks?

Fenders—mediums or hards, whatever I can get.

When did you first start playing?

Um, let me see. I've been playing about eight to ten years. Me and Al both were born in Holland. My father used to be a professional musician there.

What did he play?

Saxophone and clarinet. Yeah, he used to play for radio shows because back then they used to have live radio shows instead of records. So he got us into music real early. We both started playing piano like at the age of six or seven.

Did you take formal lessons?

Sure.

Learn to read?

Oh, yeah! Definitely. I slightly know how to read for the guitar, because I know notes. But like if I see an A or an E, I don't know which one it is in relation to the piano. But piano, yeah, I played for a long time. Got all my musical theory and stuff like that from playing piano. We used to have this old, Russian teacher that was a super concert pianist, and that's what our parents wanted us to be, was concert pianists. Started working, had a paper route. I bought myself a drum set.

Is this in Holland?

No, this was here. We moved over here about ten years ago—'67, '68, something like that—right around the Cream days. That's when we came here. Because rock and roll, man, I wasn't into it at all back there [in Holland]. There wasn't much of a scene going on. We came here, and all of a sudden Hendrix and Cream, around '68, and I said, "Fuck the piano, man! I don't want to sit down. I want to stand up and get crazy!" But before then, when we first came here, I started playing drums, and my brother was taking guitar lessons—flamenco, you know, nylon strings, stuff like that. While I was out doing my paper route so I could keep paying the payments for my drum set, he'd be playing my drums. And eventually he got better. I mean, he could play "Wipe Out," and I couldn't. [*Laughs.*] It was back in those days. So I said, "Keep the drums. I'll play a guitar." From there on, we've always played together. I've never played with another drummer.

What kind of guitar did you start on?

Teisco Del Rey—four pickups in a row. Cost seventy, eighty bucks.

Did you take lessons?

Ah, no. Not for guitar. I've always been around music all my life, so I've kind of got an ear to pick up things pretty easy.

What was your first professional gig?

Well, what do you consider professional? Just making money or the first backyard parties? [*Laughs.*] We used to do some outrageous parties.

When did you start playing parties?

With this band [Van Halen], we used to play parties too.

When did the band form?

The way the band is right now, about three-and-a-half or four years ago.

Who did you play with before that?

It used to just be just me and Al and a different bass player. We used to be called Mammoth. I got tired of singing. I used to lead sing, you know, and I couldn't stand that shit! I'd rather just play, concentrate on playing. So Dave [David Lee Roth] was in another local band, and we used to rent his PA. We said, "Fuck! It's much cheaper if we just get him in the band!" So we got Dave in the band, and then we were playing this gig with Mike's band, our bass player [original band member Michael Anthony]. A group called Snake— they opened for us. We were all tripped out, because he was lead singing for his band and fronting his own band. Dave was fronting his own band, and I was too at that time. Then we all just kind of got together.

What city was this in?

Pasadena, L.A., Arcadia. We all just kind of got stuck with each other, because by the time we graduated from high school, everyone had to go to school and be a lawyer or whatever.

How did you get from there to playing coliseums in just four years?

Oh, playing everywhere and anywhere. From backyard parties to places the size of your bathroom—you name it. Everything. And we did it all without a manager, without an agent, without a record company. I guess the main thing that really got us going was the Pasadena Civic. We used to print up flyers, with some local people helping us. But it was basically our own thing. We'd print up flyers with a picture on it and stuff like thousands of 'em in high school lockers. And the first time we played, I guess we drew maybe 900 people. The last time we did, which was almost a year ago, we drew 3,300 people at four or five bucks a head. And that was still without a record out or management or anything. It was about the only place where we could play our own music. We used to play Gazzari's and everywhere else, where you got to do the Top-40 grind, you know.

How did you get your record contract?

Ah, I was getting to that. We just kept playing, doing our Civic shows and clubs and stuff like that, and then we got into playing the Starwood and the

Whiskey because Rodney Bingenheimer, who's a big wheel in the L.A. music scene, saw us. He said, "Shit, you guys are all right. Why don't you play at the Starwood?" So we played there for maybe four or five months, and one day Marshall Berle, who's now our manager, saw us. He's Milton Berle's nephew. He brought down—well, he didn't tell us who was there. He just said, "Hey, there's some people there to see you, so play good." At that time he really had nothing to do with us. He was just working his way into having something to do with us. It ends up that we played a good set in front of no people, an empty house at the Starwood on a rainy Monday night. We got done with the set, and we're all going, "Hey, it was a good set. All right, guys!" All of a sudden Marshall walks in with [producer] Ted Templeman and [Warner Bros. executive] Mo Ostin. It was a heavy thing, man.

Ted Templeman who produced the Doobie Brothers?

Yeah. Well, he still produces them. He's done them and whoever else. I mean, it was heavy because I remember talking to other bands, and they've always been trying to get Ted to produce their records, but he only works inside of Warner Brothers. He doesn't produce other acts. And there he was. And he said, "Hey, it was great, man." And within a week we were signed. It was right out of the movies, man, because really we never . . . well, we made a tape once with Gene Simmons from Kiss. We flew to New York with him, and nothing really ever came of it, because we didn't know where in the hell to take our tape. So we had a bitchin' sounding tape—you know, the world's most expensive demo tape, which he paid for. But we didn't know where to take it. We didn't feel like walking around knocking on people's doors, pushing ourselves on them, saying, "Hey, sign us, sign us!" We just kept playing everywhere, and eventually they came to us.

How long ago was that?

A year and a half or so.

How long did it take you to cut the first album?

Three weeks. The album is very live, no overdubs—that's the magic of Ted Templeman. I'd say out of the ten songs on the record, I overdubbed the solo in two—"Runnin' With the Devil" and "Ice Cream Man." And "Jamie's Cryin'"—three songs. All the rest are live! I used the same equipment I use live, the one guitar, soloed during the rhythm track. Al just played one set of drums. [*Laughs.*] And Mike, you know. And Dave stood in the booth and sang a lot of lead vocals at the same time. The only thing we did overdub was the backing vocals, because you can't play in the same room and sing, with the amps—otherwise it will bleed onto the mikes. The music, I'd say, took a week, including "Jamie's Cryin'," which we wrote in the studio—I had the basic riffs to the song. I was just dickin' around. And my guitar solo,

"Eruption," wasn't really planned to be on the record. Me and Al were dickin' around rehearsing for a show we had to do at the Whiskey, so I was warming up, you know, practicing my solo, and Ted walks in. He goes, "Hey, what's that?" I go, "That's a little solo thing I do live." He goes, "Hey, it's great. Put it on the record." Same with "Jamie's Cryin'." The music took a week, the singing took about two weeks.

What's the difference between your studio playing and live playing?

Well, between that record and the shows we're doing now, I'd say none. [*Laughs.*] Because we were jumping around and drinking a beer and getting crazy in the studio too. There's a vibe on the record, I think, to me, because a lot of bands, they keep hacking it out and doing so many overdubs and double-tracking and shit like that, it doesn't sound real. And then a lot of bands can't pull it off live because they overdubbed so much stuff in the studio that it either doesn't sound the same, or they're standing there pushing buttons to get their tape machines working right or something. So we kept it real live, and the next record will be very much the same.

Have you already got plans for it?

Oh, for the first record we went into the studio one day with Ted, and we all just played live and laid down like forty songs. And out of those forty we picked nine and wrote one in the studio for the record. So we got plenty of songs. As a matter of fact, I'm gonna get together with Ted on Wednesday and figure out which songs off that tape that we're gonna do for the next one. But we've been writing, and we've got so many more songs since that tape, and we've got like thirty songs left just on that tape. I think we're gonna use just that tape for the next album, because Ted seems pretty sure that he's got some hit action or whatever just out of those songs. A little polish here and there, but the basic ideas are there.

What kind of practicing do you do?

I never really sit down and really practice, like shut myself in a little room and go, "All right, I'm serious now." You know, I just sit around and whenever I get bored, I play my guitar.

Do you compose with the guitar?

Sure, sure. Sometimes I don't. Mainly I'm always thinking music. I'm always trying to think of riffs, using my head. Like sometimes people think I'm spacing off, but I'm not really. I'm thinking about music.

Can you remember it later?

Sometimes yeah, sometimes no. Most of the time I'm so high, I forget. By the time I get to a guitar, I forget!

How many amps do you use?

I had four good amps that I used to use all the time, but I don't have them anymore. What I basically have is three different setups, three complete setups. I have three 100-watt tops of whatever make—right now I'm using Music Man, a couple of Laney amps, which are English, and a couple of new Marshalls. I'm just using everything right now because I lost those old amps. But I use like three 100-watt amps for the main set—what I call it—and then I do my guitar solo, and after that I change guitars and amps to setup number two. And setup number three is also again three amps, for backup.

So you have each guitar plugged . . .

Into a different setup. So if something is wrong with the first one, all I do is grab another guitar and it's completely different amps, so I don't have to worry about trying to fix the setup that I was using. With my guitars, I use one pickup in the back and the vibrato—that's the sound I'm into right now. Who knows what will happen on the next record.

What about effects?

I use two Echoplexes. I use a flanger, just for little subtle touches. I don't use it for any intros or anything, just notes here and there, like maybe I'll hit a low note [*makes growling sound*] and hit the switch, just for little subtle effects. And I use a phase shifter, a Phase 90—MXR, I think. It doesn't really phase; it just kind of gives you treble boost, which I like. Cuts through for solos. That's about it. I use a Univox echo box, and I had a different motor put in it so it will go real low and delay much slower. Like on the record, on "Eruption," on the end of my solo [*imitates the descending notes at the solo's end*], all that noise? That's a Univox echo box, which I put in the bomb. Did you see that thing?

That big torpedo you have onstage?

Yeah, it's a bomb, a practice bomb. They used to fill it with dirt and drop it on the beach for target practice or whatever. Yeah, I thought it looked cool. Usually it blows up.

What's your strategy for playing guitar within the band?

I do whatever I want. [*Laughs.*] I don't really think about it too much. I'd say that's the beauty of being in this band, that everyone pretty much does what they want. I don't know. It's not that strict. Everyone just does what they want. They throw out ideas, and whatever happens, happens.

Do you change songs for each set?

What do you mean? Like, say, if we play tomorrow, would the set be exactly the same?

Do you leave yourself room to do what you want onstage?

Oh, yeah, definitely. Half the time I forget the solos I played on the record. Everything is pretty much spontaneous, you know. It's not so set. We used to have a keyboard player, and I hated it, because you have to play everything

Jas Obrecht and Eddie Van Halen backstage in Oakland, July 23, 1978. (Jon Sievert)

exactly the same all the time with the guy. You couldn't noodle. Like in between vocal lines, you couldn't noodle because he'd be doing something to fill it up. And I didn't dig it, because I play too much. Sometimes I guess too much. But I like to play my guitar. I don't want someone else filling where I want to fill it. [*Laughs.*] I've always liked to play three-piece, because I just play too much, I guess.

What guitar players were you most influenced by?

Uh, that's a toughie, really. But I'd say the main one, believe it or not, was Eric Clapton. I mean, I know I don't sound like him . . .

You're more like Hendrix or Blackmore.

Yeah, I know. I don't know why, because Hendrix I like, but I was never into him like I was Clapton. And Clapton, man, I know every fuckin' solo he ever played, note-for-note, still to this day.

You memorized them?

Oh, yeah! I used to sit down and learn that stuff note-for-note.

Off the record?

Yeah. The live stuff, like "Spoonful," "I'm so Glad" live—all that stuff. But Hendrix too. Just like the whole band—none of us really have one main thing that we like. Like Dave our singer doesn't even own a stereo. He listens to the radio, which is a good variety. That's why we do have, like on the record, we got "Ice Cream Man," which is a change from the slam-bang loud stuff. You know, we're into melodies, melodic stuff. Most of our songs you can sing along with, even though it does have the peculiar guitar and end-of-the-world drums.

What advice would you give a young guitarist who wants to follow the route you've gone?

You just have to enjoy what you're doing. I mean, you can't pick up a guitar and say, "I want to be like him, I wanna be a rock star," just because you wanna be a rock star. You know? You have to enjoy playing guitar. If you don't enjoy playing guitar, then it's useless. Because I know a lot of people who really want to be famous or whatever, but they don't really practice guitar. They think all you do is grow your hair long and look freaky and jump around, and they neglect the actual musical end, which is tough. To learn music is like going to school to be a lawyer. But you have to enjoy it. If you don't enjoy it, then forget it.

Does reading music help?

[*Tentatively*] Uh, it would help in certain things. I don't think it really helped me that much. It doesn't help me in writing songs, you know. I can usually remember what I come up with, and I put it on tape. That's all. Unless you read charts, unless you're a studio musician, then you have to know how to read. That's what I like about rock and roll—it's more feeling than technical. That's why I hate a lot of bands, because they're so technical that there's no life to it. I like loose rock and roll with good musicians.

What's your opinion of the recent state of rock and roll?

I say it's cool. I've never given up on rock and roll. I remember people used to say, "Ah, rock and roll is dead. It's gone." Bullshit. I don't think so. It's always been there. It's still the main stadium sell-out thing.

What are your plans for the future?

Plans for the future, man, just to keep fuckin' rockin' out! You know, playing good guitar.

Are you heading into any new areas with your guitar?

Ah, sure. We got some acoustic tunes, which sound real nice.

You use an acoustic guitar?

I've never really owned one. I play it on electric, but I know it will sound much better on an acoustic, because it's acoustic type of riffs. And I play keyboards. So does my brother. So don't be surprised if you hear some piano or synthesizer or something on the next record or maybe the third one. I don't think we're gonna make any drastic changes for the next one. I think a lot of people make that mistake: They make too drastic of a change, and people go, "Ohh, I don't like 'em anymore."

How long have you had your main striped Strat?

A couple years. Before that I used to have an old, gold-top Les Paul.

What happened to it?

I painted it up and ruined it. [*Laughs.*] Nobody taught me how to do guitar work. I learned by trial and error, and I fucked up a lot of good guitars that way. But now I know what I'm doing, so now I can do whatever I want with guitars to get them the way I want them, because I hate store-bought, off-the-rack guitars. They don't do what I want them to do.

Which is?

Which is fuckin' kick ass and scream! Like the vibrato setup—you gotta know how to set the thing up so it won't go out of tune, which took me a long time to get down. I mean, no one ever told me. I used to talk to other guitarists who half-ass had it down, and they wouldn't let me know how to do it. But I figured it out, and I can just twang the fuck out of that thing now, and it won't go out of tune.

I think that's it.

Alright!

CODA: Over the years, Eddie has had his share of ups and downs—from platinum albums, sold-out stadiums, and successful endorsement deals to a high-profile divorce and battles with bandmates and drug and alcohol addiction. Through it all, he has remained intensely devoted to his music. On the cover of its June 19, 2015, issue, *Billboard* magazine declared him "The Last Guitar God."

Tom Petty performing in Mountain View, California, June 5, 1987. (Jay Blakesberg)

E ver since the Heartbreakers' first FM-radio hit, the guitar-hook-laden "Breakdown," Tom Petty has remained a law unto himself. He's been unwavering in his all-or-nothing fight to control his artistic freedom and integrity. Like his musical forebears John Lennon, Keith Richards, and the Byrds' Roger McGuinn, he is staunchly devoted to rhythm guitar. One of rock's preeminent songwriters, he has crafted enduring songs that deal with outcasts, love, heartbreak, resilience, and especially American individualism. It's fitting that when the iconic Traveling Wilburys initially came together as a "band of brothers," Tom Petty received equal billing with Bob Dylan, George Harrison, Roy Orbison, and Jeff Lynne.

Raised in Gainesville, Florida, Petty first became infatuated with music upon seeing the Beatles on *The Ed Sullivan Show*. In one of his earliest bands, Mudcrutch, he played alongside guitarist Mike Campbell and keyboardist Benmont Tench. Moving to Los Angeles in search of a record deal, Mudcrutch disbanded in the early 1970s. Petty, Campbell, and Tench regrouped as Tom Petty and the Heartbreakers, releasing their eponymous debut album in 1976. It took nearly a year for "Breakdown" to break through. Their follow-up album, *You're Gonna Get It!*, reached #23 in the *Billboard* album charts. By decade's end, their third album, *Damn the Torpedoes*, had reached #2, and "Don't Do Me Like That" had become a Top-10 single. Legal issues with record companies impeded Petty's progress early on, as did the severely broken hand he suffered after punching a wall in anger. As detailed in our interview, this injury proved fortuitous, in that his physical rehabilitation required him to expand his approach to the guitar.

Over the decades, Tom Petty has enjoyed many successes—hit singles with the Heartbreakers, as a solo artist, and in collaboration with Stevie Nicks, the Traveling Wilburys, Johnny Cash, and others. He's earned enough gold and platinum records to cover large walls. At the time of our interview, the Heartbreakers had just finished a world tour with Bob Dylan and Tom had begun work on what would become the *Let Me Up (I've Had Enough)* album.

Our conversation took place mid-afternoon on May 27, 1986, in the office of manager Elliot Roberts. I'd been warned in advance by an MCA publicist that I could only have fifteen minutes with Tom and that I was forbidden to bring up the topics of sex and drugs. A few minutes later Tom came into the room, pulled a chair so close to mine that our knees nearly touched, and shook my hand. We got right to it. He ignored the time restriction, speaking for nearly forty minutes.

People seem a little nervous that I'm gonna ask the wrong questions.
Yeah? Who's nervous? I've got nothing to hide. Ask me anything.
Um . . .
Let's talk about fucking. Who you been fuckin'?
A few here and there.
Alright! Now that's out of the way. [*Lights cigarette.*]
What is the appeal of working with Mike Campbell?
The appeal? Well, he's the best, you know. I mean, he really is the best. I've played with Michael since 1970, so I wouldn't understand playing with anybody else. I really think he's the best in rock and roll, that there is. If you asked a guitar player, they'll tell you. There's a lot of things. We're partners and we're friends and we write together and play together. We've developed a whole style of playing together, actually.

Do you consider yourself a rhythm specialist, while Mike is more of a soloist?
Yeah. Well, of course, yeah. Lately I play a lot more solos since I broke my hand. You know, when I was going through the therapy to get my hand together, I learned a lot of lead playing. I don't know why I've never done it before. When I was doing my therapy, I got into that. I play a lot more solos on this record. We have a way of playing together. A lot of times we get comments that some people thought the records were like six guitars, when there's really only two. We can make a lot of noise, the two of us.

Do you work parts out naturally, or do you sometimes tell him not to play a certain solo or does he suggest rhythms to you?
No, we never talk about that stuff. It's not that kind of band where you really have to talk about it. Nobody really knows who's going to take a solo most of the time. Maybe on a rare occasion, but this kind of band, if you're gonna work it out, it's over. It's just got to happen.

Does he inspire you?
Oh, yeah. Sure. I'd be lost without him. He's an integral part of this band.
Do you ever take solos on records?
Oh, yeah, sure. Mike does most of them. "Between Two Worlds," I played a great solo—on *Long After Dark.* I'd have to think for a minute to remember. But most of them are usually Mike or two of us at once—that sort of thing.

What does it take to be a good rhythm guitar player?
It's a dying art, I tell ya. It's a very important trip, and a lot of people miss it. A lot of these kids today, they just learn all these Ritchie Blackmore things, but they don't know a fucking chord to save their life. They don't know how to write a song, but they know how to play a solo. There's a lot to rhythm. Like, I can carry a band. I can make a band chug along. That's an important thing. If I don't play, there's a difference.

Were your musical heroes rhythm guitarists?

Well, I like a lot of guitar players. I've always liked [John] Lennon. I basically just studied Lennon's playing, even in the films, just watching his right hand and how it worked. Stuff like "And I Love Her," if you ever listen to that—that has an amazing rhythm pattern. I think I learned a lot from learning that and watching him in the film. Keith Richards is another person— I've learned a lot from him. Dylan, actually, since I've been playing with him. The two of us can play rhythm really good in sync. There's a lot to being a rhythm player. It's kind of like being the line on a football team, but I really enjoy it.

Are there other players that you'd suggest somebody listen to?

As a rhythm player? [John] Fogerty is a good rhythm player. Slim Harpo is amazing! Amazing rhythm player. If I think for a minute, I'll probably think of some more. Of course, [Jeff] Lynne and Keith. Dylan on acoustic can't be beat. You know, I played a lot of bluegrass too, and country stuff. Michael actually turned me on to that about 1970, '71. We had a little country group, one of the first ones ever with long hair. We did that, and I'm really glad we did that because we learned a lot of guitar stuff. In bluegrass, you have to play pretty fast and precise in the rhythm, so that helps a lot. If you listen to any, like, Bill Monroe, any of that stuff, there's a lot of integral rhythm patterns that are really important.

In the studio, do you play guitar and sing at the same time?

Yeah, we do everything live. This last album we've done—a double album [*Pack Up the Plantation: Live!*]—there's maybe three overdubs in the entire album. Everything's live.

But on previous studio albums, did you lay down the rhythm tracks and then sing on top of them?

No, I sing and play at the same time. I could never do it separately the right way. I mean, I've done that, but it's never as good as just doing it.

You never wanted to front a band without playing?

No, I started as a player. I started as a bass player, actually, for years. It was only when I joined the Heartbreakers that I went over to playing guitar all the time. I'd always played the guitar because I always wrote, but nobody else wanted to play the bass, so I was always playing the bass. Still do. I do a little bit of it now with Bob—all of us play the bass at one point in the show. We have to.

Has working with Bob Dylan had an impact on your own style?

I think it freed us up a bit. I think it got us back on the . . . I don't know, really—it's too early. I'm sure it has. I don't know exactly how to describe it. The main thing that's going on with us is that we took three years off, and

TOM PETTY

229

the last two we've been consistently working and playing. And with Bob, one of the things that went on there, probably at the rehearsals and the sound checks, is we've been playing four and five hours a night, just playing, playing, playing, playing. We've played *so* much together recently, we kind of feel funny if we don't play. So I think that affected this album. This album was all written on the spot in the studio, and it's probably our best album. Maybe we should have been doing that all along. I don't know.

How would you compare your rhythm style to Dylan's?

They are probably different. When I'm playing with him, what I'll try to do is get exactly in sync with what Bob's doing. That's a challenge, because it gonna change every night. It's never going to be the same. Sometimes you have to find where I [one chord] is, or what exactly this is about. But we've gotten where the two of us, especially on acoustics, can really lock up and make the band happen. And electrics.

When you write, do you come up with chord progressions first?

There's no pattern. I might, or I might have some words or I might have nothing. Never can tell.

Onstage, what determines whether you use the Strat or the Rickenbacker?

Well, I haven't used a Stratocaster in a while.

What's the appeal of the Rickenbacker?

There are two Rickenbackers that I play most of the time. One's a twelve-string, which I've played forever. It's a blonde hollowbody twelve-string [Model 360–12]. And the other one is a red hollowbody six-string [Model 365] that's a *great* rhythm guitar—more like an electric/acoustic, almost. And the rest of the time with Bob I've been using Gibson's ES-335 and what is it called? SG, a little red flat thing.

How do you route your guitars? Do you use any effects?

Nah, just a wire [cord] to a Vox AC30. We don't have any effects. We don't even like guitars that have been fucked with. I won't have any guitar that has some little switch put on it.

When did you first get into Rickenbackers?

When I was fourteen or fifteen. The first guitar I ever had, the first electric, was a Rickenbacker.

After you broke your hand, did you have to change the way you set-up your guitars?

No. I did come back playing the Rickenbacker a lot of the set because it was easy to play. Now that my hand's strong I haven't set it up any differently.

When you broke your left hand, one doctor told you that you'd probably never play again. Can you give any advice for when that happens?

If that should happen to you—and I hope it doesn't—you just have to remain optimistic. That's the only advice I can give. I never accepted that I wasn't going to play again. I refused to accept it. You can't accept that. And neither would the surgeon. He didn't want to have that attitude, although it was a reality. It was beyond playing—it was having the use of my hand at all. See this scar on the back here [*points to a scar on the back of his hand that runs from his middle knuckle toward the wrist*]—I broke all these bones in half. My hand was closed like a claw; it wouldn't open. It was like that for nine months. I have full use, some pain now and again. I have four pieces of metal and this little wire.

How did the injury affect the way you play?

I think I got better as a lead player. I went through all this therapy, and once I had the movement in my fingers, the doctor made me play guitar all day because that is what I ultimately do. And we figured that was the best therapy after the electroshock and all that awful shit. So I had to play guitar literally all day, sometimes when it hurt. All this stuff just started—I just started finding things. It was interesting—stuff that had been there all the time and I just never thought about doing it.

Do you play in any styles that never show up on any of your albums?

I think there's a lot we do that hasn't shown up on the albums. I think we're uncovering that more and more as time goes by. I can play country pretty good, you know. I'm a pretty good blues player. Actually, we played a lot of blues on this record. I think I probably play a lot more guitar that you'd notice on this record, because there are only two guitars on the record—one over here and one over there. So when one of us falls down, the other one jumps in. That's what we do with Bob, when we got three people going for a lead. You never know who's gonna play the lead, so everybody dives in and starts backing out when we realize who's got the biggest fish.

Do you play much acoustic guitar?

Constantly. All day long.

Is that what you learned on?

Not really. I had acoustic, but the strings were so high I couldn't get anywhere. So when I got an electric, I learned more. But for ten years or more, that's what I play all the time.

What's your favorite?

A J-200 acoustic, Gibson.

Do you write songs on that?

Oh, yeah! Sure. Almost all songs, except if I'm maybe writing in the studio, I might use an electric. But most of them were written on my Gibson Dove and the J-200.

What kinds of strings do you use on those?

I don't have the faintest idea. Don't know. Bugs [guitar tech Alan Weidel] puts them on. I don't like to change strings very often. On my electric, I don't like to change them the whole tour. I *never* let them change strings on my twelve-string—ever. A lot of people don't understand how to make a twelve-string work. Like, they are always up there nosing around, trying to figure out what I'm doing to it. But I'm not doing anything—it's the way I play it. Nick Lowe used to every night be up there, thinking that I had some little box somewhere; it was a running joke. But all it is is an AC30 and a Rickenbacker twelve-string, a very old one. But if you put new strings on them, there's no way you're going to control them, because they are very thin and they spread out. But when the strings are really old and thick and dead, you get that thickness.

You must not sweat a lot to corrode the strings.

Oh, yeah—they're awful. It's an embarrassment, really.

Do you own many guitars?

Yeah. I have no idea. Bugs brings around trunks of 'em. I know which ones are good, though.

In the song "The Waiting," you have one of the beautiful pure Rickenbacker tones. How do you set up your equipment to get that sound?

That's just my blonde Rickenbacker, the treble pickup. That was a Vox Super Beatle on that record.

What's your method for miking an acoustic guitar onstage?

Well, gosh. I haven't found a good one. Last tour, I had one of Bob's guitars, the Yamaha that had a pickup—the acoustic/electric. We used the same model, both of us; they look like little J-200s. Those sound pretty good. We're still looking around. I'm trying to get the J-200 amplified for this tour. Neil Young—I saw him, and he had a great rig on his Gibson; it was the best one I ever heard. It's hard to mike them in those big places—you know, football fields. It's just ridiculous.

How do you do it in the studio?

In the studio, what I've been doing is working out rather well, because I have a tendency to back away from the mike and be all over the place. So I just took a little contact mike, clipped it on to the hole. And then we put a microphone kind of around right where the neck and the body join, and we just do a split off the two. I'm not sure of the name of the mike—it's just a little tiny thing that clips on.

What has your work as a producer taught you about getting a good electric guitar sound?

Well, it's essential! The trip is, with a guitar you could stay there and bang your brains out all day, but if it ain't goin' on, it just ain't goin' on. The guitar has got to sound good right there. The secret to that, to any sound in the studio, is to have something that makes a good sound. I've seen so many people go, "This don't sound good!" Well, it don't sound good because it don't sound good, you know? You can do everything in the control room, and it's no good. Basically, you've got to have an amp and guitar that sounds good.

I've heard people say that if you play quieter in the studio, the parts sound bigger on the record. Have you found this to be true?

I think it's all down to the noise that's coming out. I just turn the amp up to where it sounds like I want it to sound. And then if everything is done right, it should sound that way inside [the control room]. I don't think there's any rules. I don't know. I don't buy that. I think if you want an exciting sound, then you've got to have the amp loud to make that sound. Maybe if you got a little amp. Everybody's got a different theory. The most successful ones are the guys that know. Like, Michael has this amp—it's an Ampeg Rocket— and he uses that quite often. It's a tube amp, and that thing sounds great. I don't care what room you put it in—turn that thing on, and it sounds like that. But when it's not going on, the best thing to do is just take a look at your equipment. Maybe you're in the wrong part of the room or something. It's the same with drums and everything. When they sound really good, it's a simple thing. Usually the problem is more in the room rather than in the control room.

Why do you like Vox amps?

I'm just used to them because I've played them all my life. They tend to work very well for us. I don't know. There's probably other good amps. We haven't had much luck with Fenders or Marshalls. These AC30s are great. They are making new AC30s now that are great. I gave one to Bob, and he's playing one now. And he can't believe it. They sound great. They make them just like the old ones. There's two different kinds. One's better than the other—I can't remember which one it is. They have a very rich sound, they have a nice tremolo and reverb, and they're very simple. The Super Beatle—I like that. I played that a long time, but it's really a loud amp and sometimes a little hard to deal with because it's just too loud, even in a big place.

What would you most like to improve about your playing?

I'd just like to keep learning more. The nice thing about the guitar is that no matter how long you play it, there's always something sitting right there. That's one thing. Like playing with Michael, sometimes I'll say, "How did you do that?" And I'll look at the way he did it, and I'll go, "God, man, I never thought about that." Maybe that will open up a whole other thing for me, just seeing one different formation or something where I'll go, "Ah, yeah!" There's always something else to learn; that's the real thrill of it.

Do you ever feel like you're in a rut or feel stale with your playing?

No. I don't think about that. I just try to get off.

Do you use a pick?

Yeah. Fender mediums. Sometimes I use my fingers if I have to, you know, with the pick as well. I'm a pretty good fingerpicker. I can do that pretty well.

Have you ever recorded outside of the Heartbreakers?

Oh, yeah. I've played on some people's albums. Remember there was a guy named Dwight Twilley? I used to play on his albums. I played on this album Bob's got coming out. But if I think for a minute, I'll probably think of a few.

If you could jam with any musicians past or present, does anyone come to mind?

Oh, well, let's think for a minute. You mean just to play with somebody that I've never played with? I've played with a lot. I'd love to play with Johnny Cash. John Lee Hooker—he just drives me crazy. I just get fever and chills. There are so many people I admire, so many good players.

Is the simplicity of rhythm guitar what appeals to you? It sounds like the musicians you admire are . . .

Well, we never think of us as rhythm and lead too much. Like, I got the freedom to play over the last couple of years. We keep it very free. If I want to start playing lead or start playing another part or something, I just do it. Or if I want to stop playing altogether, I just do it and trust that it's gonna keep goin'. And once that freedom's there, the music's much more exciting than if everybody said, "You're gonna play this, and you're gonna play that." That's a little limiting. You've got to have that discipline to know when you must do that. I think that kind of confidence in each other is real important. You hit an energy level and you try to just get lost in that. And hopefully that's going to get the song over, then the song is going to do the work. If you're playing a good song, you're alright. You're in trouble when you're not, because there's really nothing the fuck you can do about it. But if it's a good song, you get the song over. You know, we're real song-oriented. We don't think of guitar much; we think of song.

If you had children who want to be guitarists, what would you suggest that they emphasize in their learning?

Trying to have a good understanding of basic chord structures that make up most popular songs is a good place to start. Learn the old four chords—the C, A-minor, F, and G—and know what the minor is, and know that there's another minor that fits into this key. And I would just learn a lot of songs. What you have to do that most people can't do these days, most of these kids, is . . . I kind of like to think that I can pick up a guitar and sing you a song, and you won't miss anything. I think that's the test to whether you've written a song or not: you should be able to sit down at a piano or pick up a guitar and perform that song for someone. Even songs I've written like "Don't Come Around Here No More"—which is a very complex record—I can sit at the piano and play you that song and get it over to you, or play it on the guitar. The ones you can't do that with you better keep a close eye on.

Do you have much of a background in music theory?

I don't know anything about music theory at all. I've learned a lot of, like, lingo over the years. I don't know what a V [five chord] is, for instance. I hear 'em say, "Play a I, IV, V"—I don't know what that is.

Do you know a lot of chord inversions?

I know millions of chords. I couldn't tell you the names of them, but I usually know what key I'm in, which is more than [bassist] Howie [Epstein] does. You know, Howie can play anything with strings on it—literally—but he doesn't have the faintest fucking idea what the names of the notes are. You can say "G," and he's like "This one?" To this day. I'm not that bad. I've learned it. Like, from songwriting, I know things like these chords fit into this key, or I can move into this key from this key and back to this key—that kind of thing. From that, and the piano. I write a lot on the piano too, so I guess in that sense I know music theory. I've never had any instruction.

Have you ever discovered a chord progression on the guitar that instantly sparked a song?

Oh, yeah. All the time. "The Waiting"—that came with the riff you hear at the intro. I wrote that on my twelve-string. And when that came down the song was in the bag.

Do you ever get ideas when you don't have an instrument in your hand?

Yeah, sure. I can kind of hear it in my head. See, I value not knowing what I'm doing. Like, sometimes Michael says, "This song is exactly like this Buddy Holly song," or something. And I'll say, "Well, I didn't know that. I don't give a shit about that." If I get hung up worrying about that, I wouldn't do anything. So let's go on and do it, and if it's a total embarrassment, then we'll back off. But usually by the time you're done, it doesn't sound anything like that anyway. So I like not knowing.

Some musicians claim that when they go to another instrument, like from guitar to piano, they know so little that they can write stuff.

That's true. Well, it's true that in guitar, if you're in a rut, you might tend to go to the same thing all the time. You can maybe walk over to the piano and start to play that song, and with the luxury of being able to play a bass line against the chords, something else happens. My best piano songs are all based off mistakes.

Which came first for you, guitar or piano?

Guitar. I had to teach myself piano. They let me play on some of the records on piano sometimes, but I can only really play one rhythm. [*Laughs.*]

Are you working on any new guitar techniques?

I'm just trying to keep it rockin', you know. I never think in those terms of working on a guitar technique. I just think of trying to get it over—or trying to amuse myself. I try to get into what I'm playing. Something that fits with the band. I just try to lock up the band—it's my job. If it's gonna all fall in, it's my job to lock this baby up and keep it locked. And if that means upbeats or if that means flamenco or if that means calypso, that's what I gotta do.

Do you prefer playing in the studio to the stage?

Mmm. I like 'em both. They're getting to be more and more the same since we're cutting so live now anyway. I don't know. The stage always has the advantage of an audience, of feedback.

If it takes you too long to record a song, will you scrap it?

We've done this so long together. We record everything ever played in the studio, the whole session. If one guy's playing, if two guys are playing—everything's recorded. It's very rare that we ever do a take past two takes, that is kept, because it's just not the same. And I won't play the same song all night anymore either. That's nowhere. It doesn't work for us. I won't necessarily scrap it. Maybe I'll say, "Well, let's play it country," or "Let's play it as a ballad," or "Let's not play it. Let's play 'Bye Bye Johnny.'" Or "Let's play some more songs," or "Let's play some sets of this." And then all of a sudden, when no one's thinking "Well, hey, how about this one," *bang*—you get it. Or you leave it and come back to it another day. But you're never gonna get anywhere once everyone is tired and weary with it. I've never seen that work.

Do you have any favorite Mike Campbell solos?

Oh, I've got dozens and dozens. He blows my mind. [*Laughs.*] I shouldn't say that—he'll read it. I tell ya, one of my favorites is the one he plays on "So You Want to Be a Rock and Roll Star." [Roger] McGuinn and [Chris] Hillman [creators of the Byrds' original version] called me about that. That fucked 'em up. It's hard to do that on a twelve-string—it's really hard to play that way on a twelve-string. They loved it; they're big fans. Keith Richards is a big fan—he goes on and on about it. I saw Michael playing with the Rolling Stones one time, and it was really something to see. But I won't go into that. I'll tell you, he's played a lot of great solos, a lot of classic solos. He's very imitated.

I like hearing him on slide.

Yeah, he can play that thing. The solo in "Even the Losers"—I heard that on the radio the other day, and that's pretty staggering. I remember [Bruce] Springsteen was sitting there with us when we did that solo, and old Bruce just got religious. "Even the Losers" was on *Damn the Torpedoes*. I heard it on the radio, and then I remembered that whole scene with Bruce. We gave him some water and he calmed down. But that is a great solo, and it's one that was very imitated, you know. Bryan Adams and [John] Mellencamp—they make a living off Mike Campbell, don't they? If you listen to those records and that style. You know, Michael is not one to show off. He thinks as a writer a lot, which sometimes I have to kick his ass about. I want to tell him, "Go ahead and give it to me."

When you perform a song in concert, do you ever think back to whatever caused you to write it?

Certainly. Yeah. Well, you try to get into that character or that frame of mind, because you must believe it to convince the audience. It's a lot like acting, in the sense that you just have to become that character. If you don't believe what you're singing, the jig's up. You really can't fool anybody, not even in a 50,000-seater. You just can't hide that. God knows, we tried. But you can't fool 'em. So that's a real trick of performance too—getting your mind in the shape to take all that on.

Do you know when you play your best?

I think I do, yeah. I think I do. I don't know if I always do. I think I know now from producing, I know what *the* take was.

Do you know a hit when you record it?

Well, I wish I did. I have an inkling, but I'm surprised a lot of the time too.

Do you have any favorite songs you've written?

Most of my favorite ones now are ones probably no one's heard yet. They're on this new album. I have quite a few. But on the old albums, there's quite a few. "Southern Accents," I think, is one of the best songs I ever did.

A real change of pace for you.

Yeah, it was. It was either that or cut my wrist. [*Laughs.*] This new album is going to be quite a shock too, I think. "Rebels"—I was real proud of that song. Some of the ones that weren't as popular, like maybe, say, "Straight into Darkness." That's one I like quite a bit.

Since you're from Florida, I'm curious why there's not more solo guitar playing à la the Allman Brothers. That was the Southern sound for a while. Did you ever engage in that kind of . . .

Yeah, yeah. We had to play all those songs. I think we consciously didn't want to do that because we wanted to create our own style rather than kind of jump on that boat. And it's hard. Like, all you can do is just mix all your influences into a stew. And then the funny thing is that you look up and all of a sudden it's your own thing. And that's a real gas. And you can take it somewhere, you know. Do something with it.

I'm often amazed by the hooks Mike plays. He's understated, so what he says is really important.

Yeah, it's essential. The lick in "Breakdown."

I can't imagine that song without it.

Without that lick, right? Do you know the story of that lick? I'll bore you with this for a moment. When we did "Breakdown"—it must have been ten, eleven years ago now—we were doing it. I wrote that song in the studio, and the first version was like seven minutes long, with this long guitar in the end. Everyone's gone home, right? And I was sitting there listening and in walks Dwight Twilley. We were hanging around a lot at that time because we were the oddballs at the time, especially down at Shelter Records. They didn't know what to do with us. Twilley walks in, and right in the fadeout of the song, Campbell plays [*sings the song's melodic guitar hook*].

Was he playing with a slide?

No, it's just straight-on finger stuff. He played the lick once in the end. Twilley turns to me and says, "That's the fucking thing, man! How come he plays the lick once at the end of the song? It's the whole hook." And I listened back and said, "You're right." So I called them all up—4:00 in the morning— "Come back down." And we did it again around the lick. It took a couple of takes, and there it was. So he does all that kind of stuff.

He credited you with playing the solo in "Don't Do Me Like That" or "Refugee."

Yeah? Which one? I don't remember. Sometimes I come up with the solo and he plays it. Like maybe he'll have an idea and I'll say, "Nah, play something like this." Or I could sing something to him, and then he'll take it and usually improve on it quite a bit.

Does he ever suggest chord patterns or inversions for you to play?

He might. Yeah. He might say, "You know, since I'm doing this, maybe you should go up here," or maybe I should go to an open tuning or use a capo or something.

Do you ever play in open tunings?

Oh, yeah. Lots.

G?

All of them. Whatever the song requires. We use capos a lot. "Don't Come Around Here No More" is in the key of F, so we're not really showing off changing all those guitars. People are like, "Well, why do you need all that?"

Well, there's a reason you need it. Like with "Don't Come Around Here," it's an F tuned to [be played in] an E formation.

So the guitar is tuned up . . .

A step. So you can play an E formation and get the full sound, because using the barre chords isn't very effective.

When you go onstage, how many guitars are out there?

Quite a few usually, just between the tunings and the emergency factor.

How many differently tuned guitars will you have?

Well, I don't know. With Michael there's probably three or four. With me, only three.

You have one standard, one up a step . . .

Yeah. Depends on what's in the set and if there's something that I've gotta play open ended.

What are some of the songs you play in open tunings?

Oh, there's quite a few. "Dogs on the Run." We had a song called "Shadow of a Doubt"—that's all open tuning. I think those are open A. [*Long pause.*] I don't remember—I'd have to see a set list. I've got it narrowed down now to where I don't have to use too many guitars. I can usually use my 335 and the two Ricks. And then I've got this one solidbody rigged for "Don't Come Around Here," that's tuned up to F. This is on the last tour. And I think I have a Stratocaster for maybe two songs. A couple of songs I use the Strat because they just have that kind of sound. You couldn't get that out of anything else. And that's about it—that and the SG. I've started using that an awful lot, most of the time.

In the studio?

Yeah, and on the last tour we did, the Dylan stuff. It's an old 1960s-odd SG. I got it right before the tour, and it was brand-new in the case. This old '60s thing. And now Campbell's taken the motherfucker. He will. I'm sort of concerned about getting it back, because he's used it the whole album. But he's got to give it back for the tour.

He's got Red Dog [Tom's red Fender Stratocaster] *too, right?*

Yeah, he kind of took that. But I took one of his Rickenbackers. We do that. There are some guitars that the ownership isn't quite clear on [*laughs*], and there are some you can't touch.

Which is your untouchable?

Well, my red Rickenbacker is mine.

The one on the cover of Damn the Torpedoes?

No, that's actually his. That's his twelve-string that I was playing for a while. Now I'm not allowed to mess with that. He used to let me play this clear guitar he had, a Dan Armstrong, and I kept breaking it. Three times I'd run across the stage and the cord would rip all the guts out of it. On three occasions. And so that was the end of that.

Are you rough on guitars otherwise?

Bugs says we're pretty hard on them.

Do you hit it hard when you play?

Oh, yeah. We smack 'em in the amps, you know. [*Laughs.*] There's a Telecaster I played for about three tours. I just got tired of it. For variety, I put it away. I've been playing it on the album—this old white Telecaster. But that thing, I could get great sounds. I could take that thing and just go *boom* against the amp and just make this great sound.

Will there be any new directions in your playing on the album you're doing?

It's pretty wild, this album. I'll tell you, it's untamed. [*Laughs.*] It's very untamed. A lot of guitar on it. Boy, I think it's really something. I'm really excited about it. It's the most rockin'—I hate to use that word—but it's the most rockin' thing we've ever done. People always say, "You know, I wish they'd make records like they did when they were young" or whatever, but this is wilder than any of that.

How would you like to be remembered in terms of your musical life?

How would I like to be remembered? Uh, fondly.

As a songwriter, as a musician . . .

Oh, I think they'll probably remember much more than that! [*Laughs.*] I wish they could forget some of the trouble I've been in and maybe just focus on the music I've done.

Thanks, man.

Okay. Thank you! I'm glad to be here.

CODA: Since our interview, Tom Petty has, among other feats, released and/or appeared on dozens of albums, headlined world tours, played the halftime show at Super Bowl XLII, and provided the voice of Elroy "Lucky" Kleinschmidt for the animated TV series *King of the Hill*. He was inducted into the Rock and Roll Hall of Fame in 2012 and has been the subject of several biographies. With sales in excess of 80 million albums, Tom Petty ranks among the world's best-selling music artists.

As an editor for *Guitar Player* magazine, I'd often hear about superb guitarists who, for various reasons, were largely unknown outside of their hometowns. In the early 1980s, this was clearly the case with Eric Johnson. What instantly set Eric apart, though, was *who* was talking about him. Two quick examples: Jeff Baxter, studio ace and veteran of the Doobie Brothers and Steely Dan, told me in 1980: "Eric Johnson from Austin, Texas—this kid is just *amazing*! He's twenty-three. When I heard a tape of him, I went ape. This might sound silly, but if Jimi Hendrix had gone on to study with Howard Roberts for about eight years, you'd have what this kid strikes me as."[1] Steve Morse, 1982: "Eric Johnson is one of the best electric guitarists anywhere. He's so good it's ridiculous. I'm not kidding—he's better than Jeff Beck. Eric *destroys* people when he plays. We've played gigs with him, and it put a lot of pressure on me when it came our turn to play. All I can say is that if he had an album out, he'd be the first one on my list of required listening."[2]

In 1982, when Eric was entangled in a contract that curtailed his performance opportunities, I sought him out for his first nationally published interview. It was unusual for *Guitar Player* to publish a feature on a guitarist who didn't have widespread recognition or even an album to promote, but all it took was a pair of ears to hear that Johnson already was an extraordinary musician. As we spoke, what impressed me even more was Eric's humble attitude and steady focus on the spiritual and intuitive sides of musical creation. "I always try to connect myself with what I'm feeling inside and hearing inside," he explained. "I think that's the best way to try to achieve your own feel for the guitar. It's like intuition: 'intuition' is like the 'tuition from inside.' And if you get with that, your own self will show you how to play guitar."[3]

For Eric Johnson, the creation of sublime music has always been about the journey inward, an approach shared by John Coltrane, Miles Davis, Wes Montgomery, Jimi Hendrix, and others visionaries. Over the years, Johnson's unwavering devotion to perfecting his art has become as legendary as his near-fanatical attention to the minutiae of his gear. This is evident in his songs, interviews, instruments, and the way he plays guitar. As Stevie Ray Vaughan put it, "The guy has done more trying to be the best that he can be than anybody I've ever seen. He plays *all* the time, and tries to get his instrument in perfect shape all the time. He works hard on his tone, sound, techniques. He does incredible things with all kinds of guitars—electric, lap steel, acoustic, everything. Few people understand that when the guy was fifteen, he was playing Kenny Burrell and Wes Montgomery stuff, and he was doing it *right*—that's pretty cool. Eric is a wonderful cat. He's always been one of my favorite people in the world, as well as one of my favorite guitar players."[4]

Eric has released many solo albums over the years, with 1986's *Tones*, 1990's *Ah Via Musicom*, and 1996's *Venus Isle* being among the very best. Near the end of our first interview all those years ago, I asked him what he'd like to accomplish. "I'd like to have my own studio," he responded, "and be able to record albums the way I want, which is really experimenting with guitar. I'd just like to contribute some new things for guitar."[5] Eric, I am happy to report, has achieved these goals. Our mutual friend Max Crace was on hand to shoot photographs when this October 13, 2012, interview took place in Eric's spacious Saucer Sound studio in Austin, Texas.

What is it about Stratocasters from 1954, 1957, and 1958 that is so special for you?

That's a really good question. I've always wondered what it was. I think it's several things. I think that they had a shipment of wood at Fender that was real special—that was one thing. That kind of wood is really hard to get nowadays, and even though it's a solidbody guitar, it makes a difference in the way the sound travels. You know, when you go out to a restaurant and you eat a meal and you feel really good, it might have been because the person preparing the meal had all this great emotion and vibes. It's like whatever we do goes into what we do. You know what I mean? On a very subtle level we can feel that. And the other thing that's kind of undeniable is it was a point in time where the electric guitar was so new. Every week you'd hear somebody on the radio or on a record and say, "I've never heard that!" It was so new that it had that kind of birth energy to it. It's almost like when you're in the studio and you record that first track, and it's got this magic. And then you go back and do it ten times, and it's, "Oh, it's actually better now, but it's not as fun to listen to or it's not as good." So I think those two factors play into it. They're still making great instruments, but it's hard to recapture those two issues as time rolls on.

Do you think it's possible that the fact that they're more than a half-century old and have aged and become more of a unit . . .

One unit—yeah, I think so. Yeah, you're right. Definitely. That's why whenever I see a vintage instrument, I always think it's cool if somebody doesn't take all the parts off and put them in a big box and put everything back together somewhere else, because it's had forty years to be the way it is and grow into that entity. I'm kind of ridiculous about that: "Oh, make sure the screws go back in the same place," you know. And the only reason for that is because they've been there for forty years, and I think they do what you say. All these parts, because they've sat and they've had time to gestate, it turns into a complete entity. And if you do disturb that, it does affect the sound.

When you purchase an old guitar or trade for one, what do you look for?

I go for a particular thing. I like it where when you're playing with a clean tone, the sound is real crisp but it kind of punches out. But then when you go to the lead sound, it kind of sucks in, more like a Gibson does. They have more of this kind of folding-in character to them. So it's almost like you get the best of both worlds. You get that real pronounced EQ clarity for the rhythm tone, but the more you push the amp or you push the guitar, it starts folding in upon itself. It's a response of the parts and the wood and the way it resonates. Some guitars will do the exact opposite—they'll kind of be a little bit edgy-sounding on the top end when you're on the clean tone, and then as you push it more and more, they start going out, so they bloom out. As they bloom out instead of folding in, you hear every single pick attack. And it's not only the sound of the pick attack which bugs me a little bit, but it's also the fact that if you're pronouncing that pick attack so much, the note is not recovering quick enough for you to go to the next note. One way is in favor of your picking, and it's kind of more like an impulse ballet thing that breathes out and folds back in the same sync of your pick, and the other way is like you're fighting it and you're actually tripping-up your sound.

Are you careful about how the instrument sounds acoustically?

Usually when they work right, they sound better acoustically too. Yeah, you can kind of hear it sometimes.

Do you have any gear that's so precious you won't take it on the road?

You know, I do, but every once in a while I play it anyhow because I try not to get too hung up in that, because I just figure, well, the whole reason I got it is to play it. I bought this old Marshall combo that I've been using on the road, and it's really sweet and original and in great condition. The first thing I do is take it on the road and start touring with it. [*Laughs.*] I don't know if that was smart. Hey, you know, I bought it to play, so I'm just gonna play this thing. I don't know. I have some guitars that I don't typically take out, but it's just because I really haven't used them on the road that much. Most of the stuff I'll use.

Among all the guitars you have, are there any that you'd site as the two or three most precious?

Yeah. I have a 1980 [Martin] D-45 that my dad bought me, and it's real sentimental, because my dad's passed away. I got it when it was brand new.

When I had those instruments stolen in '82, he bought me this guitar to replace the acoustics I lost. It had been in Heart of Texas Music for a while. I think it was an '80 or an '81, but I got it in '82.

Did he take you to play it first, or did he just surprise you?

I went down to Heart of Texas, and they had two of them. I tried them both out for a few days, trying to decide which one to keep, and took the other one back. Yeah, so that's a real special guitar. And I have a guitar that Chet Atkins gave me that's a Del Vecchio [wood-body resophonic]. That's real special to me. You remember Bill Maddox, the drummer that was killed? In his will he had an old Strat that he willed me, so I would never . . . that's real special.

Do you have a particular guitar that you've written a lot of songs on?

That Martin I've written a lot of songs on. Let's see, what else? Yeah, that's probably the one that I have that I've written a lot on. All the acoustic songs that I do pretty much I wrote on that. Some of the electric tunes I wrote on that '54 Strat I had that I don't have any more—that I wish I had! I shouldn't have gotten rid of it.

The Virginia?

Yeah. There were four women in '54—Mary, Virginia, and I don't know who the other two were.[6]

Where would they sign the guitar?

There's a piece of masking tape right down inside here [*indicates the inside of a Fender Stratocaster's body cavity*].

So that's near the pickup selector.

Yeah. And it's only in '54 they did that. It's really interesting, man. You know, I don't even know if I want to say it because everyone will go out and say, "Oh, '54!" But they really are—they're different than the other ones. [*Smiles, adds with humor*] But they're not any good! They're horrible! [*Laughter.*] They're worth about $200, so . . .

Send them to me and I'll take them off you!

Yeah.

What are your favorite Gibson guitars?

Honestly, a 335. I know there's a Les Paul out there that I'd love to own, but I've owned so many and I've never kept a single one of them. And it's not that they're not great. There's a certain thing about my technique or something, or the weight, that I haven't quite found the right one for me. But they're great. I mean, my heroes all played them, but I've never found the right one to settle on. But I'd say a 335. And I have an SG that sounds great—I was never really a huge fan of SGs, but I stumbled on this guitar, and it has a great sound and it stays in tune, so I like it too.

Have you used it for slide, like Duane Allman?

No, I haven't.

The SG is interesting because you can easily get so high up the neck.

Yeah, yeah. They're great. I can't believe this one stays in tune, because every other one I've ever played never stayed in tune. But this one seems to.

Speaking of SGs, I understand that you enjoy Angus Young's playing.

Oh, yeah! He's great.

Doesn't he have one of the best vibratos in all of rock and roll?

Absolutely. He's awesome! I don't know how he plays running around like he does, either. He sounds like somebody that is sitting down concentrating really hard. Yeah, he's a great player.

When you think of the guitarists you admire, who would you put in the category of people who have the million-dollar vibrato?

Definitely Eric Clapton and B. B. King. Mick Taylor, like from the Mayall days. You know, in certain ways Peter Green. And then the slide stuff that Robert Johnson did, the way he would do that. And then Django Reinhardt for his own style. Oh, Albert King—definitely Albert King! Of course, that's more like he's just making big stretches. Yeah, I'd say definitely Albert King. That's where, I guess, Clapton honed his own style. I mean, Clapton's vibrato on early Cream stuff is pretty ridiculous. It's pretty great.

B. B. talks about how he developed his vibrato because he couldn't play slide well, so he decided to imitate a slide with his fingers.

Oh, wow.

He also told me that when he was a kid, strings were so hard to get that if he broke one of the Black Diamond strings, he would just tie a knot in it, restring it, put a pencil above the knot, and tie string around the pencil so it became a capo. And then he would play above the pencil until he was able to buy a new pack of strings.

Oh, my God. That's great. I thought you were gonna say just take it and just rewrap it to the ball and tie it—we used to do that as kids. But that's one step more. That's even more old-school. That's living the blues right there!

Could you describe your thoughts on the spirituality of playing music? Is it important to keep yourself pure and unmotivated by greed and ego to play at your very best?

You know, that's a great question. I've thought about that before. I think that for me to play my best, I need to have myself not modulating but more in sync and focused with that aspiration. Somehow that, for me, is the gateway to feeling at peace with myself. If you're at peace, you can travel beyond yourself. At that point, you're available for any nuances of magic that are bombarding us twenty-four hours a day anyhow—we're just too busy talking or distracted to hear it or feel it or see it. But it's always there if you can get into that focus where you're just at peace with yourself. Being like that allows me to then go pick up on something sublime. I'm always kind of searching, looking for something that's sublime, that makes me feel better or makes somebody else feel better. But it's not like "Oh, that's the only way you can make art"—I don't think it is. I think there's a real validity for art that sometimes causes angst or dissention or uncomfortable provocation of thought. But my little niche is to try to make people feel good, to say, "Oh, wow!" I think life is hard anyhow, so why not use that opportunity?

The question is really interesting to me because I'd love to say that that's necessary, but I guess it's not. Maybe what's necessary to make a really good artist is being able to turn off the switch of your self, which is just gonna just throw a bunch of paraphernalia in your path for you to trip over. Have you ever met artists and gone, "Jeez. These people are not very nice—they're really just hung up on themselves"? Or you meet a famous actor or whatever, and it's just like, "Wow! This is a high-maintenance person." But they'll walk on the set and [*snaps fingers*] bam—they'll just be in touch with this God energy, and they do this amazing performance or this amazing piece of music. Some people—regardless of how they live their life or what they like or appreciate or how they conduct themselves or relate to other people—have an ability to just [*snaps fingers*] do a switch to where they can go beyond themselves, regardless of what their self is comprised of. So I guess it's an enigma and just depends on the individual. I used to grapple with that, because I thought, "Well, that blew my theory of you've got to do all this homework." But it's important to work on that spiritual aspect. The other stuff, really, if we think it matters at the end of the day, we're totally just kidding ourselves. I don't think it does.

Do you go through a process of emptying yourself to write songs or prepare to go onstage, a letting go of the ego?

I try to, yeah. I think it gets harder as you get older. In some ways it can get easier because you're aware of the benefit of doing that. You appreciate that benefit so much more, so you're more committed to trying to get there and do that. But in some ways it gets a little harder because you have all this history of living. It's like if we only had three days, we'd have a lot of extra space in the computer to make up the alphabet of our self. But if you have forty years, it's filling up all the space, and your consciousness is that forty years. You get a little bit more solidified, you know. The more that you've solidified with all that history, you associate with it so much that it's harder to just let it go. It can be more demanding on your psyche because you have all this self. But I know that the best I ever play is always when I can put all that aside, let it all go and just show up and be available. You've got to do that to create more significant music.

What have been your easiest and your most challenging songwriting experiences?

Interestingly enough, one of the easiest was "Cliffs of Dover." That just came in five minutes. It's a hard song to play, but it's really just a silly little melody, cute little fun thing. I guess that's why people related to it, because it is that. It was more like a gift—it just came to me. And I think some of the others—I can think of songs that I worked on forever and ever and ever. I have ones that I have been working on for years that I've never written, but I know are really, really good. But I never can finish them because I never can find—I don't know how to finish them.

Where and when did "Cliffs of Dover" come to you? Do you remember the moment?

Yeah, it was like years before I recorded it—it was like the mid-'80s. I remember just sitting and practicing and getting this idea for the melody. I think I came up with [*sings opening refrain*]. I kind of like that, and then the rest is just I-IV-V-I with a real simple [*sings another line*]. It's really a pretty simple melody. And then within a few minutes, "Oh, I've got a middle eight for this."

"Zap" was another one that came quickly?

Yeah, yeah.

What do you remember about that?

I remember listening to a Frank Zappa record and it had some interesting riffs [*sings them*], almost like "Zap" a little bit. So I had that one riff [*sings part*], but I didn't have any of the rest of the song. I used to just call it my Zappa lick—"Oh, I've got that Zappa lick." So when I finished the song, I just changed it to "Zap," because it was kind of a Frank Zappa construction.

What's the backstory for "Emerald Eyes"?

I was just sitting down at a Fender Rhodes one day, just jamming around on a song, trying to come up with some chord changes. I liked the chord changes, and I just put a melody to it.

Did you know somebody with emerald eyes?

No. Actually, Jay Aaron wrote the lyrics to that.

Tell me about "Bristol Shore."

That actually was a friend of mine named Judy that I was hanging out [with] at the time. She worked for Exxon Mobil. She'd fly out on a helicopter to these oil platforms in the Gulf of Mexico. And I'd gone down to Galveston to meet her, but she had to go out. I didn't ever catch up with her. I just ended up hanging out in Galveston for the whole evening because she got an emergency call to go out to one of the platforms. So I just changed it. There's references to it, like "she's been delayed in the Gulf of Mexico." I looked around, and I couldn't say, well, "Galveston" [the title of a Glen Campbell hit]. I was looking at a map and found Bristol Bay. "Hey, that sounds cool. That's a little bit more mysterious." So I changed it to "Bristol Shore."

How did "Desert Rose" come about?

That, my friend Vince [Mariani] just named that song. He called it "Desert Rose." He gave me the idea for the title, so I started writing the lyrics.

Was that on guitar?

Yeah.

"East Wes" and "Manhattan."

"East Wes" was just kind of a simplified version of kind of a Wes Montgomery thing. "Manhattan" was an instrumental that had kind of an urban sound to it, so I just named it that.

A lot of young players who are into rock and roll have probably never heard Wes Montgomery. Why would you recommend someone seek out his music?

Well, I can think of a million reasons for me, personally, because I love his playing so much and the way it sounded. But I think any young player should have the opportunity to listen to anybody that had a really special, unique spirit that was so powerful that what you're feeling from what they're doing is not so much what they're doing, but the spirit that's coming from behind it, that's fueling it. And that happened with so many artists in a rarified way because they were so dedicated to that as they voiced their music through it that they paid homage to that. And they stayed in that place a lot. They didn't go elsewhere to get fuel for their creativity. It's important for young artists to check out any artist that was dedicated to that space almost in its entirety.

What's really interesting is that with the ones who are, there's such a symmetry between them. And that's why I say it's not really *what* they are doing, it's the spirit from behind it that fuels it. It's like the very first time I ever saw a live video of Wes Montgomery—you know, the '65 stuff—he's just kind of sitting there smiling and playing. And the first thought that came—and I know guitar, because I've played guitar my whole life—was Wes has his own sound. You wouldn't say, "Oh, yeah, he reminds me of this rock guitar player." Not at all. It's a totally different thing. But you know what the first thing that came to my mind when I watched him was? "That's another version of Jimi Hendrix," because of the spirit. When you look at the early Hendrix stuff, like Monterey Pop—before things got complicated or he had personal issues or whatever—he's just nodding his head and smiling and he's "Hey! What's going on?" and he's playing. And Wes is doing the same thing.

Eric Johnson
in Seattle,
November 8, 1996.
(Jay Blakesberg)

That same energy was fueling Wes' playing, and that same energy was fueling Jimi's playing. With Louis Armstrong, you can pick up that same thing. It's all the same. You find people that are so different, there's something that you're picking up in your heart. And I think it's because they stay real close; they're fueling themselves off that really rarified space that is the best place. And it becomes more of a spirit that infuses it. It's bigger than what it is. All kids should seek out people that really are committed to that.

Would you put John Coltrane and Miles Davis there?

Yeah, absolutely. Yeah.

When you listen to Wes, do you prefer the beautiful, melodic "Down Here on the Ground" type of material over when he's going further out and pushing the boundaries?

You know, I love it both. I like it both. At one point I tried to say, "No, okay,

I'm not gonna like *Down Here on the Ground* anymore. I'm only gonna like the Riverside recordings and *Movin' Wes* and *Smokin' at the Half Note* and the Wynton Kelly stuff. I've only got to like that. I can't . . ." I'm sorry, I like *Down Here on the Ground*. It's got an incredible vibe. If you put on *Down Here on the Ground* and you drive around at night, it's just great. And it's another thing. It's got that spirit. They're great songs, regardless. Yeah, it is on CTI and it is pop and it's homogenized and all that, but so? Music is music. There's great music. There's some killer songs on *The King and I* soundtrack. I'm not gonna argue if somebody says, "Well, that's a Broadway thing and there's no blowing on that, and there's no . . ." You know what I mean? "Yeah, and? What's your point?" I'm not gonna go see a John Wayne movie and be bummed because there were no spaceships in it, you know. You get what you get from something, if you're open enough. But that record, *Down Here in the Ground* and the vibe of Herbie Hancock—I mean, his playing on that is just so . . . the way he plays to support Wes. It's crazy. And Ron Carter. It's just a beautiful-sounding record. They are limiting themselves to just songs, and there's not a lot of blowing, but what a great-sounding record to just chill out and listen to songs and music. So I think there's a place for it all.

It's transporting.

To me, it is. I mean, it's one of my favorite Wes records. I don't go to it to look for, "Okay, Wes. I wanna see you shred your buns off and be blowing." There are other records where he does that more, and it's incredible. But it just has a vibe.

Do you prefer the softer side of Coltrane?

I kind of do, but that's just my personal preference. I like the edgy Miles stuff, and I like the softer *Kind of Blue* Miles stuff too. I think "Naima" and some of that stuff—it seemed Coltrane played on the edge, tonality wise. It was almost like he purposely played a little sharp or something, which is really cool on some of the more hard stuff. It's still great. But it wouldn't be my go-to as much as more of the lyric stuff, I guess.

Are there parts of the Hendrix catalog you prefer over others?

Oh, absolutely. People don't ask me about that and I don't even bring it up, but I'm not a real fan of, like, releasing 160 records on Jimi Hendrix— "Oh, here he is in his house, playing the E chord." I don't think he would have wanted that. But he's become such a commodity that there's endless records that get released on him. And, you know, there is some stuff in there— recently maybe they've been trying harder to dig—but there's some pretty cool stuff. Like there was a recent record that had a take of the Bob Dylan tune "Like a Rolling Stone." Have you heard it? It's not the one from Monterey. It's killer! It's great. There are some gems, and there are some stuff that really warrant it, but I think that there's a lot of stuff that just because it has the name Jimi Hendrix, they're gonna put it out. And I think, ultimately, would Hendrix have wanted this out? And I think that's why kids should really go and listen to the records that Hendrix made, and not just hear the aftermath recordings that he didn't necessarily want.

I always come to Electric Ladyland, *because that's the one album he produced. That's as close as we're ever going to come to knowing his own concept of how his music should sound. For me, that's the most complete picture of Hendrix in existence.*

It really is. It's amazing. I listened to that record recently because we did the Hendrix tour, and I had to learn some songs I didn't know. And yeah, he did that in 1968 too—it's unbelievable! It was really ahead of its time. Everything's great on it. I like it all.

How far back do you go with guitar players? Are you familiar with Charlie Christian, Eddie Lang . . .

Eddie Lang. Yeah, I've heard him. I don't listen to him regularly. But Charlie Christian, I have his recordings. I listen to him. Who's the other guy—not Eddie Lang, but . . . Lonnie Johnson. Yeah. B. B. really liked him a lot. Roy Smeck was cool too. He was a great player, but he's from more like the '50s and '60s, I guess. Those are the main ones. Robert Johnson, of course.

What appeals to you about Johnson?

He was just a great technician. I mean, he just really nailed it all. The singing and the playing was just scary. And he didn't have a lot of guitarists to listen to for that kind of level of playing.

I once asked Eddie Van Halen how he became so good at such a young age. He said that he came home from school, sat on the edge of his bed, and played guitar until he went to sleep. He didn't go to parties or socialize very often. Did you find it necessary to make sacrifices and get rid of distraction that got in the way of accomplishing your musical goals?

Yeah. And then there's that trade-off. You've got to be sure that you still have your life with your family and your loved ones. So it is delicate balance. Yeah, what you're saying is so true. That's what I did too. I'd come home from school and that's all I did. I just played and played and played and played and played. It is a discipline and you've got to sacrifice all these things to do it, but you have to find that sweet spot, whatever it is, with music—like, if we're talking about music and guitars. You have to find that sweet spot that's going to spark a passion and an excitement for you so that you want to make that sacrifice. A lot of people who go to guitar school are, "Okay, I'm gonna go to school and I'm gonna practice, practice." And it's like licking a stone. It works—you'll get mileage out of that—but I can't help but think maybe next week, maybe next month, ten years, you're gonna quit or get disillusioned, because you're just sitting there *ehh*—it's like grinding a stone. I think that Eddie Van Halen did that, or you did that with literature and journalism, and I did that with guitar because we couldn't wait. It's like, "It's 3:15! I don't care about . . . I'm gonna go home and play. I love it! It's great!" I remember my fingers bleeding. I didn't like it, but I was like, "Oh, I've got to keep practicing!" I mean, I could hardly let them heal, because I loved it! I just loved it.

I was at the right place at the right time to develop a love for it. My parents loved music. My dad loved music more than anything in the world, so I wanted to be like my dad. When I was five years old, I'd look at him and he would just be crying and laughing because of music. And then I was lucky to be born at a time when the Beatles—there's absolutely great music now— but there was a certain fire close to the original inception of rock and roll, where you have people like Clapton and Hendrix. It was all a new sound. It was an inspiration to last a lifetime. You'd hear it and just go, "My God!" You couldn't wait to discover this and that. The guitar wasn't a household appliance at the time. I sometimes notice at sound checks. When I was a kid, I'd be at sound check. If I had a cool lick, the whole place would turn around— the guys setting up the chairs would go, "Wow! What was that?" I could play the greatest lick in the world now when they're putting the seats in the theater, and they're not even gonna turn around, usually. They've heard it.

These things [*points to guitar*] sit in every kitchen in the world. You see it on the front of magazines when you're flying on an airplane—you know, the Strat. The Hard Rock logo is a Les Paul. We've been completely saturated by it. So I think I was lucky. At the time, it was like it came from another planet. And people that really interpreted it well and played it well were just so rare. It was such an inspiration. It can still be found today, but you have to dig a little harder to find it amidst all the cacophony. Having that gift to have such a love and passion for it allowed me to want to do that, to make that sacrifice. I don't know if I'd have made that sacrifice if I hadn't have been so impassioned and so blown away with how much it excited me.

So I think what kids need to do, if they want to play an instrument, guitar, you've got to create a vision of where you want to be, and then figure out a way to remove the obstacles to make it happen, rather than go, "Well, I've got this way I do it." You create that vision. And when you create that vision, you've got to create it in a way that the sound or the playing is the way you want to do it. Even if it seems totally out of balance and impossible, you just like dream it. "Oh, I can hear this sound, I can hear this part! If I could do that, that'd be great!" You start developing a passion for that vision you have.

Then you have the recipe and the fuel that's going to make you want to make that sacrifice. Those four hours [*snaps fingers*] are gonna go like that as you practice, rather than, "Oh, God. It's 3:00, I got another hour," and you're sitting there killing yourself because you're studying music in some school and you've got to do this. You've got to figure out a way to streamline that with making it fun. And a lot of times that will mean a certain type of music or a certain thing, rather than trying to talk myself into "Oh, I don't like *Down Here on the Ground.* I've got to just do this." Me, personally, if I had done that and it was only about playing guitar and playing licks, I'd probably put it away and not play. But it is about songs, and sometimes the simpler songs make you feel good. You don't want to take for granted or belittle the things that give you that excitement of the heart, you know, because that's the fuel that will keep the discipline fun, and then you'll want to do the discipline.

Are you still making breakthroughs? Do you have an agenda of what you'd like to accomplish with the instrument?

Yeah, I want to learn more about harmony and chord changes and being freer to play melodies and solos over chords. I think there's a lot there that would open up things for me if I would get more well versed and freer with that. So I've been working on that a lot lately, trying to get that together.

Have you ever noticed that sometimes the first pass is the best? You can cut a solo eighteen times . . .

Oh, yeah. Absolutely. A lot of people have given me criticism over the years, like, "Oh, Eric, you're better live. You do nice records, but they don't have the vibe, they're too polished, they're too . . ." You know what I mean? "Oh, it sounds like you beat 'em to death." And you know, I think there's a little bit of truth in all criticism, whether it's 98 percent or 1 percent. I went back and listened to some of my records and I'm kind of late to the party, but finally, at fifty-eight, I started hearing what they're talking about. You listen to the old blues records or the Wes records or all the records we love—God, like the '50s Ray Charles stuff? I mean, forget it. I started really listening a little closer to that, letting that issue be prominent, and I can't even listen to some of my recordings now. It's like, yeah, it sounds like I went in there with a lab coat and a scalpel.

*This is post-*Tones?

Yeah, yeah. I mean, there are songs that have been recorded a million times, and they're great. There's a couple of Hendrix tunes that were supposedly done over and over for edits, and they're great. But I think as a general rule—like you were saying—that aspect of making music needs to be a big part of your headspace as you're making music. It certainly is when you play live. So why throw it out the window when you're not playing live? So I think if we all want to grow and we all want to go forward and get better at what we do, we have to take inventory of what it is about ourselves that *we* can do to make this better. Some people, they're so live and spontaneous that they never tune their guitar. It's completely out of tune and they're horrible, you know. But with me, it's the opposite. It's like, "Wow. Take 1 percent of that criticism." If I do want to get better—not better in the sense of faster, but if I want to learn to make deeper, more significant music—I need to take inventory of what I need to do. And I think what you say—you can't put enough emphasis on that. You know, if you went to your wife and you're teary-eyed and you say, "Honey, I just really love you. Okay. Wait—I'm gonna go out of the room, I'm gonna come back in, and I'm gonna do it again." You still mean it, but it might not have the same thing as when you just said it in the moment as you spontaneously spoke. Why should it be different with what I play on the guitar or what somebody else does? It's just living.

To really make your mark as a musician—if you're lucky enough to do it—it seems that you have to make an inward journey and base your music on that which is uniquely you.

Yeah.

You could never play Van Halen better than Van Halen, you can never play Billy Gibbons better than Billy Gibbons, and the list goes on forever. I wonder about the wisdom of spending so much time learning to play "Cliffs of Dover" or "Electric Ladyland" or "Voodoo Child" versus turning that stuff off and pulling out what's you.

Yeah. I think if it's a stop on the way to somewhere, it's good. I went through a period where I sounded so much like Eric Clapton people were just making fun of me. But it was okay as long as I didn't stay there. I learned so much about the way to pick the string and the muting and setting the amp. I loved his playing, and I had to ingest the whole concept and vocabulary of how he did it. And by that, you get to the point where you say, "Oh, I get it. I see how he did that." If you just do that, I think it's a dead-end street. But you can use it as a learning tool to just keep going forward and then let it go. As essential as it is to digest your heroes so that you understand technically what they are doing, it's more important, when the time is necessary, to let it go and be yourself. You have to do that. I don't think you only have to do that as an individual in art. You have to do that with yourself. *I* need to let go of "Cliffs of Dover." If I want to keep my career blossoming, I need to be big enough and brave enough to let go of that. I can play it the rest of my life, but as far as conceptually, musically, and artistically, I need to be big enough to drop this history that I think is Eric, and open the window to see what can happen.

It's interesting you say that, because I remember when I toured with B. B. King. I think it was during a sound check, and I was so stoked I was playing with B. B. King. I was running through all these blues songs I play—I'm not a blues guitarist, but I can play a blues style. I grew up on it, and I can do it. But that's not the point. Where's your space that's unique to the world, where you really shine? You could write like Shakespeare if you wanted or whoever, but it might not be Jas Obrecht. I remember B. B. brought me into his trailer and he said, "What are you doing?" I said, "Well, I'm just doing my thing." He said, "Well, that's great, but you need to be *you*." When people ask me, "What's the best advice a guitarist you admire gave you," it was him. He said, "You know, just do what you do that's unique to the world."

CODA: In the years following our 2012 conversation, Eric Johnson has continued to release albums and tour extensively. Following his 2013 concert recording *Europe Live*, he collaborated with Mike Stern on *Eclectic*, and he then participated in the 2014 Experience Hendrix Tour, re-creating the music of his main guitar inspiration. As this book was going to press, Eric was finalizing *EJ*, his first all-acoustic album.

Joe Satriani in Berkeley, California, October 16, 1992. (Jay Blakesberg)

The guitar instrumental, a staple of early rock-and-roll and surf music, came roaring back in the 1980s and early 1990s. Whereas the pioneering instrumentals of Link Wray, Lonnie Mack, Dick Dale, the Ventures, and others in the 1950s and 1960s tended to utilize simple, straightforward melodies and one or two predominant guitar tones, metal-era instrumentalists sculpted their music from a much broader array of tones, techniques, and influences. Their styles ranged all the way from the studied, Paganini- and Bach-influenced "neo-classical" approach of Yngwie Malmsteen to the bold deconstructing and reconstructing of players such as Steve Vai and Buckethead. Among the new generation of guitar instrumentalists, none have eclipsed Joe Satriani. With sales in excess of 10 million albums, he claims the record for being "the world's most commercially successful solo guitar performer."[1]

Joe Satriani grew up in Westbury, New York. He took up guitar in high school, advanced quickly, and gave guitar lessons to fourteen-year-old Steve Vai. Moving to the San Francisco Bay Area, Joe continued to give lessons to up-and-coming young players—Metallica's Kirk Hammett and Testament's Alex Skolnick among them. He played in a new wave band called the Squares and in 1984 released his self-financed *Joe Satriani* EP, to little fanfare. His next releases, *Not of This Earth* and *Surfing with the Alien*, on Relativity Records, skyrocketed him to the forefront of instrumental guitar rock. Poignant, lyrical, and provocative, the albums showcased music that Joe himself accurately described as ranging from "full-tilt boogie to ambient bliss, tongue-in-cheek psycho Western to dire metallic adagio, cerebral cool to visceral hot, two-handed fantasies to foot-stomping wanged and wah-wahed surf and roll, and possibly the only heavy metal instrumental about an insect!"[2] Fittingly, he named his publishing company Strange Beautiful Music.

In 1987 Joe sent me a rough demo of *Not of This Earth*. Popping it into my cassette player, I recognized within moments that this was fresh, innovative, extraordinary music. The other editors at *Guitar Player* shared my view, and we offered Joe his first national cover story interview. My conversation with Joe took place at Hyde Street Studios in San Francisco on the morning of September 6, 1987. When I arrived, he and his producer, John Cuniberti, were mixing "The Crush of Love."

I was thinking of headlining this interview with a parody of the Star Trek *intro.*

[*Joe laughs.*]

"Space Guitar—The Final Frontier. These Are the Voyages of Joe Satriani . . ."

I like that!

His Lifetime Mission . . ." How would I finish it?

Lifetime mission? "To boldly go where no man has gone before! To seek peace and harmony." Yeah, I suppose. In my own way, I suppose that's what I'm trying to seek—peace and harmony.

What's your favorite part of playing?

Favorite part of playing? Being paid. You mean in the process of learning how to play something or writing it or playing it, recording, performing—what's my favorite?

Yeah.

When I finally write it. The first time I write it—the thrill of hearing it. The thrill of hearing myself play something that seems to have come from within. You know, without sounding spacey, it comes from I don't know what, but it seems like it's something that has to come out. And then when I finally hear it, it's an unbelievable experience. The only close second to that is probably playing it live and seeing people really like it. Or just sitting there playing it and saying to myself, "Oh, my God—that's it! That's it!" And then it fades after you've perfected and you start to worry about, "Well, how am I going to record it?" Because in my head, it sounds completely different.

Do you tend to work on one composition at a time?

I've got hundreds of songs going all the time. Some songs I can finish in an hour, some songs would take me take a year, some songs I'm still working on that I started writing, I don't know, maybe fifteen years ago. If I can't seem to please myself with it, I'll put it on the shelf. I'll bring it back; I'll try again.

Do you sometimes think of the mathematics of music theory as you're composing?

Well, I wouldn't really call it mathematics, although I am thinking of numbers. I'm not purely coming up with a numerical phrase and playing like that. If someone says to me or if it comes to my mind, "root, third, fifth," I instantly know what that is because I was trained to tag that information onto the sound. So I have a memory of what that is. I don't know. It's very possible that some of the things that I'm writing or playing are starting out mathematical. I don't know. I really don't know. It's quite automatic now.

Does your knowledge of keyboards affect the way you play? Your left hand, especially?

Hmm. That technique wouldn't affect me at all, because I'm a terrible keyboard player. Maybe. Maybe at some point the idea of the piano having the range that it has allowed me to experiment with consonance and dissonance and how that changes when it's spread out over many octaves. How a D chord on top of a C chord sounds really awful when they're right next to each other, but when those chords are spread out two or three or four octaves, it becomes more and more consonant—at least to my ears. That seems to be the application. And so when I realized that, then that helped me think about things, how I could actually play chords way up here [*indicates the higher range of his fingerboard*] while I had a basis. So I guess so.

Do you listen to much non-Western music?

Yeah. I listen to quite a lot of what was originally called Oriental music and Asian music—anything from Arabian music all the way to Chinese and Japanese and Southeast Asian. You know, I was exposed to a lot of things as I was growing up. It just seemed very natural for me to like it for what it was and, as a result, to reflect it, I suppose, in my style.

When you first start imagining a song or finding it on the guitar, how much of the final product can you hear?

That varies, differs from song to song.

Have any come to you fully realized?

Yes. Songs like "Brother John," "Headless Horseman." "Satch Boogie"— when I clicked on the idea of how I wanted the song to go, I knew exactly what it was going to sound like. Then, of course, John beefed it up quite a bit. [*Laughs.*] Sometimes I come in with an idea that I think is really heavy, and I'll show it to John and he'll [*snaps fingers*] really click with it. He'll take it to the next logical dimension that will exceed my expectations.

Where did the idea for the middle of "Satch Boogie" come from—when everyone quiets down and you do the unusual solo?

It just seemed . . .

JOHN CUNIBERTI: Controversial.

JOE: The controversial section! Boy, oh boy, was it ever!

JOHN: We have people sending us tapes that have it cut out, suggesting that these would be good edits.

JOE: And we did that. When we did our first mix of that, for just a sampler for Relativity, we actually had three mixes: where the entire track was flanged during that middle part, where just the guitars were flanged and the only reverbs were on the kick and snare, and then where the entire part was missing.

Which version got on the record?

Another one altogether that had the entire solo in the middle.

Is that a left-hand finger-tapping solo?

Um, a two-handed piece. Pretty conventional, physically, although the chord pattern is very unusual. And it works out to a pitch-axis idea where the A is the constant note, but all these chords change around. But yeah, I think every time I've gone back and listen to the thing, that middle part makes it for me.

Me too. It almost starts out as a kind of supercharged blues, and then the middle section puts it in another dimension.

That's exactly how we felt about it. Except without it, it wasn't us. It wasn't the *Surfing with the Alien* record. It was just a blues, a boogie. We didn't think that we were mocking it. We just thought, "Now hear this!" You know? "Take this! Now take that!" And I just love the groove. I just thought it was a crazy groove.

Can you play most of your stuff onstage without another guitarist?

Yeah, sure. The only difficult part is, like, if I'm doing "Ice 9," I can't get that exact ice guitar sound for the two chords. [*Demonstrates.*]

What chords are those?

You might think of it—it's hard to really describe—you might call it a Csus4 to a Bsus4. I should say Csus4 with a major seventh to a Bsus4. Or, since it's over the C-sharp, I think of it as a C#maj7 augmented 11 to a C#m7 with an added 11. That's how I hear it in my head.

I've heard people say they were disturbed by some of your music.

Oh, really? [*Laughs.*] We did something right then.

Some of it almost has a sinister kind of feel.

Yeah. I can definitely say "The Enigmatic" is sinister. "Ice 9" definitely has an edge to it.

Is "Ice 9" a reference to Kurt Vonnegut?

Yeah. Yeah. I'm a great fan of his.

Are you a science fiction fan?

Not so much. I'm not very well read with science fiction. I know there are some stories by Harlan Ellison I really like.

What was the inspiration for "Rubina"?

Just pure love for my wife.

Let's talk about this song you're currently working on, "The Crush of Love."

That was a real intense feeling. It sounds more like a pop song, in a way, but it's extremely lyrical. It was just so perfect—the writing of it, the way that I felt at that moment was just so complete.

What was happening at the time? If you can say . . .

It was one of those situations where I was sort of feeding off of a very simple emotion and I kind of blew it up into something that it wasn't—on purpose, just to really *feel* it. We had finished doing *Surfing*. After not being around home for such a long time, just working on the record, working on the record, finally I get to be home. My wife had a very intense work schedule at the time, and so it was just one of those nights where I really wished that we were together. But she had to work late, so there I am, just kind of feeling sorry for myself, and I just kind of went with it and went with it until it got way out of proportion. It didn't resemble what the original emotion was, but that sort of got me in the mood and I just went with it, as I usually do, just as a way to really feel something. I got this progression down—it just happened very quickly, just in the space of hours. I must have stayed up twenty hours because I had to go back to the tape recorder and listen to it one more time. [*Laughs.*] Louder, slower. I'd slow it down really slow. I'd play it really fast. I'd listen to it from every possible vantage point to get every last drop out of it. I love that.

What has experience taught you about getting a great guitar sound on record?

[*Joe laughs.*]

JOHN: The secret weapon.

What's that?

JOE: Our Neve preamp. You explain it, John.

JOHN: It's a microphone preamplifier and an equalizer. The signal goes right to the tape recorder, so we bypass that console, basically.

You go direct from the Neve onto tape?

Yeah, right onto the tape recorder.

Does this mean you don't need amplifiers?

No. Microphones plug into this, essentially.

JOE: So if we're recording, like, for "Satch Boogie," using Marshalls with a Chandler tube driver and a wah-wah pedal and stuff like that, it will be a few mikes, but they'll all eventually run through that. It just gives it . . .

JOHN: It has a sound to it you can't find anywhere on anything. It's a unique kind of sound.

JOE: And then when we go direct—"Midnight" was done direct—we went into that. It's really just a beautiful sound, and it's different. And you can make it sound fat or skinny or obnoxious.

JOHN: It's ideal for guitar because it's not electronic-sounding in any way. It's very pleasing-sounding.

Is it a tube unit?

JOHN: No, it's not a tube. It's all discrete, though. It's all Class A, so it's all transistors. There's no ICs [integrated circuits] in it. This does not sound electronic-sounding is the best way I can put it. It's very pleasing-sounding. In fact, this record we just did, everything was recorded through it. The whole record. We can't afford to have a console that's got like fifty of those in it—those are very expensive. They're a couple of thousand dollars apiece, each channel. So to have fifty inputs in the console would cost a fortune. In fact [*points to device*], that came out of a console in London. They built these consoles that became very expensive—too expensive to build anymore, because now they're all automated. So they made the consoles cheaper so they can have them automated and bigger, but they couldn't afford to make them sound like that [*points to the Neve*]. And so what people are doing is getting the consoles and they're breaking them all up into individual modules, and engineers like myself buy the modules and then do the recording through those and then do the playback through the normal computerized console.

Do you use much direct signals on records?

JOE: Oh, yeah. All the synthesizer stuff, all the bass guitar.

JOHN: Most of the clean stuff.

Would that be like the chords in "The Snake"?

JOE: Yes. That was flat direct, as a matter of fact. Preamp right into the board. Other times we'll use a Rockman. Sometimes we don't. With "Midnight" we had a version recorded with the Rockman, but we just didn't like the overall sound.

JOHN: We really try avoiding the Rockman when we can. If we can find something that sounds as good or better, we'll go with it.

Did you use an electric sitar on "Lords of Karma"?

JOE: Yeah, a Coral.

Does "The Enigmatic" have an altered harmonic minor scale?

No, it does not. The basis of the song is the enigmatic mode, which is a root, a flatted 2nd, major 3rd, raised 4th, raised 5th, raised 6th, and major 7th. I discovered that scale in a John McLaughlin book—*Birds of Fire* songbook. Years ago, I was just looking through the music store and I saw it and said, "Yeah, I like that name!"

Do you think there's an inherent mood in every key and every scale?

Not just one, no. I think in the hands of an artist, it's almost limitless what you can do. I definitely operate on that assumption, because that's why I've always adored major keys. Because I've heard so much beautiful music done in major keys, and yet very little of it is in heavy rock, exploratory jazz-fusion—whatever you want to call this sort of thing we're doing. Most of the stuff is Dorian, minor key, or else it's more "ethnic"-oriented. "Ethnic" maybe isn't the best word, but that's how it's printed up in most books. You know, like they'll call a Phrygian dominant mode a "Jewish" or "Spanish" scale. To answer that question, no, I think one scale can sound a lot of different ways, and that's one thing on the last two records I've really tried to work with, like with "Always with Me, Always with You" and "Rubina," trying to use those major scales to be tender and sharp and haunting—a whole bunch of things.

Is it the same approach with chords?

Yes, most definitely. Yeah, yeah. The fewer notes in the chords, the easier it gets. In my mind, I see the melodies and the solos and the rhythms as being in the chords. Maybe other people may think simply of the rhythm guitar part as the chord, and they write from that way. But I think in terms of, like, with "Ice 9," it's in sort of a Dorian mode, but at the end of that solo there, I just flip it around and use a major third because there's no third being played. I've just tricked you into assuming that I wasn't going to do that. And that way you can play the note. With playing with small amounts of harmonic information, you get more mileage. You get more freedom as far as writing the melody and the solos.

Do you hear melodies in your imagination before you find them on the instrument?

Yeah. It's sort of like it comes to me. I hear it as being laid out, as being pretty obvious. But I do spend quite a lot of time editing. Like for "Always with Me," I edited the hell out of that one, because it intrigued me how beautiful it was. I wanted the song to start with a melody, go into a slight improvisation, give a counter melody, go back to the original melody, do a little improvisation, go back to the melody. I wanted to be as cool as a sax player you'd see in a nice jazz club where there's a piano player, bass player, and a drummer with brushes. And this guy just stands up with his sax. He plays the melody, he does the solo, he plays the melody, and the song's over. No big rush, no ego solo, no exploding things, you know what I mean? I felt like, "Wouldn't it be great just to play the song like that?" It took me a while to get all the little subtleties down to where I felt this was natural. I had to find that sort of player in me, those sensibilities, and figure out the technique— like how do you get notes that die out when you've got a lot of sustain, a lot of gain? It was hard. We actually sat here for quite a while. We used the Pultec and maybe the GML in combination with a Marshall, the Chandler Tube Driver, and the Rockman, just to get this particular technique to work, just so if I lifted my finger off the note would die out or if I kept it there it would keep going. And we played with how loud the monitor should be as I did this playing, because it had to be one long thing that was just one statement.

Are recording solos one of the most difficult aspects of the recording process?

Sometimes yes, sometimes no. Things like "Surfing [with the Alien]" and "Ice 9" were fun, because we'd fire up the amp, we'd get a sound, we'd be excited. Boom—we'd go and it would be there, and we'd go, "Oh my God, that's great! Let's do the next one!" We'd just kind of go through. And then other times, like "Always with Me," to me, is a type of a solo that's different from the other solos in the other songs in how it's arranged. That took a lot of care. I didn't even start recording that until hours went by. I was just playing little phrases and readjusting them, getting to the point where I could do those funny things with my fingers that I can't usually do. So sometimes they come very quick—literally first takes. And other times it takes a long time to find it, and all of a sudden, bam!

Do you ever do splicing?

Splicing of solos? No. The only time we do splicing is when the two of us can't physically mix something from one part to the next, like "Circles." It was just impossible to turn off the rock band and bring in the ECM guys for the transition, or the vice versa.

Did you record the second album any differently than the first? Had experience taught you anything?

Yes! *Surfing with the Alien* was recorded with Dolby SR noise reduction, and the first record [the *Joe Satriani* EP], we didn't use any noise reduction whatsoever.

JOHN: Hell, we didn't know we were making a record when we made it!

JOE: Yeah. Joe's credit-card project—that's what it was. That's exactly what happened. I didn't actually even consider going through the humiliating process of sending it to record companies until I'd sent it to Steve [Vai], and Steve said, "I'm gonna send it to this guy Cliff Cultreri. I know he's gonna love it." So Steve sent it to Cliff, and Cliff called me back and said, "I do love it. It's really wild. I'm gonna work it out." And Cliff got together with his record company, Relativity, and we worked it out.

I have to admire that. You must have had a lot of dedication and feeling that you're going to make it to do an album on a credit card.

[*Laughs.*] It was a sign from God! I wanted to do a project, and they mailed it to me—just completely at random. "Mr. Satriani: You have been selected because of your blank, blank, blank, blank, blank." So this little light bulb went off in my head.

Have you had offers to play in a major band or is this something you'd consider doing?

It's something I would consider doing, but I really would like to bring the Joe Satriani live experience around the world once. I would really like to.

An instrumental band?

Yeah. I really would like to do that. If people are ready to see us play and just have a really good time and be very live, then I'm into doing that.

Do you feel competitive with other guitar players?

No.

Does it bother you to see less inventive players gather a lot of success? It must be hard to have that talent but not have the audience for it at the right time.

Yeah. But over the years, it seems like I see success and failure as both impostors. They cannot be what you use for your standard operating procedure—how to write music, how to play. At least for me.

What's important for you?

The songs, the music, what I'm feeling. I know that I'm not good if I'm really not into what I'm playing. If I don't believe in what I'm playing, if I'm not excited about it, I couldn't come here for twelve hours a day and be inspired.

Can you play all of your repertoire cold, or do you have to be in the right mood to play certain pieces?

Right now I'm ready to play. I've been psyched for years to do this. It really gets a bit more aggressive live, most definitely. People have told us that. Like when you saw us [at the 1987 Chicago NAMM show], it was the first or second time we ever played together. The shows in Japan were a lot better because Jonathan [Mover] and Stuart [Hamm] both had a little bit more time to see how they were gonna think about *Not of This Earth* and *Surfing with the Alien*. It was complete for these dates. When we played in Chicago and New York, the record wasn't really done. They hadn't even heard it, really. They'd just heard some rough mixes and stuff. I think live the stuff really opens up and becomes more interesting, and I'm always ready for that. It seems like I've got an enormous burst of energy when we're about to go on because I really want to get to all these songs. And they're always telling me, "Let's do this one! Yeah, let's do this one!" And it's like, "Okay, but maybe we should have rehearsed it," you know? Because we're doing it as a three-piece. If we go to do "Echo," we don't have a piano player there or a Nashville-tuned guitar to strum some of the ambient things. But Stuart is really good at covering that ground.

Can you give players suggestions for unorthodox approaches to guitar? Things they can do to open up sounds?

Yeah, yeah. One is a very practical musical way. And that is to pick something you hear on the radio that you like, perhaps just for one particular element, like if a guitar player is more of the heavy rock player but he's wondering about blues or soul or how these players feel a solo element. Get a tape recorder—get a four-track. I think this helps a lot, because we're in the age of recording. People's sounds are built around their records, not so much their live performances. They're lasting impressions. So put down a mock soul piece and retain your personality, but try to go with the track. And then pick out lots of different things. I just used those two different styles as an example. And it's similar to someone who plays B-boy music or stuff like that wanting to get involved with stuff that he hears, let's say, Ralph Towner play or maybe some thrash band or something that he's heard—Possessed or something, where the whole band is just really killing a speed groove. The thing to do is to just set up a little parameter, a little fake song, and just work on it until you find your own voice in that particular form of music. It will be at first maybe a little unusual, but eventually once you make an association with it, that's *your* approach to it. It's like—what was the old phrase?— "copping a feel," if I can use it that way. It's more of just sort of finding out how you can find a personal voice through all styles, because it's music. You have to think of it simply as music.

What advice would you give players who spend all their time on techniques? How can they get more feeling in their playing and become more distinctive? The young Yngwie clones and people like that.

Yeah. Well, on one hand I really admire anybody who puts a lot of time into practicing and comes out with such a good result. It's *really* amazing that there are guitar players like Yngwie Malmsteen and guys like him. It's really good guitar playing. It's hard to say anything negative about it, because it's just so incredible.

I meant people who spend all their time mimicking one player.

Yeah, yeah. I understand. Gee, I don't know. I've always tried to go the other way. Sometimes I think it comes down to personality—if people are open to lots of ideas, lots of different ideas and views, if they have an open mind with what comes by them in life in general and they try to keep themselves interested.

Were you raised with that?

Yes.

Was anyone in your family a musician?

My mother and my three sisters and my brother—as a matter of fact, quite a few. Except for my father, everybody. But no one took it seriously. One of my older sisters, Marion, was probably my first influence on guitar. She was a folk guitar player and singer, but it was just for fun. She played in school and stuff like that. I have three older sisters, and the oldest of the three, Joan and Carol, were schooled on piano, so there was a piano in the house and my mother can play. My brother and I were the only ones spared music lessons. By the time we came around, my parents had given up trying to force the kids to learn how to play. And so my brother and I used to sit down and we used to play something called "Constrati and orchestra," which was a little game we invented. Constrati was this ridiculous, pompous conductor. We made him up. And we would sit down and go, "Ladies and gentlemen, Constrati on piano!" And we would just bang away together on the piano.

That's as far as it went. My brother went on to play blues harp and flute and a little bit of guitar, and I stuck with the piano, but my technique was just awful. Instant tendonitis, you know, with the left hand. So I can only play bass and chords. I can't play like real keyboard players, but I know the keyboard. And guitar was just quite natural. I just fell into it because I was just completely floored by Hendrix. The first time I ever heard him on the radio, it was like a psychedelic event. And I was just a little kid, but it just seemed like the whole room was spinning when I heard the music.

Something was really different about the music.

Yeah. Yeah, all at once. It was wonderful. He was one of those guys who, from song to song, would change his guitar sound or change direction. Those first two records were very radical in terms of how eclectic they were, and the variety. It was great. It was such a great stroke for a new type of technique. I'm sure guys like Harry Partch must have loved Hendrix.

Harry Partch?

Harry Partch is an experimental composer and instrument builder of this century. I think he's dead now. Harry thought that our system of music was just awful. It was a prison, and getting people to practice was the worst thing that you could ever do—it crushed all forms of human expression through music. So he went about building a lot of instruments and writing his own way. And when Hendrix came along—if you look at all the other guitar players who had come up, let's say, for twenty years up until him, all these really smoking jazz guys—very few of them touched me. Wes Montgomery, to me, was *perfect*. The first time I ever heard him, it was like I needed no convincing, no introduction. My mother and father used to play these records, and I said, "I love this! What's this guy doing? It's beautiful!" And Hendrix, to me, sounded exactly the same way. It was like he took all the technique out and he said, "Man, I'm just gonna play the way that it comes." I don't know these guys, so I don't know what they went through, but as a listener, it just hit me as so natural and so off the wall and so anti-technique that I loved it. It sort of gets back to your question about the people who may try to sound like Yngwie Malmsteen. Yngwie is Yngwie. I mean, Yngwie is a person, and his personality drives him to sound the way he does, to write the kind of music he does. That's what's so great about him—when you put on an Yngwie record, you get *Yngwie*, and it's great. It [copying Yngwie] is pointless. It would be almost as if upon hearing Hendrix I decided that I'm gonna become Hendrix—it's a dead end.

Were you playing guitar at the time you first heard Hendrix?

No. I was playing drums. I played drums and then I quit music for about a year. I decided to start playing when Hendrix died. I actually quit the football team the same day, which was great because I was a lousy player—a little guy, destined to be destroyed! [*Laughs.*] It was a great excuse, a great time.

So you decided on September 18, 1970.

Yeah. A lot of people did. I've found so many people who just made the decision like [*snaps fingers*]. I knew: "That's it. I've had it now. If there isn't that one guy left in the world to make me feel alright, then I've got to do something about it." That's what it felt like to me.

Were you inspired from the beginning to find your own way?

Yes! I think my parents encouraged my brother and my sisters all to be individual as much as possible. To seek out what it is you want to do and don't give up no matter what.

What effect did your teacher Bill Westcott have?

Tremendous.

Did he come along in your life right when you started playing?

Before. It must have been before. Oh, I was a snotty little kid. In high school I gave him a hard time. I think he had just come to Carle Place High School in Long Island. I quit the first year of music theory—I believe it was ninth grade or something. I just couldn't sit still. I just couldn't. I said, "What is this stuff you're playing for me? What does this mean?!" I think I was there for three days and I said, "This isn't for me, bud." I stayed in the chorus, how-ever, singing in the chorus, because I did enjoy singing. It made no sense, because I was wearing big motorcycle boots and beat-up denims and a big floppy hat and I had hair that was way too long. But I liked singing in the chorus and I had a good time doing that, but I couldn't sit still for his theory class.

The next year, though, I sat through it. He is an amazing teacher because of what he was able to transfer to me as far as feeling about music goes. And at the same time, he taught me, hands down, all the theory that there is—how to read, what's music theory, what modes sound like. He brought to my attention Harry Partch, the best of Bartók and Erik Satie and Chopin and Handel, everybody. And he could sit down and play it. But when he played it, he'd look at you. You'd sit next to him and he'd get into it. And that's what was great: you could be with him and you'd see him get into it and you could feel him get into what he was doing. To me, it was like, "*That's* how you play!" I never played piano like Bill, but he said you could *feel* this way about music, you can write this way. He said early on, "You know, Joe, it may turn out that you're not really gifted on the guitar, but don't let it stop you from writing and imagining whatever it is you want." And so he would introduce techniques, mental ways of approaching writing or just getting out pieces of paper and writing total nonsense, putting it away, and picking it up the next day and reading it and then fixing it. It was a way of second-guessing yourself or surprising yourself with things. He was just Mr. Inspiration. And plus he taught me all there is to know to get 90s in band theory and pass the Regents exam in New York and feel very confident—to the point where when I got to music college, there was no point, absolutely no point, in being there.

What did Lennie Tristano give you?

Oh, wow. He was another guy that was great just to be next to because he was so intense. What Lennie showed me was that technique was not music. But when you're practicing technique, don't fool around. You just do it right or you're doing it wrong. And don't play things until you're ready to play them. And if you play it and you make a mistake, it's because you weren't ready to play it and you shouldn't have played it in the first place.

Did timing come naturally for you or did you have to teach yourself?

I taught myself, I'm sure. I think timing is natural, but I think you have to practice it. You have to work it to convince yourself that it's there so you can find it. When I was a young kid listening to the Beatles and the Stones or something, I didn't say, "Boy, you know, he could have played groups of five there." I wasn't thinking about that. But once you get exposed to it and a knowledgeable person says, "You can feel groups of five and you'll like it and you may use it with discretion and taste." Timing comes later. Plus, I've learned a lot from other people's timing, like the timing of Hendrix or the timing of Stevie Wonder or Larry Graham, who I'm copying right there [*indicates "The Crush of Love," which is playing over the studio speakers*] for this Sly Stone groove. You go back and you listen and you say, "Yeah. They're late here and they're early here, and that creates a sound. Some people push the beat when they're creating this kind of a song. Some people drag, some people are right in the pocket." I think as you get better with your sense of time, the idea of a beat, instead of being a little dot, becomes this huge circle or this line—however you want to look at it. But it's a big thing, and you see that you can play with it and you can use that as a tool to get a song to come off a certain way, to evoke a certain emotion—especially with bass.

How long have you been playing bass?

About as long as I've been playing guitar, but it's a casual thing. I did teach bass for a while, but I always told my students, "There will be a time very soon where you will be as competent as myself, and I urge you to move on to a real bass player." But I have found very few good bass players who are really good teachers who teach steady. I don't know why. I think it's the nature of the instrument and how it's used in the music world. To be a guitar player, you really have to work on being exceptional to be popular. Being a

JOE SATRIANI

269

bass player, you just have to be really good. You have to be solid, and you'll work forever. So as a result, it would appear on the surface that there isn't much to learn. I would disagree with that, because I know the difference between myself playing a groove perfectly and someone like Stu Hamm playing it perfectly—it's something I can't even come close to. He has it. He is bass incarnate. And certain bass players are like that, and if I was a serious bass player, I'd find those people. I'd hang around with those people and I'd take lessons, just to kind of absorb what it is that makes them *think* so bass-like and always find the right place to be.

At what point in your development did you start giving guitar lessons?

Very early. Steve was one of my first students. I'd been playing only a few years, although I've only taught a few people. Steve, his friend, maybe two other friends, something like that.

Some of your music seems to have its closest equivalent in some of Steve Vai's Flex-Able *material.*

Yeah. We share a certain sense of the absurd, I guess. And then at the same time, some of the most tender things I've ever heard out of any guitar player have been some of Steve's playing. That energy, that intensity, can go in any direction. It's frightening. He keeps getting more and more amazing. [*Laughs.*] He's great!

Where was Steve at as a player when you met him?

He was a complete beginner. Guitar in one hand, no strings, and a pack of strings in the other. [*Laughs.*]

By the time he left, where was he?

By his last lesson, he was doing things that I wasn't doing. And I'm sure he could play as fast as I could. And at the time, I was on this campaign just not to play fast anymore. I had just gotten so sick of it.

Was he doing a lot of whammy by then?

Yeah. We had gone crazy with the whammy. He was getting into the whammy a lot, and he was doing two-handed stuff. Our lessons were long. You know, the last lessons were just these long jams because he'd developed so quickly into a confident player and a really good improviser. He could just sit there in a room, and before you know it, we'd be playing, and before you know it an hour would go by and we'd have gone through all these things.

Did he strike you as being a special musician?

Right away.

What was it?

His ability to hear notes to tune his guitar, his choice of music, and his personality. He was just completely honest and straightforward. And he was just a little kid. I mean, I was a young guy, but he was really little compared to me. I think he was like fourteen or something—that's pretty young.

He has an amazing mind.

He does! He does. And it seemed to me that was there. Because he would bring in music or I would play him something, and I would think to myself, "Oh, I just played this for some other kid, and it went right over his head." Steve would hear *exactly* what it was that I wanted him to hear, and he'd say, "Wow! This part is great," or, "This thing they're doing . . ." Or he'd come up with a question that was *the* perfect question, that was the reason why I put the record on in the first place.

Did a lot of kids come in with parts they wanted to know from Van Halen or whomever?

Back then, definitely not, because it was the early '70s. Steve—what was he into? Bad Company, Kiss, Bachman-Turner Overdrive, Hendrix, Led Zeppelin, of course—all that stuff. I had lots of strange records. I think I played Zappa a few times, and then he slowly got into Zappa—or quickly, I don't know, but it seemed like all of a sudden he was really *hearing* something.

Would you slow down records to hear parts?

No, I couldn't do that on my deck. I never had the ability to do that. Bill Westcott trained my ear and taught me how to complete the training by just singing scales.

Why don't you sing on records?

Listen to this. [*As Joe said this, the solo on "The Crush of Love" came over the studio speaker.*] I can't sing as good as that. You know what I mean? To me, that's a voice. When I go to open my mouth, I've got to convince myself. Like John says, if it's not right, I just freak out. It may take me a while to write the kind of songs that I think I can do justice to with the vocals.

Were you experimenting with finger taps before Van Halen came along?

Sure! Oh, there were a lot of people who were. A lot of people. Yeah. But I'm a huge Van Halen fan. When I first heard their first record, I just loved it. I just love that thing! I thought, "Wow! This is great." It was sort of like saying, "This is *exactly* what I wanted to hear that I haven't heard."

The sound of that record when you first heard it was amazing. No one had a sound like that.

And he put together that little double hammer-on thing, two-handed thing in such a great way.

"Eruption"?

Yeah. It was so gutsy. It wasn't progressive rock. It was really like a go-for-the-throat kind of thing.

He could make a song like "You Really Got Me" sound brand new.

Yeah. Really great. As a matter of fact, all of their records I find really special. He always does something. I find their records to be unusual—the way they do the drums, and how he uses some of the guitar and bass sounds and stuff like that. I *really* like that. I think that he must be definitely crazy, and I like that. And they must try unusual things that people must have said, "No, you can't do that," and they went ahead with it anyway. [*Laughs.*]

Do you ever play acoustic guitar?

Yeah, I do, although I've never owned one that I've been very happy with. They've all been nightmares with their intonation. And they always seem to be completely unbalanced as far as low-end, high-end. And then I don't get the range I like. I have so many complaints about it, but when I hear other people play their kind of music, I love it. Who that's guy that was on your cover a while ago?

Michael Hedges?

Yeah. Amazing. Amazing sound he gets out of that. It would take me years to get that kind of power.

What do you do when you practice?

Most recently it's been with specific things. When you start doing records, you wind up with deadlines. You come up with a great idea and you say, "I've got to practice this because I want it to be killing so I can put it on this record by such-and-such a date." And so sometimes I'll play one one-minute piece for eight hours a day every day. I won't play anything else. Other times I'll only play rhythm and the bass and fool around with the synthesizer or drum machine, just because I'm thinking about music. Sometimes I'll put down the guitar and I just won't play it because I'm being too repetitive with myself or angry with myself for being so stubborn, for not moving on. I'll just say, "Okay, I'm just not gonna play it then." And then I'll pick it up and I'll hear something that I didn't hear before and it'll go on. And then other times it's just non-stop and Rubina will have to come and say, "You better stop playing. You're playing too much."

Do melodies ever come to you at odd times, such as when you're sleeping or without an instrument?

Yes. Most definitely. I've had songs come to me in the middle of guitar lessons, in the shower. I've had them come to me in dreams.

Do you write them down?

Yeah. There's a song called "Saying Goodbye" that I knew what I wanted to write, but I didn't know what it was as far as melody. And I've never been able to do this—so it's not any kind of special Joe power or anything—but I just said, "I'm going to dream this. I'm going to go to sleep with the idea that

I'm going to wake up and play it." Sure enough, I woke up the next day, and there it was. I just got right up out of bed, went to the guitar, and wrote this thing down.

You have to be in sync with your spirit to do that.

I think so, yeah. It's been rare with me that I've been able to do that with sleeping. Usually dreams are really bizarre. I'll write from them, but they're not musical dreams.

Do you have to do anything special to protect or engender your creativity? Are there sacrifices involved?

Yeah. Yeah. I probably seem like a recluse or an eccentric to some people at certain times. And then they wonder why at other times I'm suddenly not a recluse anymore. So I guess that's just because when I put my mind to something, that's the only thing that I'm gonna do. And if it's a song, I will stay in and I'll do nothing but play the song over and over again for hours and hours a day. I will disregard time frames of night and day—you know, "Now is when you get up and eat lunch" or something like that. I'll just forget about that whole thing, and I'll just operate on my own schedule. When you do that, of course, you can't go out with people. You do different things. And so when you say, "No. I'm staying home and listening to a tape," they say, "Well, listen to it when you get back or in the car." They don't understand. It's got to be under strange circumstances. They don't realize that I play things in multiple speeds and I change things. I will listen to a song and watch any TV program and every commercial go back and listen to the song. Sometimes I'll just listen to it once. Other times I'll listen to it for three hours and go back. I just need the freedom not to be bothered.

CODA: In 2015, Joe Satriani wrote his recollections of this interview: "It was Jas Obrecht who first contacted me about doing an interview. I was still giving lessons at Second Hand Guitars in Berkeley and recording solo guitar music at night. The interview experience was so exciting because the journalist asked all the cool questions. They don't do that anymore. When *GP* put me on the cover and had my new song 'The Crush of Love' inside on the Soundpage, it had an enormously positive effect on my career. The song went on to become a radio hit for me, and *GP* can take credit for 'breaking it'!"[3] Today, Joe Satriani retains his position as one of America's foremost rock guitarists. He's received fifteen Grammy Award nominations, and in 2014 he published the autobiographical *Strange Beautiful Music: A Musical Memoir* (BenBella Books).

Ben Harper in San Francisco, May 3, 1994. (Jay Blakesberg)

With his 1994 debut album, *Welcome to the Cruel World*, Ben Harper revealed himself to be both a forward-looking singer/songwriter and a passionate advocate for roots American music from the era of 78s and wind-up Victrolas. For starters, he conjured his lonesome, overtone-laden slide sound on a Style 4 Hawaiian koa guitar built by Hermann Weissenborn during the 1920s. His playing technique, with the guitar held flat on his lap, harkened to the Hawaiian musicians of the early twentieth century and the very first recordings of blues guitar.

With slide songs such as "Whipping Boy," Harper seemed to conjure the spirit of Blind Willie Johnson, whom he readily acknowledged as his primary musical inspiration: "That's it," Ben confirmed when I asked him about it soon after the album's release. "When I'm sleeping, I hear Blind Willie Johnson. I hear him all the time. My other heroes are Blind Willie McTell, Robert Johnson, Taj Mahal, Lowell George—oh, man!—and Chris Darrow, who played with David Lindley. And even great rhythm players, like Bob Marley, with his chunk rhythm heartbeat, and Jimi Hendrix—God, all day, you know?"[1]

Born in 1969, Ben grew up surrounded by music. His family owned the Folk Music Center, a music store in Claremont, California, and his grandparents weaned him on their collection of blues 78s. After some musical experimentation, at age sixteen he found the technique that suited him best. "I found I was able to express myself on slide guitar," he recalled. "I started playing bottleneck a lot—I still do—but the attack and the sound I was trying to attain used a different musical formation, so I switched to playing lap-style."[2] He invented his own tunings. Before signing with Virgin Records, Ben sharpened his playing in Taj Mahal's road band.

In our 1994 interview, Ben was guarded about his recording techniques and the open tunings he used for slide. This was not the case when we had our next interview, on June 5, 1997. At the time of this conversation, he was celebrating the release of his third album, *The Will to Live*.

You have an uplifting message in a lot of your music.

Thank you for feeling that. It's nice to be behind the guitar in that spirit.

To me, a song like "Homeless Child" has everything that made "Rollin' and Tumblin'" great.

Ah, bless your heart!

I hear it coming out of that spirit of "get in the trance and ride that lick as far as you can" kind of music, especially with that jangly background rhythm.

It's almost like that old Eddie Head music, "Lord, I'm the True Vine," and those other songs from the 1930s.

Absolutely. You know how hard it is to bring something new to roots blues. I mean, what's brought to blues and the spirit of blues today is really nothing but barroom. And the barroom blues, for me, just doesn't move my heart. And so it's been a huge challenge and it's the first time I feel strongly that I'm bringing a contribution to the blues. And I hope I have done the spirit of roots blues music justice through that song. I mean, I write a lot of blues songs and Jas, I gotta tell you: I put 'em away. They haven't been strong enough and I just set them aside and I use the lyrics from the blues songs for other songs and things. And I feel privileged to have written a song that, from your words, reaffirms my feeling of *contributing* to that spirit and not taking from it.

That song of yours "I Want to Be Ready" sounds even older, like it could have been a Southern spiritual before the Civil War.

Yeah.

Where did that song come from?

It just came into my mind. And, you know, around the house there was a lot of roots gospel music played, because of my family and how much they love roots and gospel music. And "I Want to Be Ready" and "Long White Robe," they've been used in early Delta blues and gospel music phrases that are maybe not exactly that, but in that vein. And it's from that tradition—directly. Definitely. "I want to be ready to wear my robe" or "my long white robe"—that type of lyrical usage as far as life's redemption to a higher level of existence after life. I mean, that's used as a reference in gospel music constantly. It was something I felt and wrote the song at once—it came at one time: "How I am strong just to know what makes me weak, how I am found just to know just whom I seek." It just came out.

Did "Homeless Child" evolve over time?

The first two verses of "Homeless Child" and that lick—that came straight up. And then the last verse just came later. And it just came in one *wow*!

There's a certain sense of melancholy in a number of your songs. I wonder if you feel some spiritual link or subconscious connection to people from the past who've been oppressed.

When you feel your ancestral heritage, you feel it whether you're conscious of it or unconscious of it, whether you act upon it or not. I feel that strong. That's a large part of my expression.

Do you feel it when you pick up an instrument?

Every time! When I pick up an instrument, for me, I go somewhere. You know what I mean? I go somewhere it takes me. I can't say where. I don't even want to know where. And then I try to bring the people with me to where it trips me out to. Then it's a good show.

You have some wonderful old instruments. Have you ever intuitively felt something about the previous owner or felt anything about the kind of music the instrument may have played fifty or sixty years ago?

Definitely, definitely. Oh, yeah. You pick it up and every instrument speaks in its own voice, which is why every instrument has an infinite [amount] of songs within it. Every instrument! And it's to that player to tap into that inspiration of the instrument itself. And that comes from the instrument itself, it comes from the maker, it comes from previous players. Sure. That's why sometimes when you get a new guitar with old strings, you don't want to change them real quick because you don't know what songs are in those strings. I mean, I'm so drastic, Jas, that even pens have songs in them. If I have a pen and it doesn't write a song in a week, I throw it away.

That's amazing!

Yeah. I don't mess around with this stuff, man.

What engenders your songwriting? What's the kind of condition where it's most likely to occur?

There's no condition but life's condition. You know, people say, "Oh, I gotta be around the house. I gotta be at home and comfortable." Man, you get to the house, the phone's always ringing, take out the trash, blah blah blah. Music is inspiration is eternal. Inspiration doesn't stop for man, man has to catch up with inspiration and keep up with inspiration, because it's always moving.

Had you played much standard steel-string guitar?

Yeah, I woodshedded on bottleneck—for years, hours a day. Just hours and hours, to where morning would turn to night. And I did that for years, man. For years! From the time I was eighteen to twenty—two years, just playing and really trying to learn Robert Johnson tunes. Breaking strings, because I didn't know Robert played slide with a capo. So I was trying to tune the strings way up. Oh, it was a mess. And Mississippi John Hurt—of course, Elizabeth Cotten—and just working those songs out. Because once that music hit me when I was at a conscious level of age—when you're fourteen, fifteen, sixteen, seventeen, when you're in your teens, you listen to things differently. And so when I was at an age where I was opening up musically, Mississippi John Hurt just hit me like a truck. And at that point, that was something I *had* to play and be a part of. I woodshedded eighteen, nineteen, twenty, and Taj called me up. He had heard me play and said, "Man, come on the road with me." And I went on the road with Taj for a while, and that was great. And then I really started getting into my own things.

Then lyrical inspiration came and I started writing, and that's when I started making records.

Is there anything you've learned making the second and third album that you wished you knew when you made the first record?

I have to say no, because the only way you learn to make records is by making records. And I feel now more than ever I am able to make the studio as musical as an instrument itself. And that's with the help of my producer and dear friend, J. P. Plunier. He and I produced the first two records together. But you know what, man? He has shown me stronger than anyone how to get out of my own way for the first two records—not that I was in my own way, but I needed to learn about production for those records. But for this record, it took every drop of my blood sweat to get this record to where it is. I mean, realize, Jas, like on "Faded" and on "Will to Live," you're hearing an acoustic Weissenborn run through a Groove Tube Solo 150-watt and a 4x10 Marshall with an Expandora together with an Ibanez Tube Screamer. And, man, it has taken me *years* of experimentation to get to *that* sound. Also run through the Sunrise 12. I go through those pedals, and you lose a little bit of the line signal from those pedals. But then I go into the Sunrise 12—not the tube preamp, but the 12 dB—and then I go into the amp.

This is with an ancient Weissenborn?

This is with a Weissenborn, man.

I've never heard of anyone doing something like that.

Oh. And to come out on the positive end of that experimentation is overwhelmingly positive for me.

It's such a big, angry sound.

And you can tell. People say, "Oh, Ben Harper has gone electric!" No. It sounds it, but you can tell it's not a Tele, it's not a Strat, it's not one of the Rickenbackers. You can tell it has its own thing—I hope! I hope that its own sound is coming through.

I was wondering if it might be a lap steel.

No, no. It's a Weissenborn with a Sunrise, run through those effects.

Then the sound in the guitar's acoustic body must be driving a lot of the distortion.

Well, the Sunrise picks up the movement of the top and the air from the sound hole, and so it's still acoustic, yet it's run through that different chain.

Did you use the same setup on something cut at lower volume, like "Homeless Child"?

"Homeless Child" was straight acoustic. No, no. What we did on that—see, we always run the amp in a separate room, so it's isolated. And then we run a clean send from the pickup itself to the board, and then we mike it in the sweet spot. And so we have three channels to either combine into one or pick whichever one fits the song best. And so that's a combination of a Fender Champ amp—a '58 Champ, tweed—and a mike sound.

To my ears, it sounds like that track was recorded about 1952.

Amen! And then we ran the whole track back through the Champ, and then miked the Champ and mastered it from there. Sounds like a damn 78, doesn't it?

Yeah, it does.

I'm so glad to hear you say that, man. And that was J. P.'s masterpiece. He just came up some incredible ideas. And that's where we come full circle. I had to get out of my own way so I could focus on the playing and the singing and step it up to another level, and not have to think about different ideas and running behind and saying, "Was that a good take?" No. I had to just say, "Hey, man, it's on you. Tell me what's best." It took everything I had to just concentrate on the music itself.

Isn't it great to give it up?

Oh, it's so great! God.

There are so many players I wish would do that.

Yeah, yeah. Man, I'm so glad you recognize that too. But thank you for saying so, because it's a big step for me.

Hearing you play nylon-string classical guitar is a treat. I don't associate you with that at all.

What song is that on?

There's a break in the middle of "Faded."

You know who that is? It's gonna blow you away, and Jas, you gotta cover this guy. You've got to do a specific article on him, because he's a genius. On "Jah Work," the guitar playing is done by Al Anderson, [Bob] Marley's first guitarist. From *Natty Dread* on, that's Al Anderson. And he's just a wealth of reggae music knowledge. From Ernest Ranglin, he revolutionized. He took it another step and brought blues into reggae music. I don't play skank. I don't play reggae guitar. So I had to call. Al's just been down with the music and the lyrics, and he's been coming to shows. And I called him up, said, "Man, 'Jah Work Is Never Done.' Who better to pay on 'Jah Work Is Never Done' than Bob Marley's guitar player?" And he also played that nylon blues guitar in the breakdown, and he and I played together. I played Turkish saz—it sort of sounds like a twelve-string. In "Jah Work" Al was on a small-bodied Guild twelve-string and a Gibson G-2 [Gibson LG-2 acoustic]. He's a genius. And the thing is, he heard the song maybe twice, if not once—I don't know if he rewound the rough mix—and he just went in and *dropped it*. He's a genius, man. You gotta talk to Al.

It must have brought a great vibe to the session.

Didn't it? And then the stuff he laid down on "Faded," I played saz while he played a ninety-dollar nylon-string Prelude guitar. Good mike—had a good mike on it.

I've been telling people for a long time: It's in the hands. It ain't in the instrument.

Proof there!

Were there other guests guitarists, or did you do the rest of it?

I did the rest of it. Just Al.

What's the secret for getting that beautiful, crisp, immaculate sound of an acoustic rhythm guitar?

It's found in patience and in the instrument itself. Well, it starts in the instrument itself, but great-sounding instruments don't always go to tape easily. I thank mighty God I have had the pleasure of being able now to try different [techniques]. At the same time, it's easy to say about early Robert Johnson, those guys, "Oh, they didn't care about what mike," but you know what? Those old roots cats who were recording for RCA, they were geniuses too. And they had a selection of mikes. In the early Columbia Blind Willie Johnson stuff—those guys weren't joking around. They probably tried six different mikes before the one that was right for Blind Willie's sound came up.

With Blind Willie McTell, you can hear the differences from session to session day to day.

Totally. Can't you, though?

Or you can imagine where he was positioned in the room at different times.

Or certain rooms have a certain life. You don't want to record guitars in a certain room for a certain song—and that's how drastic it gets. Every instrument, different guitars, sound different in different rooms. And you've got to be sensitive to that kind of thing to give the song its strongest voice.

What's your favorite room to play in? Do you have one?

Yeah. My favorite room to play in is the room at Grandmaster Studios. It's on Cahuenga, just north of Sunset [in Hollywood]. That's where we recorded *Fight for Your Mind* and *The Will to Live*. And it's the wood room there. The guy started building the studio at the front door and tuned it all the way in to the recording room, and it is just a *beautiful* room. Allen Dixon owns it. Black Crowes—*Shake Your Money Maker*, that was recorded there in that room. It's just a great room. It's a real magic room. If you're ever in L.A. and we time it right where I'm there, I am bringing you through there first thing. You'll know what I mean when we walk in the door and you start talking in the room. You just get a chill.

Keith Richards told me that he can walk into a studio room, snap his fingers, and know right away if it's going to be good or not.

Yeah. You just know. Ah, Keith. Man, thank God Keith is still around making music.

Listening to "Ashes" and "Widow of a Living Man," it sounds like you have a very light attack on acoustic.

Yeah, I like to take it easy when it's time to take it easy. I think that you have to respect the lyrics and the guitar work. It takes a gentle, gentle brushing of the guitar. A lot of people, especially people in the folk tradition, man, they want to just get on there and just hammer away. It's insulting to the instrument and to the song. You really gotta take it easy.

Isn't it tougher to record at such a quiet volume?

Ah, man! People say, "It must be hard to record those fast slide licks and things," but it's harder, because those were all recorded vocal-guitar at once. And it's a challenge to get that right feeling at that right moment. The softer songs are *way* harder to record than the band ones. They're much more delicate.

If you're recording guitar and voice at the same time, what's the best mike to be singing into? Does it matter?

You know what? It could be a really cheap old RCA mike, or even a cheap beta—you know, a Shure—or it could be a C-12 or a U-47. Tube or solid-state. It just depends on the tune and the sound you're going for.

Do you always play fingerstyle?

Yeah. I don't use picks. I have—I used picks on the songs "Welcome to the Cruel World" and "Give a Man a Home," but my thumb, thank goodness, is blistered to a rock. So I can sting the string like Albert King.

What did you use for the solo on "Glory and Consequence"?

I gotta tell you. For the basic track, it's that same Guild twelve-string on "Jah Work" and "Roses." I think that's over on the left side [of the mix]. And then it's the Gibson G-2 sunburst for the rhythm acoustic track, and then it was done. The song was done. And then J. P. said, "Man, you gotta try electric guitar on this song." J. P. has a '63 Tele, cream, and I have a '58 Twin, which I like to run for recording. I won't take it on the road, but I like to record with that, the high-powered Twin tweed. That's on the solo for "Will to Live." He brought it in to the studio to play during break time—he'd go in and play the Tele when we'd take breaks. And he said, "You gotta try electric on this song. I think it would work." I said, "J. P., man, you know I'm not a solidbody player. I like to mess around." He said, "Just try it." I said, "Nope." He said, "For me. Please." I said, "Alright, man. I plugged it into the high-powered

Twin '58—boom. "We're gonna roll tape." I said, "Alright, man. I'll throw the headphone on." I threw the headphones on, I took one pass all the way down the song, and that was it. That's what's on tape. That's how Ben plays the electric guitar. And then I put it up. I said, "Okay. I'm not doing it again."

Who did the wah-wah in "Mama's Trippin'"?

That's me. That's a Gibson G-2 acoustic with a Vox wah-wah. [*Both of us laugh.*] Isn't that a trip?

It's funny, the stuff you came up with.

[*Laughs.*] It's crazy! I'm having so much fun with this stuff.

What are your main tunings now?

My main tuning is DADDAD—"dad dad." And I'll go a whole-step below that and a whole-step above that.

What's the advantage of playing in that tuning?

It just opens up all kinds of chord possibilities and single-note lead possibilities. It's just endless. It opens me up to be able to play pretty much anything on the slide guitar. You can go all the way up the neck and have a workable open chord. And it also works as a really cool drone when necessary.

It has a beautiful sound.

Thank you.

Is that the tuning we hear on the record a lot?

Yeah, definitely. Definitely.

Is there backwards guitar on The Will to Live? *Sometimes you have a strange attack.*

On "Roses from My Friends," it's eight to ten backwards slide guitar tracks on the intro. And backwards slide is a trip! It falls so different than fretted backwards guitar because it's almost like playing backwards cello or something.

The attack is so bizarre.

Yeah, and it lands in such a strange place. But finding the place where it finally drops and works is such a joy. In the solo section on "Roses from My Friends," it's backwards slide guitar, backwards [Fender] Rhodes [electric piano], and then a bed of forwards Rhodes. And then on "Will to Live" it's just one solo from beginning to end—you know, of the solo section—and there's a drone that I do on the low string at the twelfth fret on the teardrop Weissenborn. It's a feedback, and I adjust the volume pedal during the drone, so it takes off into a higher feedback and then lower as I push forward or lessen the thrust of the power through the chord. I did that twice and panned it, and then took the solo over it. So there's a drone all the while behind the solo. And that had a great effect, I think. I'm really happy with the way that effect came out for that song.

I like how the music works as an entire album—the journey it takes.

Oh, good, good. Because we spent so much time sequencing the record. I mean, some people, I guess, maybe just throw a record together. We take a *lot* of time—months, really—getting the order of the songs. Not only the order, but the space between the tunes too.

Are all Weissenborns good-sounding instruments, or do you have to look for one?

I'll tell you what: all Weissenborns are good-sounding instruments. I've never heard a dog, Jas. Ever. Ever! Even the ones with loose ribs. Even the ones with no ribs! They *all* sound amazing. Not all the remakes do, but all the Weissen ones do.

Have you acquired any extras in the last couple of years?

Yeah. I've gotten a nice collection together of Konas and Weissenborns.

Does any particular one stand out?

The teardrop. Because, man, the teardrop can sound like the hourglass-shape. The teardrop can sound like a National or a Dobro. Dobros and Nationals run and hide when the teardrop comes out. They just duck.

What songs have come out of that one?

It's my main writing slide guitar. I've had this one for six years.

Do you know what year it was made?

I believe early '20s.

When you hit the stage, do you have a mission beyond playing well?

[*Long pause.*] If I play well, all other missions that I may have, conscious or unconscious, are fulfilled.

When are you happiest?

When my sound is together and the shows go strong.

Have any musicians given you valuable advice?

John Lee Hooker's magic words, the first time I ever met him—at the Sweetwater, opening up—he said [*imitates Hooker*], "Man, I like your slide playing. You wanna be a great guitar player? Do you wanna?" "Heck, yeah, man!" He said, "Well, man, you gotta take all them notes you're playin' and play *half* as many. And you'll be gettin' somewhere." Well, Jesus Christ, that's the best damn advice, and I took it to heart, man. Isn't that something? "Play half as many"!

CODA: As of 2016, Ben Harper has released a dozen studio albums. His 2004 release *There Will Be a Light* brought him Grammy Awards for Best Traditional Soul Gospel Album and for Best Pop Instrumental Performance. Issued by Stax Records, his 2013 collaboration with harmonica ace Charlie Musselwhite, *Get Up!*, earned him another Grammy for Best Blues Album.

First and foremost, my appreciation goes to the guitarists whose interviews appear in this book. Your music has enriched us all, your words continue to inspire. I also give thanks to the loved ones of those who have gone before us: Duane Allman, Clarence "Gatemouth" Brown, Jerry Garcia, James Gurley, Barney Kessel, Nick Lucas, Rick Nelson, Roebuck "Pops" Staples, Stevie Ray Vaughan, and Johnny Winter.

I thank Jon Sievert, my companion on many of these interviews, and Jay Blakesberg for allowing me to use their wonderful photographs. Dick Spottswood generously shared his research on the earliest American guitar recordings and fact-checked the "Guitarchaeology" chapter. Lynn Wheelwright, an expert on the early evolution of the electric guitar, also provided valuable details. Their astute edits greatly improved this section of the manuscript, as did the suggestions of Tom Wheeler, author of several enduring books on American guitar history. Kudos to the UC Santa Barbara Library for their online Discography of American Historical Recordings, and to the Library of Congress for making available many historical guitar recordings.

The insights of many others have informed and bettered these pages: Galadrielle Allman, Sam Andrew, Jeff Baxter, John Burks, Walter Carter, John Cuniberti, Eddie Durham, David Evans, Leonard Feather, Tony Glover, Wayne Goins, Benny Goodman, Tim Gracyk, George Gruhn, John Hammond, George Kanahele, Rich Kienzle, John and Twiggs Lyndon, Barry Melton, Steve Morse, Opal Louis Nations, Les Paul, John Renbourn, Malcolm Rockwell, James Rooney, Steve Rosen, James Sallis, Larry Sepulvado, Eldon Shamblin, Joel A. Siegel, Mavis Staples, George Van Eps, Bob Weir, Jerry Wexler, and Joel Whitburn. Over the decades, dozens of publicists, artist managers, record company executives, and booking agents helped make these interviews happen. A big thanks to you all, with a special shout-out to Cary Baker, Mike Kappus, Dennis McNally, Bob Merlis, Joe Priesnitz, Elliot Roberts, and Teddy Slatus.

I salute my colleagues during the early years of guitar journalism: the staff of GPI Publications, especially Don Menn, who gave me my start as a music journalist; Jim Crockett, the visionary publisher of *Guitar Player* and *Frets* magazines; and my friends and fellow staffers Jim Aikin, David Alzofon, Janine Cooper Ayers, Tom Brislane, Carla Carlberg, Tom Darter, Bud and Maxine Eastman, Rick Eberly, Andy Ellis, Judie Eremo, Clara and Rebecca Erickson, Dan Erlewine, Jim Ferguson, Dan Forte, Dennis and Cheryl Fullerton, Lonni Elrod Gauss, Chris Gill, Joe Gore, Jesse Gress, Jim and Terri Hatlo, Saroyan Humphrey, Richard Johnston, Chris and Liz Ledgerwood, Rich Leeds, David Leishman, John Lescroart, Kyle Kevorkian McCann, Dominic Milano, Tom Mulhern, Matt Resnicoff, James Rotondi, Jim Schwartz, Peggy

Shea, Jon Sievert, Roger Siminoff, Sherry Thomas-Zon, Tom Wheeler, and Bill Yaryan. I thank Jim O'Neal and Amy van Singel, the cofounding editors of *Living Blues* magazine, and Jann Wenner, Ben Fong-Torres, Dave Marsh, and other first-generation editors at *Rolling Stone*. Your interviewing excellence provided enduring inspiration. I am also grateful to the current *Guitar Player* staff, especially Michael Molenda, Art Thompson, and Matt Blackett.

I send my thanks and love to those who nurtured, taught, and inspired me during the years in which most of the interviews in this book took place: Jason Becker, Paul Burlison, Brian Carroll, Craig Chaquico, Rory Gallagher, Billy Gibbons, Arvella Gray, Stefan Grossman, Buddy Guy, James "Al" Hendrix, Troy Leo Hendrix, Bonita Hertz, Steve Hilla, Mitch Holder, John Lee Hooker, Paul Hostetter, Matthew Kallie, Nina Dagostini Kasbow, Jorma Kaukonen, Phil Keaggy, B. B. King, Donald Kinsey, Peter Redvers Lee, Alan Lomax, Steve Lukather, Jim Marshall, Curtis Mayfield, Maureen Nesta Meek, Elmer and Margaret Pitcher, Michael Pitcher, Keith Richards, Howard Roberts, Rebecca Roper, George and Marie Staley, David Swaddell, Tommy Tedesco, Liz Tihista, Larry Townsend, Barbara Tyler, Steve Vai, Joe Walsh, Gayle Dean Wardlow, and Leslie West. I send a smile of appreciation to my friends and fellow writers who supported and encouraged me as I worked on the manuscript: Jessica Bibbee, Marco Bruschtein, Rosalie Denenfeld, Ira Fried, Mike Gentry, Roger Gonda, David Horowitz, Rod Johnson, Janet Kavanagh, Carrie Krantz, Diane Laboda, Teresa DeRuntz Leonard, Pauline Lowenhardt, Michael Moriarty, Nancy Nelson, Richard Rae, Helena Solano, Dave Solo, Lori Tucker-Sullivan, Jessica Wynn, and Tom Zimmerman. You've been pals!

This book would not have happened without the help of three fine gentlemen from the University of North Carolina at Chapel Hill: my friend, mentor, and folklorist extraordinaire William Ferris; my editor Mark Simpson-Vos; and Steve Weiss, curator of the Southern Folklife Collection. I am also grateful to Brian Paulson for preparing the audio that accompanies this book, as well as to editors Jay Mazzocchi and Matthew Somoroff.

I express my love and appreciation for my family: my parents Arthur and Rozanne; my beloved sister Nancy Jean Wakefield, gone but never forgotten; my brothers Tom and John and sisters-in-law Kathy and Mary Ellen; my nieces and nephews Greg, Annie, Liz, Sean, Kevin, and Paul Obrecht; my mother-in-law and sisters-in-law Antoinette, Viana, and Maria La Place; and Sheridan and Betsey Warrick. Blessings upon you all. My deepest gratitude goes to my wife, Michelle, and our daughter, Ava—as Richard Rodgers taught us to sing, "You make me smile with my heart."

INTRODUCTION

1. *The 2014 NAMM Global Report*, 10. Retrieved online at https://www.namm.org /files/ihdp-viewer/global-report-2014/A7352D 4907B25A95B2CE27A075D3956F/2014MusicU SA_final.pdf.

2. Ry Cooder, interview with the author, August 1993.

3. These interviews, and others, appear in *Blues Guitar: The Men Who Made the Music*, ed. Jas Obrecht (San Francisco: Miller Freeman Books, 1993); and *Rollin' and Tumblin': The Postwar Blues Guitarists*, ed. Jas Obrecht (San Francisco: Miller Freeman, 2000).

1. GUITARCHAEOLOGY

1. Dick Spottswood, email correspondence with the author, January 1, 2016.

2. John Renbourn, correspondence with the author, 1992. For more on this subject, visit "Spanish Fandango and Sebastopol," Jas Obrecht Music Archive, http://jasobrecht .com/blues-origins-spanish-fandango-and -sebastopol/.

3. *Edison Phonograph Monthly*, June 1905, accessed December 31, 2015, https://archive .org/stream/edisonphonograph03moor /edisonphonograph03moor_djvu.txt

4. Dick Spottswood, "Guitar on 78s and Cylinders: A Survey of Pioneering Efforts," *Victrola and 78 Journal* 7 (Winter 1996): 12. The original quote was updated via email correspondence, January 1, 2016.

5. *Discography of American Historical Recordings*, s.v. "Ossman-Dudley Trio (Musical group)," accessed January 4, 2016, http://adp .library.ucsb.edu/index.php/talent/detail /22244/Ossman-Dudley_Trio_Musical_group.

6. *Discography of American Historical Recordings*, s.v. "Octaviano Yañes (instrumentalist: guitar)," accessed January 4, 2016, http:// adp.library.ucsb.edu/index.php/talent/detail /41647/Yaes_Octaviano_instrumentalist _guitar.

7. Tim Gracyk, "The First Solo Guitar Recording?," *Victrola and 78 Journal* 3 (Winter 1994): 10.

8. Dick Spottswood clarifies: "Pre-1909 Hawaiian records, including a number of tracks made in Hawaii, have no slide guitars. The Toots/Kekuku cylinders are the first, as far as I know," email correspondence with the author, January 1, 2016.

9. George S. Kanahele, *Hawaiian Music and Musicians: An Illustrated History* (Honolulu: University Press of Hawaii, 1979), 367.

10. Tim Gracyk, *The Encyclopedia of Popular American Recording Pioneers: 1895–1925* (Granite Bay, Calif.: Victrola and 78 Journal Press, 1999), 114.

11. Ibid., 115.

12. Dick Spottswood, email correspondence with the author, January 3, 2016.

13. Gracyk, *The Encyclopedia of Popular American Recording Pioneers*, 115.

14. Nick Lucas rerecorded "Pickin' the Guitar" and "Teasin' the Frets" for Brunswick in 1923 and 1932.

15. This recording is available on the Library of Congress website, http://www.loc .gov/jukebox/recordings/detail/id/8009/.

16. "George Van Eps on Eddie Lang," as told to Jim Ferguson, *Guitar Player*, August 1983, 85.

17. Ry Cooder, interview with the author, February 25, 1990.

18. For detailed accounts of the lives and music of these and other 1920s bluesmen, see Jas Obrecht, *Early Blues: The First Stars of Blues Guitar* (Minneapolis: University of Minnesota Press, 2015).

19. Spottswood, email correspondence.

20. David Evans, liner notes for *Atlanta Blues 1933: A Collection of Previously Unreleased Recordings by Blind Willie McTell, Curley Weaver, and Buddy Moss*, John Edwards Memorial Foundation, JEMF-106, 1979, 13.

21. Dick Spottswood, "When the Wolf Knocked on Victor's Door," *78 Quarterly* 1, no. 5 (1990): 70.

22. Ibid., 64.

23. Transcribed from a scan of the *Music Trade Review* article provided by Lynn Wheelwright via email, January 4, 2016.

24. Lynn Wheelwright, email correspondence with the author, January 4, 2016.

25. George Gruhn and Walter Carter, *Electric Guitars and Basses: A Photographic History* (San Francisco: GPI Books, 1994), 6.

26. Ibid., 9.

27. Ibid., 10.

28. Wheelwright, email correspondence.

29. Ibid.

30. Ibid.

31. Ibid.

32. Ibid.

33. Gruhn and Carter, *Electric Guitars and Basses*, 49.

34. Lynn Wheelwright, interview with the author, May 2011.

35. Dick Spottswood, email correspondence with the author, January 1, 2016.

36. Kanahele, *Hawaiian Music and Musicians*, 372.

37. Rich Kienzle, "The Electric Guitar in Country Music: Its Evolution and Development," *Guitar Player*, November 1979, 30.

38. Dick Spottswood, "Birth of the Blast: The First Electric Guitars on Record," *Guitar Player*, April 1995, 65–66. Additional information provided via email correspondence with the author, January 3, 2016.

39. Joel A. Siegel and Jas Obrecht, "Eddie Durham: Charlie Christian's Mentor, Pioneer of the Amplified Guitar," *Guitar Player*, August 1979, 60.

40. Ibid.

41. Dick Spottswood, email correspondence with the author, January 1, 2016.

42. Richard Lieberson, "Western Swing Lives on in Eldon Shamblin," *Guitar Player*, April 1975, 35–36.

43. John Hammond, interview with the author, November 24, 1981.

44. "Leonard Feather: The Guitar in Jazz," *The Guitar in Jazz: An Anthology*," ed. by James Sallis (Lincoln: University of Nebraska Press, 1996), 5.

45. Benny Goodman, interview with the author, November 20, 1981.

3. RY COODER

1. In July 1990, I ran excerpts of the Blind Willie Johnson and Robert Johnson parts of this interview in *Guitar Player* magazine. About a year later, the April 1991 issue of *Progressive Architecture* magazine arrived in the mail. Inside, Technics editor Kenneth Labs had tested Cooder's theory about Robert Johnson facing the wall to achieve a certain sound. After four full pages of charts, diagrams, and technological analysis, Lab concluded, "Cooder is probably right."

5. CLARENCE "GATEMOUTH" BROWN

1. Interview with the author, May 19, 1992.

2. Jas Obrecht, "Clarence 'Gatemouth' Brown: 40 Years on the Road as Picker, Fiddler, Bluesman, Jazzer," *Guitar Player*, May 1979, 44.

6. ROEBUCK "POPS" STAPLES

1. Opal Louis Nations, *Uncloudy Day* liner notes, Mississippi Records, MRP 075, 2014.

2. Rev. Thomas A. Dorsey passed away on January 23, 1993.

7. RICKY NELSON

1. Between 1957 and 1959, the Burnette brothers wrote the Ricky Nelson hits "Waitin' in School," "Believe What You Say," and "It's Late," while Baker Knight composed "Lonesome Town," "I Got a Feeling," and "I Wanna Be Loved," among others.

8. CAROL KAYE

1. Brian Wilson, transcribed from the film documentary *The Wrecking Crew*, dir. Denny Tedesco (Lunch Box Entertainment, 2008).

2. Toni Ballard, "Berklee Welcomes Carol Kaye for BassDayze," Berklee press release, October 18, 2000. Retrieved from https://www

.berklee.edu/news/4554/berklee-welcomes-carol-kaye-for-bassdayze.

3. The T-Bones were actually members of the Wrecking Crew. The name was used to credit a variety of instrumental singles and albums, notably the 1965 hit "No Matter What Shape (Your Stomach's In)," which was used as the soundtrack for an Alka-Seltzer ad. This group did not tour, nor was it related to the British band of the same name.

4. Carol is likely referring to the 1960s "Teaberry Shuffle" ad, also for chewing gum.

10. JAMES GURLEY

1. Sam Andrew, interview with the author, September 30, 1978. Quoted in Jas Obrecht's "Turn On, Turn Up, Trip Out: The Rise & Fall of San Francisco Psychedelia," *Guitar Player*, February 1997, 70.

2. Barry Melton, interview with the author, November 1996. Quoted in Obrecht, "Turn On, Turn Up, Trip Out," 75. Yuri Gargarin, a Soviet cosmonaut, was the first human to journey into outer space.

3. Andrew interview, 75.

4. Ibid., 76.

5. Joel Whitburn, *The Billboard Book of Top 40 Albums*, revised and enlarged edition (New York: Billboard Books, 1991), 40.

11. JERRY GARCIA

1. Bob Weir interview with the author, October 1996. Quoted in Jas Obrecht's "Turn On, Turn Up, Trip Out: The Rise & Fall of San Francisco Psychedelia," *Guitar Player*, February 1997, 71.

2. Jon Sievert, email correspondence with the author, April 2010.

3. Django Reinhardt's fretting hand was injured in a caravan fire.

12. JOHNNY WINTER

1. James Rooney, *Bossmen: Bill Monroe & Muddy Waters* (New York: Da Capo, 1971), 145.

2. Larry Sepulvado and John Burks, "Tribute to the Lone Star State: Dispossessed Men and Mothers of Texas," *Rolling Stone*, December 7, 1968. Retrieved online from http://www.rollingstone.com/music/news/tribute-to-the-lone-star-state-dispossessed-men-and-mothers-of-texas-19681207.

3. Transcribed by the author from the film documentary *Johnny Winter: Down and Dirty*, dir. Greg Olliver (Secret Weapons Films, 2014).

4. While it's true Duane Allman played slide in standard tuning for "Dreams" and "Mountain Jam," most of his other slide songs were in open E.

13. GREGG ALLMAN

1. Tony Glover, liner notes booklet, *Duane Allman: An Anthology* (Capricorn Records, 2CP 0108, 1972), 10–11.

2. The photograph Gregg's referring to was taken by Jim Marshall, who shot the covers of *At Fillmore East*.

3. Ten days after my interview with Gregg Allman, I asked Dickey Betts about the guitars Duane used for slide. Betts responded, "When we first started out, he used to just tune his Les Paul onstage. When we got ready to do a slide tune, he'd just tune the guitar to a straight E chord and play slide right on the guitar that he'd been playing all night, rather than switching. As he got more advanced and got into it more as a couple of years went by, he started using a Gibson SG. He liked that because of the long neck, and you can get way down to the bottom frets without any trouble."

4. Twiggs Lyndon, road manager for the Allman Brothers Band and the Dixie Dregs, perished in a free-fall accident on November 16, 1979.

18. ERIC JOHNSON

1. Jeff Baxter, interview with the author, October 1980.

2. Steve Morse, interview with the author, May 1982.

3. Eric Johnson, interview with the author, September 27, 1982.

4. Stevie Ray Vaughan, interview with the author, February 1986.

5. Johnson interview.

6. Here Eric is referring to the 1954 Fender Stratocaster used on many of his albums. Inside the body cavity, it bears the signature of a Fender inspector named Virginia.

19. JOE SATRIANI

1. "Joe Satriani: Just the Facts," www.satriani.com/about/

2. Quoted in Jas Obrecht's "Space Rock—the Final Frontier. These Are the Voyages of Joe Satriani," *Guitar Player*, February 1988, 79.

3. "Joe Satriani," in *Guitar Player: The Inside Story of the First Two Decades of the Most Successful Guitar Magazine Ever*, ed. Jim Crockett with Dara Crockett (Milwaukee: Backbeat Books, 2015), 181–82.

20. BEN HARPER

1. Ben Harper, interview with the author, March 1994. Quoted in Jas Obrecht's "Ben Harper: The Importance of One Note," *Guitar Player*, June 1994, 65.

2. Ibid.

Page numbers in italics indicate illustrations.

The *Talking Guitar* CD presents audio excerpts from each interview featured in the book. Since the original tapes are, in essence, field recordings made over the course of more than three decades, the sonic quality varies from track to track. The master tapes for these and many other Jas Obrecht interviews are part of the Southern Folklife Collection, housed in the Louis Round Wilson Special Collections Library at the University of North Carolina at Chapel Hill. For information about accessing these interviews and other holdings of the Southern Folklife Collection, visit http://library.unc.edu/wilson/sfc/.

1. Nick Lucas: Recording the First Essential American Guitar Solos [2:29]
2. Ry Cooder: Robert Johnson's Recording Strategy [2:49]
3. Barney Kessel: Charlie Christian's Contributions to the Electric Guitar [3:09]
4. Clarence "Gatemouth" Brown: Meeting with T-Bone Walker [2:25]
5. Roebuck "Pops" Staples: Sing Songs That Unite Us [2:45]
6. Ricky Nelson: How Rockabilly Records Were Made [2:31]
7. Carol Kaye: Wrecking Crew Sessions with the Beach Boys [3:07]
8. Stevie Ray Vaughan: "Floorboarding" to Jimi Hendrix [2:06]
9. James Gurley: John Coltrane Influenced Psychedelic Guitar [2:17]
10. Jerry Garcia: Creativity and the Music No One Ever Hears [6:40]
11. Johnny Winter: Getting Started on Slide Guitar [2:42]
12. Gregg Allman: Duane Allman Was the Mothership of the Band [2:16]
13. Carlos Santana: How to Project Emotion in Your Playing [3:55]
14. Neil Young: The Power of the One-Note Solo [2:31]
15. Eddie Van Halen: How "Eruption" Made It onto Record [2:46]
16. Tom Petty: The Art of Rhythm Guitar [3:09]
17. Eric Johnson: Stories behind the Songs [3:08]
18. Joe Satriani: The Guitar's Limitless Potential for Expression [2:12]
19. Ben Harper: The Songs within Each Instrument [2:31]